JOHN LAURENCE

The History of
Capital Punishment

Including "A Comment on Capital Punishment"
by Clarence Darrow

CITADEL PRESS   **SECAUCUS, N.J.**

Second paperbound printing
Copyright © 1960 by The Citadel Press
All rights reserved
Published by Citadel Press
A division of Lyle Stuart Inc.
120 Enterprise Avenue, Secaucus, N.J. 07094
Manufactured in the United States of America
ISBN 0-8065-0840-X

DEDICATORY

"And we command that Christian men be not on any account for altogether too little condemned to death, but rather let gentle punishments be decreed for the benefit of the people; and not be destroyed for little God's handywork, as His own purchase which He dearly bought."

Laws of Canute.

PREFACE

THIS book does not state the pros and cons for Capital Punishment. It is an outline of scaffold history. Some day the full history of the scaffold may be written. It will not be in one volume but in many. A full, annotated bibliography of capital punishment alone would fill a volume.

The accuracy of the printed, the written, or the spoken word is always in doubt, for added to the bias of the author or the speaker is the native inability to record with photographic and gramophonic fidelity what is seen and heard. And for that matter the camera and the gramophone are not above suspicion. The art of faking photographs is as much one of the fine arts as the higher forms of murder.

The scaffold does not suffer less from the difficulties of historical accuracy than any other subject. In some ways it suffers more. The owners of the printing presses of an earlier day found that in last dying speeches and confessions there was a source of revenue which appeared to be a new Golconda. The circulations of the broadsides of a popular murder and execution in the early nineteenth century would make many a modern printer green with envy. The value of murder, of scenes in court when sentence of death is pronounced, and the final execution, in its meagre details, is not overlooked by the modern printer. The *Newgate Calendars* in part form were the forerunners of the weekly and fortnightly educational encyclopædias of the twentieth century, and it is a debatable point which are the more interesting or the more accurate of the two.

The artists and authors of an earlier day, no less than the journalists, were not able to record any more accurately contemporary events than they can now. Newspapers, books, tracts, private papers and State papers have been consulted for the material of this book, and in the course of such research many discrepancies have been discovered and reconciled to the best of the author's judgment.

To give an example, one particularly circumstantial account of the execution of Mary Blandy shows her being hanged from the "triple tree" made infamous for all time at Tyburn. Actually she was hanged from a beam slung between two trees.

Interest in crime is a fundamental one in human nature. The wicked still stand in slippery places, and the most venerated of all the commandments is the eleventh. To be found out is to provide popular entertainment that those who read may run, many hopefully to some country where the extradition laws are not so rigorous as those of their own land.

The story of a nation's crime is national history. The scaffold has made and altered history. If capital punishment had been as rigorously taboo in the twenty centuries of the Christian era as has been the encouragement of education, it is not a matter for doubt that the history of the world would not be what it is. The rope has done more than break men's necks. It has numbed the brains of the living, and men's thoughts have remained inarticulate from fear of the freely falling knife and the headsman's axe.

"It is a sharp medicine," said Sir Walter Raleigh, as he tested the keen edge of the axe while waiting execution.

To-day we have changed the medicine, but it is a moot point whether we are any farther on the road to cure those diseases for which our forefathers administered the sharpest medicine in the legal pharmacopeia.

Philosophically, psychologically and legally the scaffold has ceased to produce any new arguments for or against its use. As an intellectual pastime its pros and cons have ceased to interest all those who are not prejudiced.

Here the plain story is told, and draw what conclusions you may from it according to your leanings. But remember, other times other manners.

CONTENTS

LIST OF ILLUSTRATIONS

A COMMENT ON CAPITAL PUNISHMENT

BY CLARENCE DARROW

In 1922 Clarence Darrow published Crime: Its Cause and Treatment. *The book included a chapter entitled, "Capital Punishment," which clearly set forth the great lawyer's attitude on the controversial subject. It read as follows:*

The question of capital punishment has been the subject of endless discussion and will probably never be settled so long as men believe in punishment. Some states have abolished and then reinstated it; some have enjoyed capital punishment for long periods of time and finally prohibited the use of it. The reasons why it cannot be settled are plain. There is first of all no agreement as to the objects of punishment. Next there is no way to determine the results of punishment. If the object is assumed it is a matter of conjecture as to what will be most likely to bring the result. If it could be shown that any form of punishment would bring the immediate result, it would be impossible to show its indirect result although indirect results are as certain as direct ones. Even if all of this could be clearly proven, the world would be no nearer the solution. Questions of this sort, or perhaps of any sort, are not settled by reason; they are settled by prejudices and sentiments or by emotion. When they are settled they do not stay settled, for the emotions change as new stimuli are applied to the machine.

A state may provide for life imprisonment in place of death. Some especially atrocious murder may occur and be fully exploited in the press. Public feeling will be fanned to a flame. Bitter hatred will be aroused against the murderer. It is perfectly obvious to the multitude that if other men had been hanged for murder, this victim would not have been killed. A legislature meets before the hatred has had time to cool and the law is changed. Again, a community may have capital punishment and nothing notable happens. Now and then hangings occur. Juries acquit because of the severity of the penalty. A feeling of shame or some bungling execution may arouse a community against it. A deep-seated doubt may arise as to the guilt of a man who has been put to death. The sentimental people triumph. The law is changed. Nothing has been found out; no question has been settled; science has made no contribution; the public has changed its mind, or, speaking more correctly, has had another emotion and passed another law.

In the main, the controversy over capital punishment has been one between emotional and unemotional people. Now and then the emotionalist is reinforced by some who have a religious conviction against capital punishment, based perhaps on the rather trite expression that "God gave life and only God should take it away." Such a statement is plausible but not capable of proof. In the main religious people believe in capital punishment. The advocates of capital punishment dispose of the question by saying that it is the "sentimentalist" or, rather, the "maudlin sentimentalist" who is against it. Sentimentalist really implies "maudlin."

But emotion too has its biological origin and is a subject of scientific definition. A really "sentimental" person, in the sense used, is one who has sympathy. This, in turn, comes from imagination which is probably the result of a sensitive nervous system, one that quickly and easily responds to stimuli. Those who have weak emotions do not respond so readily to impressions. Their assumption of superior wisdom has its basis only in a nervous system which is sluggish and phlegmatic to stimuli. Such impressions as each system makes are registered on the brain and become the material for recollection and comparison, which go to form opinion. The correctness of the mental processes depends upon the correctness of the senses that receive the impression, the nerves that transmit the correctness of the registration, and the character of the brain. It does not follow that the stoic has a better brain than the despised "sentimentalist." Either one of them may have a good one, and either one of them a poor one. Still, charity and kindliness probably come from the sensitive system which imagines itself in the place of the object that it pities. All pity is really pain engendered by the feelings that translate one into the place of another. Both hate and love are biologically necessary to life and its processes.

Many people urge that the penalty of imprisonment for life would be all right if the culprit could be kept in prison during life, but in the course of time he is pardoned. This to me is an excellent reason why his life should be saved. It is proof that the feeling of hatred that inspired judge and jury has spent itself and that they can look at the murderer as a man. Which decision is the more righteous, the one where hatred and fear affect the judgment and sentence, or the one where these emotions have spent their force?

Everyone who advocates capital punishment is really ashamed of the practice for which he is responsible. Instead of urging public executions, the most advanced and sensitive who believe in killing by the state are now advocating that even the newspapers should not publish the details and that the killing should be done in darkness and silence. In that event no one would be deterred by the cruelty of the state. That capital punishment is horrible and cruel is the reason for its existence. That men should be taught not to take life is the purpose of judicial killings. But the spectacle of the state taking life must tend to cheapen it. This must be evident to all who believe in suggestion. Constant association and familiarity tend to lessen the shock of any act however revolting. If men regarded the murderer as one who acted from some all-sufficient cause and who was simply an instrument in an endless sequence of cause and effect, would anyone say he should be put to death?

It is not easy to estimate values correctly. It may be that life is not important. Nature seems extravagantly profligate in her giving and pitiless in her taking away. Yet death has something of the same shock today that was felt when men first gazed upon the dead with awe and wonder and terror. Constantly meeting it and seeing it and procuring it will doubtless make it more commonplace. To the seasoned soldier in the army it means less than it did before he became a soldier. Probably the undertaker thinks less of death than almost any other man. He is so accustomed to it that his mind must involuntarily turn from its horror to a contemplation of how much he makes out of the burial. If the civilized savages have their way and make hangings common, we shall probably recover from some of our instinctive fear of death and the extravagant value that we place on life. The social organism is like the individual organism: it can be so often shocked that it grows accustomed and weary and no longer manifests resistance or surprise.

So far as we can reason on questions of life and death and the effect of stimuli upon human organisms, the circle is like this: Frequent executions dull the sensibilities toward the taking of life. This makes it easier for men to kill and increases murders, which in turn increase hangings, which in turn increase murders, and so on, around the vicious circle.

In the absence of any solid starting point on which an argument can be based; in the absence of any reliable figures; in the absence of any way to interpret the figures; in the absence of any way to ascertain the indirect results of judicial killings, even if the direct ones could be shown; in the impossibility through life, experience or philosophy of fixing relative values, the question must remain where it has always been, a conflict between the emotional and unemotional; the "sentimental" and the stolid; the imaginative and the unimaginative; the sympathetic and the unsympathetic. Personally, being inclined to a purely mechanistic view of life and to the belief that all conduct is the result of certain stimuli upon a human machine, I can only say that the stimuli of seeing and reading of capital punishment, applied to my machine, is revolting and horrible. Perhaps as the world improves, the sympathetic and imaginative nature will survive the stolid and selfish. At least one can well believe that this is the line of progress if there shall be progress, a matter still open to question and doubt.

Two years after Crime: Its Cause and Treatment *was published, Darrow engaged in a public debate with Judge Alfred J. Talley, Court of General Sessions, New York City, on the topic: "Resolved: That Capital Punishment is a Wise*

*Public Policy." The debate took place on September 23, 1924
in New York's Manhattan Opera House under the auspices
of The League for Public Discussion. Darrow, who took the
negative, was introduced by Chairman Louis Marshall as
one who "is known from the Atlantic to the Pacific as a
lawyer, as a defender of unpopular causes, as an essayist and
as a great orator." In the course of his presentation and ref-
utation, Darrow made the following main points:*

Every human being that believes in capital punishment
loves killing, and the only reason they believe in capital punishment is because they get a kick out of it. Nobody kills anyone
for love, unless they get over it temporarily or otherwise. But
they kill the one they hate. And before you can get a trial to
hang somebody or electrocute him, you must first hate him and
then get a satisfaction over his death. . . .

I shall not follow my friend into the labyrinth of statistics.
Statistics are a pleasant indoor sport—not so good as cross-
word puzzles—and they prove nothing to any sensible person
who is familiar with statistics.

I might just observe, in passing, that in all of these states
where the mortality by homicide is great, they have capital
punishment and always have had it. A logical man, when he
found out that the death rate increased under capital punishment, would suggest some other way of dealing with it.

I undertake to say—and you can look them up yourselves,
for I haven't time to bother with it (and there is nothing that
lies like statistics)—I will guarantee to take any set of statistics and take a little time to it and prove they mean directly the
opposite of what is claimed. But I will undertake to say that
you can show by statistics that the states in which there was no
capital punishment have a very much smaller percentage of
homicides.

I know it is true. That doesn't prove anything, because, as a
rule, they are states with a less diverse population, without as
many large cities, without as much mixture of all sorts of elements which go to add to the general gaiety—and homicide is a
product of that. There is no sort of question but what those
states in the United States where there is no capital punish-

ment have a lower percentage than the others. But that doesn't prove the question. It is a question that cannot be proven one way or the other by statistics. It rests upon things, upon feelings and emotions and arguments, much deeper than statistics.

The death rate from homicide in Memphis and in some other Southern cities is high. Why? Well, it is an afternoon's pleasure to kill a Negro—that is about all. Everybody knows it.

The death rate recently in the United States and all over the world has increased. Why? The same thing has happened that has happened in every country in the world since time began. A great war always increases death rates.

We teach people to kill, and the State is the one that teaches them. If the State wishes that its citizens respect human life, then the State should stop killing. It can be done in no other way, and it will perhaps not be fully done that way. There are infinite reasons for killing. There are infinite circumstances under which there are more or less deaths. It never did depend and never can depend upon the severity of the punishment. . . .

I don't want to dispute about the right of the State to kill people. Of course, they have got a right to kill them. That is about all we do. The great industry of the world for four long years was killing. They have got a right to kill, of course, that is, they have got the power. And you have got a right to do what you get away with. The words power and right, so far as this is concerned, mean exactly the same thing. So nobody who has any knowledge of philosophy would pretend to say that the State had not the right to kill.

But why not do a good job of it? If you want to get rid of killings by hanging people or electrocuting them because these are so terrible, why not make a punishment that is terrible? This isn't so much. It lasts but a short time. There is no physical torture in it. Why not boil them in oil, as they used to do? Why not burn them at the stake? Why not sew them into a bag with serpents and throw them out to sea? Why not take them out on the sand and let them be eaten by ants? Why not break every bone in their body on the rack, as has been done for such serious offenses as heresy and witch-craft?

Those were the good old days in which the Judge should have held court. Glorious days, when you could kill them by the millions because they worshiped God in a different way from that which the State provided, or when you could kill old women for witchcraft! There might be some sense in it if you could kill young ones, but not old ones. Those were the glorious days of capital punishment. And there wasn't a judge or a preacher who didn't think that the life of the State depended upon their right to hang old women for witchcraft and to persecute others for worshiping God in the wrong way.

Why, our capital punishment isn't worth talking about, so far as its being a preventive is concerned. It isn't worth discussing. Why not call back from the dead and barbarous past the hundred and sixty- or seventy-odd crimes that were punishable by death in England? Why not once more re-enact the Blue Laws of our own country and kill people right? Why not resort to all the tortures that the world has always resorted to to keep men in the straight and narrow path? Why reduce it to a paltry question of murder?

Everybody in this world has some pet aversion to something, and on account of that pet aversion they would like to hang somebody. If the prohibitionists made the law, they would be in favor of hanging you for taking a drink, or certainly for bootlegging, because to them that is the most heinous crime there is. . . .

There is just one thing in all this question. It is a question of how you feel, that is all. It is all inside of you. If you love the thought of somebody being killed, why, you are for it. If you hate the thought of somebody being killed, you are against it.

Let me just take a little brief review of what has happened in this world. They used to hang people on the crossways and on a high hill, so that everybody would be awed into goodness by the sight. They have tortured them in every way that the brain of man could conceive. They have provided every torture known or that could be imagined for one who believed differently from his fellow-man—and still the belief persisted. They have maimed and scarred and starved and killed human beings since man began penning his fellow-man. Why? Because we hate him. And what has added to it is that they have done it under the false ideal of self-righteousness.

I have heard parents punish their children and tell their children it hurt the parents more than it did the child. I don't believe it. I have tried it both ways, and I don't believe it. I know better.

Gradually, the world has been lopping off these punishments. Why? Because we have grown a little more sensitive, a little more imaginative, a little kindlier, that is all.

Why not re-enact the code of Blackstone's day? Why, the judges were all for it—every one of them—and the only way we got rid of these laws was because juries were too humane to obey the courts.

That is the only way we got rid of punishing old women, of hanging old women in New England—because, in spite of all the courts, the juries would no longer convict them for a crime that never existed. And in that way they have cut down the crimes in England for punishment by death from one hundred and seventy to two. What is going to happen if we get rid of them? Is the world coming to an end? The earth has been here ages and ages before man came. It will be here ages and ages after he disappears, and the amount of people you hang won't make the slightest difference with it.

Now, why am I opposed to capital punishment? It is too horrible a thing for a State to undertake. We are told by my friend, "Oh, the killer does it; why shouldn't the State?" I would hate to live in a State that I didn't think was better than a murderer.

But I told you the real reason. The people of the State kill a man because he killed someone else—that is all—without the slightest logic, without the slightest application to life, simply from anger, nothing else!

I am against it because I believe it is inhuman, because I believe that as the hearts of men have softened they have gradually gotten rid of brutal punishment, because I believe that it will only be a few years until it will be banished forever from every civilized country—even New York; because I believe that it has no effect whatever to stop murder. . . .

There isn't, I submit, a single admissible argument in favor of capital punishment. Nature loves life. We believe that life should be protected and preserved. The thing that keeps one from killing is the emotion they have against it; and the greater the sanctity that the State pays to life, the greater the feeling of sanctity the individual has for life.

There is nothing in the history of the world that ever cheapened human life like our great war; next to that, the indiscriminate killing of men by the States.

My friend says a man must be proven guilty first. Does anybody know whether anybody is guilty? There is a great deal implied in that. For me to do something or for you to do something is one thing; for some other man to do something quite another. To know what one deserves requires infinite study, which no one can give to it. No one can determine the condition of the brain that did the act. It is out of the question.

All people are products of two things, and two things only —their heredity and their environment. And they act in exact accord with the heredity which they took from all the past, and for which they are in no wise responsible, and the environment, which reaches out to the farthest limit of all life that can influence them. We all act from the same way. And it ought to teach us to be charitable and kindly and understanding of our fellowman. . . .

In the end, this question is simply one of the humane feelings against the brutal feelings. One who likes to see suffering, out of what he thinks is a righteous indignation, or any other, will hold fast to capital punishment. One who has sympathy, imagination, kindness and understanding, will hate it and detest it as he hates and detests death.

A BARBAROUS FORM OF PUNISHMENT

EDITORIAL, *New York Herald Tribune*, MAY 3, 1960

Caryl Chessman died well, as befitted a man well aware that the world's eyes were on his dying. Other and nobler men have also died well, but few deaths have so dramatized the ugly absurdity of capital punishment in a society that should have outgrown it.

For Chessman succeeded in making himself a world-wide symbol of the fight against the death penalty. The struggle to live has universal appeal, and Chessman managed to personalize the fight of one man against all that the "little green room" has come to represent.

He may or may not have been guilty, twelve years ago, of robbery and sexual assault (called kidnapping by a strange quirk of California law). The courts found him guilty; to the end he maintained his innocence, and the germ of doubt thus left will continue to cloud the case. But certainly the man killed yesterday by the sovereign state of California was not the same man whom that state's courts originally sentenced.

By dint of hard work and a quick intelligence, the young hoodlum on death row had made himself an international celebrity; he had won millions of persons to his cause; he had matured, and he gave every impression of feeling and respecting the responsibility that his self-won position in the limelight laid inescapably on him.

California sentenced a young thug; it killed a man who had learned law, and probably citizenship, the hard way.

Californians are no safer today than before Chessman died, and respect for law—which is different from fear of its power—is no stronger.

The law should inculcate respect for life by itself respecting the sanctity of life. The state should not, as California did yesterday, put itself in the position of the errant father telling his wayward son, "Do as I say, not as I do."

Death is final. It leaves no room for second thoughts, or for correction of the errors that are a mathematical certainty in a system of justice based on fallible human judgment. And the quintessential premeditation which judicial killing represents makes it more coldly vicious than a crime of passion.

The very concept of a death chamber is antithetical to the ideals of Western civilization. If hangings in the market place would be abhorrent today, executions in the chill green solitude of the gas chamber should be recognized as no less so. Chessman is dead, but those who rallied to his cause because of a belief that capital punishment is wrong still have a job to do.

A HISTORY
OF CAPITAL PUNISHMENT

CHAPTER I

A GENERAL HISTORICAL REVIEW

THE taking of life was the primitive and supreme satisfying of personal vengeance. The most expert fighter, the one who killed oftenest, was the one ultimately most feared, the one who took the leadership in early communities. In the beginning such a man slew his enemies through his personal prowess or cunning. Leadership would bring him the power, on occasion, of delegating slaying to others.

From the earliest times death as a deterrent to others must have been common. It was the final means of ensuring respect, of instilling terror among those for whom the struggle for existence was acute. Man kept his possessions by brute force, and before the idea of the State became dominant, death was the only real deterrent to the covetous. The dead, at any rate, could not steal; but the living could, whatever bodily punishment had been inflicted on them, and they could also harbour vengeance.

It was not until comparatively recent times that the punishment of death was specifically reserved for murder and other major offences, although as far back as the time of Moses the right of the State over the individual in the case of capital offences was recognised.

Among the earliest records we find mention in the Ancient Laws of China of beheading as the prescribed mode of capital punishment. In early Egypt and Assyria the axe was used, and in some very early records it is stated that malefactors were ordered to kill themselves, usually by taking poison. One of the officials of the Court of the

Pharaohs was certainly put to death by poisoning. It is recorded that the Egyptians refused burial to executed criminals and gave their bodies to the birds and beasts. The Greeks also refused decent burial to infamous persons and criminals.

For the oldest death sentence extant we have to search in the Amherst papyri, which contains the accounts of the trials of State criminals in Egypt some fifteen hundred years before Christ. The criminal condemned was found guilty of "magic" and was sentenced to death. The exact mode of his death was left to the culprit, who was his own executioner.

In England we have no record of capital punishment earlier than 450 B.C., when it was the custom to throw those condemned to die into a quagmire.

The Mosaic law is full of mention of the punishment of death, the principal mode of execution being stoning, though hanging seems to have been recognised, as is shown from the fact that in Deuteronomy xxi (His body shall not remain all night upon the tree, but thou shalt in any wise bury him that day; for he that is hanged is accursed of God) instructions are given to the effect that when a man has been hanged his body is to be cut down before nightfall and not left dangling on the tree throughout the hours of darkness. Beheading seems to have been considered a more honourable death, and it was the punishment generally meted out to enemies. Crucifixion was a mode of punishment copied from the Romans. Burning alive was probably (Genesis xxxviii. 24) practised, and was a form of punishment sanctioned by Mosaic law and used for incendiaries. Throwing the criminal from a rock was recognised by the Jews and the Twelve Tables of the Romans.

The pouring of molten lead on the criminal; starvation in dungeons; tearing to death by red-hot pincers; sawing asunder—a mode of punishment practised, by the way, by the Jews against the conquered in Palestine; and many other forms of capital punishment were common in early times.

The IDLE 'PRENTICE Executed at Tyburn.

THE IDLE 'PRENTICE

From the painting by William Hogarth

William Hogarth (1697–1764) sought his models roaming about the streets of London, and we are indebted to his works for many remarkable scenes of his period. The "Idle 'Prentice" was one of a series of paintings *Industry and Idleness*, the latter culminating in the scaffold scene shown here.

[*Face page 2*

BURNING A WOMAN FOR TREASON
(*From an old print*)

Women were burnt alive in the olden days for high treason and petty treason,
that is the murder of their husbands. Usually before the faggots were lighted
round them they were strangled at the stake.

Burial alive was the fate meted out under the Roman republic for vestal virgins who violated their vows of chastity. At the passing into law by the Decemviri of the Twelve Tables (451–450 B.C.) the following were also recognised as crimes to be punished by death:

Publishing libels and insulting songs.
Furtively cutting or causing to be grazed crops raised by ploughing, by an adult.
Knowingly and maliciously burning a house or a stack of corn near a house.
Theft by a slave who is taken in the act.
Cheating, by a Patron, of his client.
Perjury.
Wilful murder of a freeman.
Wilful murder of a parent.
Making disturbances in the City at night.

During the Republic the death penalty was enacted for these and many more crimes, abolished for citizens in 299 B.C., and restored again later.

In the time of Paul, crucifixion, burning and decapitation were in use among the Assyrians, Persians, Egyptians, Carthaginians and Greeks, but were abolished by Constantine, on his adoption of Christianity, throughout the Roman Empire. One of the cruelties inflicted by Nero on those sentenced to death was impalement, and is referred to by Juvenal. Such an atrocity was practised as late as 1876 in the Balkan peninsula, while under Charles V criminals were thrown into their open graves and impaled by pointed stakes.

The Romans had a curious punishment for parricides. They were thrown into the water in a sack, which contained also a dog, a cock, a viper and an ape. This superstitious form of punishment persisted, in some countries, into the Middle Ages. The parricide has always been singled out for special punishment in all countries and ages.

The Romans also inflicted the death penalty by drowning at sea; precipitation from the Tarpeian rock; burial alive and beating to death.

In all countries capital punishment was, with comparatively rare exceptions, public.

"When criminals are executed," says Quintillian, "the most public places are chosen, where there will be the greatest number of spectators, and so the most for the fear of punishment to work upon them."

Again, Seneca, following the same line of argument, says, "The more public the punishments are, the greater the effect they will produce upon the reformation of others."

The argument is a doubtful one, and the ultimate effect of public executions will be referred to on various occasions throughout this book. History bears out that the very publicity involved defeated its object, and that the gallows became in course of time a scene of merry-making at its worst, and the resort of thieves and other criminals at the best. As a deterrent, publicity undoubtedly failed, a fact not universally recognised until the nineteenth century.

From the *Vocabulary of Archbishop Alfric* of the tenth century, and from early illuminated MSS., we find that the gallows was the usual method of capital punishment in Anglo-Saxon times. But in addition to hanging, beheading, burning, drowning, stoning and casting from rocks were common forms of death meted out to criminals under Saxon and Danish kings. The king had the right of choosing the form of death.

William the Conqueror was averse from taking life except in warfare, and ordered that no person should be hanged or otherwise put to death for any offence whatever, but that did not prevent criminals being mutilated. Fighting men were too valuable to be hanged for minor offences. William Rufus was also opposed to the infliction of the death penalty, but Henry I substituted to a great extent death by the axe or the rope for the long and painful one of mortification, after maiming, which was the practical result of mutilation.

Within the next two hundred years the penalty of death began to be awarded a little less indiscriminately than before and was, to a large extent, confined to certain recognised offences. High and petty treason were capital;

so were all felonies, except mayhem and petty larceny, i.e., theft of property worth less than one shilling. It follows that murder, manslaughter, arson, highway robbery, burglary and larceny were all punishable by death. All statutory felonies, indeed, were so unless the statute laid down otherwise.

With the approach of the Middle Ages, not only did the number of capital crimes increase, but the mode of inflicting the last penalty became more cruel. Torture appeared to be a necessary part of even the simplest form of execution, while the actual methods of killing were increased in number and devilish ingenuity. The death penalty was extended to heretics under the writ *de heretico comburendo*, which was lawfully issuable under statute in England from 1382 until 1677. For this purpose the legislature had adopted the civil law of the Roman Empire, which was not a part of the English common law. The law was the subject of the grossest abuse, and there was a rapid increase of capital punishment in England.

Most barons had a drowning pit as well as a gallows. The owner of Baynard's Castle, London, in the reign of King John, had the right to drown traitors in the Thames.

The Church not only offered sanctuary to the criminal, but many of its representatives possessed certain rights in respect of capital punishment. The Abbot of Battle Abbey had the right to spare the life of any condemned about to be executed, a right granted by William the Conqueror. Similarly, the Bishop of Lincoln at one time had the right of executing criminals, a right once disputed by the Abbot of Peterborough, who set up his own private gallows for the purpose of hanging a thief. The Bishop of Lincoln's authority was shown to be supreme, undoubtedly much to his satisfaction, since such authority included the right to the chattels of the criminal executed within his jurisdiction.

The number of executions increased steadily each year from the time of the death of William the Conqueror. Human life was of less value than that of many animals, for the latter could be made to work for something less than a fair share of food. In 1279, for example, it is recorded that two hundred and eighty Jews were hanged for clipping coin. This was regarded as a serious offence in many countries for centuries. That human life was but lightly thought of is well seen from the execution of the mayor of Exeter and the porter of the south gate of the town during the reign of Edward I. Both men were condemned because the gate of the city had not been closed in time to prevent the escape of a murderer.

As burning was the punishment in England for high treason for women, where hanging or beheading by the axe were not inflicted, men were punished for the same offence by hanging, drawing and quartering. The axe for gentlemen and the rope for the common herd were the modes of execution until the reign of Edward III, when hanging, drawing and quartering was made legal. Beheading was generally accepted as an honourable mode of death, indeed, and was used only for the higher classes.

Hanging, drawing and quartering was invented for the express benefit of a William Maurice, the son of a nobleman, who was convicted, not of treason but of piracy. He suffered in 1241.

The sentence passed on David, the last native Prince of Wales, at Shrewsbury in 1283, ordered him "to be drawn to the gallows as a traitor to the king who made him a knight, to be hanged as the murderer of the gentleman taken in the Castle of Hawarden, to have his limbs burnt because he had profaned by assassination the solemnity of Christ's Passion, and to have his quarters dispersed through the country because he had in different places compassed the death of his lord the king."

The Church, from the earliest times, was jealous of the authority of the king and the judges. By the fourth Canon of the Fifth Council of Paris, A.D. 615, no judge was allowed to try any ecclesiastic without first giving notice to the ordinary. From that time the power of the Church in different countries slowly increased.

In 1220 the Emperor Frederick II decreed that no one might drag a clerk before a secular tribunal. Similar laws were made by the Emperor Charles IV, and the right to clerical immunity was reasserted at the twenty-fifth session of the General Council of Trent in 1563.

In 1350 in England the statute Pro Clero read . . . "all manner of clerks, as well secular as religious, which shall be from henceforth convicted before the secular justices aforesaid for any treasons or felonies touching other persons than the King himself or his royal majesty, shall from henceforth freely have and enjoy the privilege of Holy Church, and shall be, without any impeachment or delay, delivered to the ordinaries demanding them."

In practice this came to mean immunity for all who could read. Anyone could claim benefit of clergy and was examined as to his scholarship. This examination consisted in the reading of a passage, usually from the 51st Psalm, which was appropriately called "the neck verse." In 1705 the necessity for reading the neck verse was abolished.

The Church claimed all clerics accused of any crimes except those of high treason, highway marauding, deliberate house burning, offences against the laws of the forest, e.g., hunting the king's deer, and certain minor offences. Clerics came to include all who were tonsured or had their hair cut in clerical fashion. The privilege of clergy was only allowed in case of a first conviction after 1487, and to prevent a second claim it was the practice to brand murderers with the letter M upon the brawn of the left thumb, and other felons with the Tyburn T. Ben Jonson was, in 1598, so marked for manslaughter. An ordained priest could appeal to his Church again.

The Church naturally did not extend its protection to heretics, who were burnt alive. Heresy had a very wide meaning. In 1222 a deacon was burned at Oxford for embracing Judaism in order to marry a Jewess, and many who lived with Jewesses were sentenced to death for having committed an unnatural offence.

Benefit of clergy from the sixteenth century onwards gradually lessened in importance as the law took greater cognisance of the difference between offences, and less of that between offenders. But it was not finally abolished until

1827 as to all persons not having privilege of peerage, and in 1841 as to peers and peeresses.

The number of executions, despite various methods of evasion, however, reached an appalling percentage of the population, and reflected the spirit of the times. Writers have remarked on the triviality of the offences for which death was the punishment in the eighteenth century, but two and three hundred years before we find similar records.

As late as 1450, by the old Admiralty law relative to the Humber, there was an ordinance that any man who stole ropes, nets, cords, etc., amounting to the value of nine-pence, should at low water mark have his hands and feet bound, his throat cut, his tongue pulled out, and his body thrown into the sea. Any man who removed the anchor from any ship, or cut the cable of a ship while she was riding at anchor, was liable to be hanged at low water mark.

Prisoners who refused to plead under these harsh laws were starved to death, or until the pangs of hunger brought them to a different frame of mind. In 1426, a humane [*sic*] law altered the starving into *peine forte et dure*. By this penalty the prisoner was placed on his back in a low, dark room, with only a cloth round his loins. As many weights as he could bear without his ribs being actually crushed in, were placed on him. He was given a small quantity of bad bread the first day, a small drink of foul water the next, and so on. And "so shall he continue till he die."

Henry VIII not only created a record, according to Stow, by executing 72,000 of his liege subjects, but it was in his reign that boiling to death was made legal. The Act was passed in 1531. The preamble of the statute dealt with one Richard Roose, or Coke, a cook, who was accused of trying to poison, with a brew of hemlock and other fatal herbs, the Bishop of Rochester's household, and the poor of the parish in which the palace was situate. The poisoning seems to have been successful to the extent that several people became seriously ill, and two died.

Accordingly, the cook was publicly boiled to death at Smithfield in a huge cauldron suspended from a strong iron tripod over a pile of logs. He suffered for two hours in agony before he succumbed.

In the same year King's Lynn saw the boiling to death in the market place of a servant who had poisoned her mistress. Margaret Davy, another servant, met a like fate at Smithfield, in 1542.

Edward VI did not permit this form of punishment to be legal for long. In 1547 the law was repealed, the Act substituting hanging, except in the case of women who poisoned husband or child, when the penalty was burning. In Brittany, in 1580, coining was punished by first boiling and then hanging the offender.

Apart from the burning of heretics, burning was a not uncommon form of capital punishment at one period. It continued until 1790 to be the punishment inflicted on women for high or petty treason. As late as 1783 a woman was burned at Ipswich for murdering her husband.

It has been remarked that women were burnt for high treason, instead of being hanged, drawn and quartered, as were men guilty of the same crime, and a curious instance of mistaken thinking is to be found in Blackstone's apology for burning women. "For as decency due to the sex forbids the exposing and publicly mangling their bodies," he says, "their sentence, is, to be drawn to the gallows, and there to be burnt alive."

It was customary, when a woman was burnt for petty treason, that is the murder of her husband, to tie a rope round her neck when she was fastened to the stake, and strangle her before the flames reached her. In the case of Catherine Hayes, burnt at Tyburn in 1726, however, she "was literally burnt alive; for the executioner, letting go the rope sooner than usual in consequence of the flames reaching his hands, the fire burnt fiercely round her, and the spectators beheld her pushing the faggots from her, while she rent the air with her cries and lamentations. Other faggots were instantly thrown on her, but she survived amidst the flames for a considerable time, and her body was not perfectly reduced to ashes in less than three hours."

The latest instance of burning alive was in 1789, when Christian Murphy was burned alive for coining. On June 5th, 1790, the act which substituted hanging came into force.

The last instance of a woman being burnt for high treason was in 1685, when Elizabeth Gaunt was found guilty of having assisted one Burton, who was concerned in the Rye House Plot, to escape. Burton was dastard enough to appear as the chief witness against the poor woman. While she was actually being burned at the stake there came a heavy downpour of rain and the crowd which had assembled to witness the scene interpreted this as a sign of Divine wrath at the brutal punishment.

In many countries burning alive was the punishment especially inflicted on witches. The witch of Endor and the command: "Thou shalt not allow a witch to live," were responsible for many atrocities. A German writer in 1845 says that "From the fifteenth to the beginning of the eighteenth century some thousands of wretched witches were burnt, and all on their own confession, a confession usually obtained by torture." Michelet, in his *History of France*, gives numberless instances of how commonly this crime was so punished. Remigius, in his *Daemonolatraiae Ribritres*, relates that in the space of sixteen years eight hundred witches and wizards were burned. W. F. Poole, in *Salem Witchcraft*, puts the witch death roll in Europe during the sixteenth and seventeenth centuries at the amazing total of 200,000. Zachary Gray, who edited an edition of *Hudibras*, claims that during the Long Parliament five hundred witches a year was executed. It is recorded that a woman was burned to death for witchcraft at Dornoch in Sutherland in 1722.

Ducking and drowning were punishments inflicted on witches in England and Scotland in addition to burning. In 1623 eleven gipsy women were condemned to be drowned at Edinburgh, and on May 11th, 1685, Margaret M'Lachlan, aged sixty-three, and Margaret Wilson, a girl of eighteen, were drowned in the Blednoch, for denying that James VII of Scotland was entitled to rule the Church according to his pleasure. In 1697 the last authentic case of legal drowning occurred, when a woman convicted of theft was sentenced in Scotland to be drowned in the Loch of Spyne.

It is asserted that when the lake was drained in the first decade of the nineteenth century the skeleton of the unfortunate woman was found in the bed, and was identified by means of a ring on one of the fleshless fingers. Drowning was continued in France as late as 1793.

In the reign of Elizabeth the recusant priests were hanged, drawn and quartered, and the queen occasionally gave orders that the victims should be quite conscious when the disembowelling process began. The punishment was finally settled by the Statute of Treason of 25 Edward III, 1351.

The sentence was "that the traitor is to be taken from prison and laid on a hurdle (in earlier days he was dragged along the ground, tied to the tail of a horse), and drawn to the gallows, then hanged by the neck until he was nearly dead, then cut down; then his entrails were to be cut out of his body and burnt by the executioner; then his head to be cut off, his body divided into four quarters, and afterwards set up in some open place as directed."

Lord Coke found justification for this brutality in a collection of Bible texts, and hence it was called "godly butchery."

"In treason," says Lord Bacon, "it has been an ancient use and favour for the kings of this realm to pardon the execution of hanging, drawing and quartering, and to make warrant for their beheading." This, however, could only be done where the striking off of the head was part of the sentence, in which case the king, by his prerogative had the power of pardoning all the rest. By the statute 54 George III, c. 146, the cruel and disgusting part of the ordinary mode of execution for treason was removed.

Mr. Justice Blackstone says (*Commen.* Vol. IV, p. 377) "there are but few instances, and those accidental or by negligence, of persons being disembowelled till previously deprived of sensation by strangling." There are, however several instances on record in which the sentence has been executed in all its literal rigour. The conspirators in Babington's plot in 1586 were all disembowelled alive; some of them looking on while the horrible details of the execution took place upon their companions. (Howell, *State Trials*, Vol. I, p. 1158.)

The punishment for high treason differed from that inflicted for murder in several important particulars. The head was necessarily severed from the body after the hanging, and the criminal must be drawn to the gallows, not being allowed to walk. He was to be cut down alive and his entrails taken out and burnt before his face. Then the head was cut off, " headed," and the body quartered, the head and quarters remaining at the King's disposal. The quarters were parboiled to preserve them and the various parts distributed in different places and hung up to the public gaze.

Meiklejohn, in his *History*, states that after the Monmouth Rebellion " the pitch cauldron was constantly boiling in the assize towns and the heads and limbs preserved in it were distributed over the lovely western country, where, for years after, in spite of storms and crows and foxes, they frightened the village labourer as he passed to his cottage in the evening gloom." Macaulay says, "The peasant who had consented to perform this hideous office returned to his plough. But a mark like that of Cain was upon him. He was known throughout the village by the horrible name of William Boilman."

Among the notable early victims of the sentence were Wallace, 1395; the elder and younger Despencers, 1326; and Hotspur, 1403. The Chancellor's Roll states that the cost of Wallace's execution and transmitting the quarters to Scotland was 61s. 10d.

In a minor way similar modes of execution were put into force in England as a warning to others. In 1688 one Philip Standsfield, found guilty of treason for cursing his father and being concerned in his murder, was sentenced to be hanged at the Mercat Cross till he was dead, his tongue to be cut out and burnt upon a scaffold, his right hand to be cut off and affixed on the East Port of Haddington, and his body to be carried—not drawn—to the "Gallowee between Leith and Edinburgh," and there to be hanged in chains, and his name, fame, memory and honours to be extinct, and his arms to be riven forth and delete out of the book of arms." This punishment, partly special to parricide, was carried out in all its rigorousness.

The number of offences punishable by death steadily increased. Of the appalling total of 160 capital offences referred to by Blackstone, four-fifths were made so during the reigns of the first three Georges, and the number rose to 222 before reforms began. Among the offences which involved sentence of death may be mentioned stealing in a dwelling house to the amount of 40 shillings (Act of 1713); stealing privately from a shop goods of the value of five shillings (Act of 1698); counterfeiting the stamps used for the sale of perfumery and for hair powder; robbing a rabbit warren; cutting down a tree (the " Black Act," 1723); personating a Greenwich pensioner; or harbouring an offender against the Revenue Acts. At the beginning of the nineteenth century there were more than 200 offences in the State book for which capital punishment might be inflicted. Property, even more than person, was under the guardianship of the gallows.

But the law was more severe in theory than in practice, thanks to the reluctance of juries more than the clemency of judges, and during the preceding three-quarters of a century there were only twenty-five offences for which anyone actually suffered death. In 1823 five statutes, exempting from the death penalty about a hundred felonies, were passed into law.

"About the year 1818," says George Cruikshank, "I was returning home between 8 and 9 a.m. down Ludgate Hill, and saw several human beings hanging opposite Newgate, and to my horror two of them were women. On inquiring, I was informed that it was for passing forged one pound notes! It had a great effect on me, and I determined, if possible, to put a stop to this shocking destruction of life for merely obtaining a few shillings by fraud. I felt sure that in many cases the rascals who had forged the notes induced these poor, ignorant women to go into the gin shops and get 'something to drink,' and then *pass* the notes and hand them the change."

He at once made a powerful sketch of a " Bank-note not to be Imitated," which Hone published, and it caused such a sensation that the Bank Directors issued no more one pound notes. Soon after, Peel revised the penal code, and death for minor offences was abolished. In 1820 no fewer than forty-six persons were hanged for forging Bank of England notes, some of which were afterwards found to be good. It was not until 1832 that the punishment of death for forgery was abolished.

The abolition between 1820 and 1860 of over 190 capital offences had its precedent in the greater sweep made in Rome by the passing of the Lex Porcia. Not merely were capital offences then reduced from about two hundred to four, but practically the whole penalty was abolished for Roman citizens. No such citizen—unless, having been banished, he returned in battle against his fatherland—could be put to death.

Though there were many offences carrying capital punishment, and though many were sentenced to death, the actual number of executions in the latter part of the eighteenth and the first half of the nineteenth century was small compared with the death sentences. Thus, from May, 1827, to May, 1830, four hundred and fifty-one persons were condemned to death and only fifty-five executed.

Dymond records that in 1829 twenty-four persons were hanged in London, not one of whom had committed murder. From 1832 to 1837 a large number of capital offences were swept away. In 1840, for the first time in the history of Parliament, a resolution for the abolition of capital punishment was brought in, and over ninety members voted in favour of this resolution.

Arson was long punishable by death, even when no lives were lost. On August 12th, 1851, at Gloucester Assizes, a man named Jordan was found guilty and sentenced to death for setting fire to his mother's house " with intent to do her grievous harm." On July 26th, 1861, at the Maidstone Assizes, Henry Sherry was condemned to death for wilfully setting fire to his father's house and barn. An Act of Parliament, passed later in the same year, abolished capital punishment for this offence if no lives had been lost. But the offence was still capital when loss of life occurred, and in May, 1881, William Nash was sentenced to death for setting fire to his own house at Notting Hill, London, and causing the loss of six lives. Setting fire to any of his Majesty's ships is still a felony punishable by death.

But horrible, degrading and inhuman as were the punishments in England and Scotland during the general period under review, those in other countries were worse, for torture was added to many as a matter of course, and the death penalty was inflicted for even more trivial offences than in England.

Quartering alive, tearing to pieces by horses, and disembowelling were common punishments on the Continent. In Germany military punishments included hunting and spearing to death of the condemned by his fellow soldiers; making him run the gauntlet of rods until dead, flogging to death with the knout, etc. The last two forms of execution were practised in Russia until late into the nineteenth century. The last instance of burning at the stake in Germany occurred in Berlin on August 18th, 1786. In the same year the last example of breaking on the wheel was carried out in Vienna.

During a long period in France the capital sentence was accompanied by torturing. Death was inflicted, not only for murder or conspiracy against the State, but for fraudulent bankruptcy, forgery, smuggling, false marks on jewellery, theft, duelling and many other offences. In 1127 Louis the Bulky ordered Bertholde, the murderer of Charles the Righteous, to be crucified, and the punishment was inflicted to some extent on Jews and heretics. Decapitation by the sword was notoriously common in the time of Richelieu. The stake was used in France as late as the seventeenth century, and the year 1757 witnessed the last sentence in that country of quartering. That year Damiens, who attempted the life of Louis XV, was literally pulled in four pieces by horses. Breaking on the wheel was not abolished for another thirty-two years, and this terrible punishment was more frequently used in France than in most countries.

In France sorcerers and witches were put to death by drowning, and Philippe Auguste inflicted this punishment on persons who swore. Drowning was the penalty for sedition under Charles VI and this form of capital punishment did not disappear until the end of Louis XI's reign. The sentence was often carried out by fastening the criminal in a sack of leather, before hurling him into the water.

Flaying alive flourished at one time in the same country, and it is recorded that in 1366 the Count de Rouci was flayed alive for betraying Laon to the English. Boiling in oil or water were other methods of putting criminals and others to death. These were specially inflicted on those who passed false coin, and this form of execution was not legally abolished until 1791.

A Swedish ordinance of May 1, 1563, says:

"We decree that henceforth the following crimes shall not be punished by fine or imprisonment, to wit, blasphemy, treason, assassination, open adultery, incest, rape, sodomy and other similar crimes, for as much as Almighty God has Himself decreed, and nature and reason agree that those who commit such crimes should not escape death. Further, too, divers scourges such as plague and famine come to punish men for their sins to such an extent that it often happens that a whole country is devastated and suffers for the crime of one man. It is therefore necessary, in order to avoid the anger of God, that such Malefactors should not be spared."

In 1681, by another Swedish ordinance, it was enacted that women suspected of murdering their illegitimate children should be condemned to death on simple presumptive evidence.

". . . because this crime, which is becoming frequent, ought to be as severely punished as possible in order that the anger of God be averted."

In the definite case of child murder, the mother of an illegitimate child used to be punished inflexibly with death, as being "the only method of putting an end to so horrible a crime, and as being the only way of securing the safety of child life."

By the Swedish Code of 1734, capital punishment was inflicted for sixty-eight crimes, and the methods of its infliction were: (1) Decapitation (for blasphemy, murder, sorcery, treason, adultery, conspiracy, bigamy, arson, abortion, etc.; (2) Decapitation, followed by exposure or or burning of the body (for sorcery resulting in the death of the person spelled, sodomy, murder of a superior, poisoning, etc.). (3) Amputation of hand, followed by decapitation (for some sorts of treason, arson in a State building, infanticide, murdering of a master by a servant, brigandage, etc.).

There are now only five crimes—other than offences against military or Air Force law or naval discipline—which are punishable in England with death, viz.: high treason, murder, piracy with violence; destruction of public arsenals and dockyards, and setting fire to a ship in the Port of London. In the last two the sentence is only recorded. In Scotland the death penalty can be imposed only for treason, murder and offences against 10 Geo. IV c. 38, i.e., wilful shooting, stabbing, strangling or throwing corrosives with intent to murder or to do grievous bodily harm, in all cases where if death had ensued the offence would have been murder. Before 1887, rape, robbery, wilful fire raising, incest and many other crimes were also capital offences. In Ireland in the Free State, capital punishment is on similar lines to that in England.

In 1931, in the Irish Free State an emergency Act was passed under which a military tribunal of five was appointed and had the power of passing sentence of death from which there was no appeal, to deal with the widespread attempts to overthrow the Government.

It was not until 1908 that Acts relating to children were put on a sound basis and consolidated. Under the Act of this year a child is defined as being a person under the age of fourteen. A child under the age of seven is considered incapable of committing any crime, and between the ages of seven and fourteen he or she is considered *doli capax*, on proof that he or she had *mens rea*, i.e., a guilty knowledge that he or she was doing wrong. Above the age of fourteen years a person is fully responsible, unless proved to be of unsound mind or subject to some disability, e.g., coercion. Under the Act the death sentence is abolished for all persons under the age of sixteen.[1]

Cases are on record of children of ten and even eight years old having been hanged. When, in the year 1890, Richard Davies was hanged for the murder of his father at Crewe, there was a great outcry at the barbarity of inflicting the extreme penalty of the law on one so young, for he was but nineteen. In the early part of the nineteenth century, however, age mattered little where the death penalty was concerned, and the legal infant, who was held to be utterly incapable of knowing what he was doing when he signed his name to a receipt, or gave an order for goods, was considered perfectly equal to understanding the heinousness of every offence against the law of the land. Elizabeth Marsh, who was executed in 1794, at Dorchester, for the murder of her grandfather, was only fifteen.

As late as 1831 a boy of nine years was publicly hanged at Chelmsford for having set fire to a house at Witham. In the days of George II it was no uncommon thing for children under the age of ten years to be hanged, and on one occasion ten of them were strung up together, as a warning to men and a spectacle for the angels. In 1833 the death sentence was passed on a boy of nine for housebreaking, but at the earnest solicitation of the people of Maidstone the sentence was not carried out. In 1808 Michael Hamond and his sister aged seven and eleven respectively, were hanged at Lynn for felony.

In the British Dominions and possessions, under the Indian Penal Code, sentence of death may be passed for waging war against the King, and for murder. The sentence of death for murder is alternative, unless the accused is already under sentence of transportation for life, when it must be imposed. The Code is substantially in force in India, Ceylon, Straits Settlements, Hong Kong and the Sudan.

Wilful murder, high treason and piracy with violence are punishable by death in most other British Dominions. In New South Wales and Victoria capital punishment may also

[1] As this book goes to press a Bill to raise these ages is before Parliament.

BANK OF ENGLAND NOTE
(*Not to be imitated*)

George Cruikshank, the famous artist, was so horrified at seeing a number of persons being hanged for passing forged one pound Bank of England notes, that he drew this note, and its powerful appeal resulted in the Bank of England withdrawing them.

[*Face page* 18

BURNING OF CATHERINE HAYES
(*From an old print*)

Catherine Hayes was convicted of the murder of her husband and was burnt
alive at Tyburn in 1726. The executioner let go of the rope used for strangling
before burning so that Catherine Hayes was literally burnt alive.

Face page 19]

be inflicted for rape and criminal abuse of girls under ten years of age. Under the Canadian Criminal Code death may also be meted out upon any subjects of a friendly power who levy war on the King in Canada. Canadian judges are bound by statute to report on all death sentences, and the date of execution is so fixed that ample time is allowed for the consideration of this report.

The criminal law of South Africa is based on the Roman Dutch law under which capital punishment is liable for treason, murder and rape. Though hanging is the method of inflicting the death penalty in Cape Colony, it is worthy of mention that the Roman Dutch modes of executing the sentence, by decapitation of breaking on the wheel, have not been formally abolished.

In the United States each State has jurisdiction over its own territory as regards capital punishment, and in consequence the laws vary considerably. Capital punishment may be inflicted for treason, arson, rape, piracy, robbery of the mails with jeopardy to the lives of persons in charge, rescue of a convict going to execution, burning a vessel of war and corruptly destroying a private vessel. In Arizona, Michigan, Minnesota, North Dakota, Rhode Island, Iowa, Maine, Tennessee, Wisconsin and Kansas, capital punishment has been abolished. In Iowa the death penalty was abolished in 1872 and restored in 1876.

Under the Federal laws sentence of death may be passed for treason against the United States and for piracy and for murder within the Federal jurisdiction.

In 1789 one hundred and fifteen crimes were capital in France. Under the penal code of 1810, amended in 1832 and in 1871, thirty offences remained punishable by death. It may still be inflicted for wounding a public official with intent to murder, assassination, parricide, poisoning and killing to commit a crime or escape from justice. French juries exercise freely the power of acquitting in capital cases, or by finding extenuating circumstances which do not allow the court to inflict the death penalty.

Capital punishment has been abolished in many countries. No comment is offered here upon the effect of such abolition.

It may be remarked, however, that the generally published statistics of the number of murders which have taken place immediately before the abolition of the death penalty and during the years immediately following are misleading, in that they leave out the factor that the attitude of society steadily changes in what may be called its criminal outlook. Education, better environment, new methods of communication, the publicity of the newspapers, and the like, are all factors in the prevention of crimes of violence for which little or no allowance is made in such statistics by the partisans of either side.

In Holland the death penalty was abolished in 1870, and in Belgium, though the penalty is formally retained under the 1867 code, in the latter country for high treason, assassination and parricide by poisoning, it is never carried out and there has been no execution since 1863.

The Ordonnance of 1777 in Sweden, lightened punishments all round, and did away with the death penalty, excepting for a few cases. By the Ordonnance of 1864 an alternative is given in all cases. "Que le coupable perde la vie ou soit condamné anu travaux forcés à perpétuité." Capital punishment was finally abolished in Sweden on June 3rd, 1921.

In Finland, up to 1918, there had been no execution since 1826, though the death penalty existed for assassination, and for wilful murder. In 1918 a number of Communists were executed for treason, but the penalty has not been inflicted for murder.

In Italy the abolition or retention of capital punishment was long a burning question, and from that country has come the chief opposition to the penalty. In 1872 a congress of jurors at Rome unanimously demanded the abolition of capital punishment, and four years later the magistrates of Italy, by a large majority, seconded the demand. The Chamber of Deputies in 1877 passed a Bill for the purpose, with but one dissenting vote; but it failed in the Senate. One year later the new Ministry adopted the plan of systematically and uniformly commuting every death sentence to lifelong imprisonment; and since 1879 no judicial execution has taken place in Italy. After nearly ten years of this practice, the Government and Parliamentary Commission united in asking Parliament to enact a Code which should do away formally with the death penalty. The Penal Code of 1888 abolished capital punishment for all crimes, including regicide. Under Mussolini, in 1928-31, the death penalty has been restored for particularly atrocious crimes and high treason.

In Switzerland the death sentence was abolished in 1874, but in 1879 the separate cantons recovered the right to re-establish it in their respective territories. Seven cantons voted for capital punishment and the remaining fifteen have abolished it.

In what was formally Austria-Hungary capital punishment was for a time abolished in 1787, but was enforced in 1795 for high treason, and in 1803 for other crimes. Under the Penal Code of 1906 it might be inflicted for high treason, murder, killing by robbers, public violence, incendiarism and criminal use of explosives. Capital punishment was abolished in Austria in 1919.

Denmark still retains the power the inflict the death penalty for most forms of high treason, aggravated cases of murder, rape and piracy.

The Norwegian Code of 1905 abolished capital punishment, which had been in force for the crimes of murder with premeditation and certain other crimes.

Portugal abolished the supreme penalty in 1867, and Rumania three years earlier. Under the Spanish Code of 1870, inducing a foreign power to declare war against Spain, killing the sovereign, parricide and assassination are capital crimes. In 1931 the whole Code was revised under the Republic.

Under the Imperial Criminal Code of 1872 and the laws of 1885 and 1895, the death penalty was inflicted in Germany for attempts on the life of the emperor, or the sovereign of any federal State in which the offender happened to be, for deliberate homicide (as opposed to intentional homicide without deliberation) and for certain treasonable acts committed when a state of siege has been proclaimed.

Under the law of July 21st, 1922, the death penalty may also be inflicted for certain acts against the Republic or the Government.

Hanging is by far the most common mode of infliction of the death penalty. It obtains in England, Scotland and Ireland, most of the States of America, Canada, the British Dominions and many European and Asiatic countries, including Japan.

Both hanging and decapitation are employed in Germany. Prussia still retains the old-fashioned headsman with his axe and block, and the axe is still the official mode of inflicting the death penalty in Denmark, though the actual penalty has not been enforced for many years in that country.

France makes use of the guillotine, and this instrument is also in use (nominally) in Belgium and in certain parts of Germany. Decapitation is also the usual Chinese method of capital punishment, but the instrument used is the sword.

The method employed in Spain is execution in public by the garrote, though it is now rarely imposed, but was replaced by hanging in the Spanish possessions taken over by the United States following the Spanish-American war.

In the United States, electrocution, the passing through the body of a current of electricity, is used as well as hanging.

Sentence of death in Russia is carried out by shooting, beheading or hanging, the first method being the most commonly used under the Soviet regime.

The scaffold did not always see the end of the punishment. The body of the malefactor was often exhibited as a warning to those left behind, and this aspect of capital punishment is dealt with in Chapter III.

By 25 Geo. II, any person convicted of murder was to be executed on the next day but one after sentence, but if sentenced on a Friday he was to be hanged on the following Monday. His body, after death, was to be either dissected or hanged in chains. By laws passed in 1832–4 the bodies of murderers were no longer to be anatomized or hung in chains, but to be buried in the precincts of the prison in which they were last confined before execution. This regulation, repeated in 24 and 25 Vict., is now in force.

In Scotland, not fewer than fifteen days or more than twenty-one days after judgment, if south of the Forth, and not fewer than twenty or more than twenty-seven days if north of the Forth, are the periods of time fixed by statute for the sentence to be carried out.

The regulation decreeing that the criminal sentenced on a Friday should not be hanged until the following Monday, was made to avoid executions on Sundays. That day has always been a *dies non* for capital punishment throughout the United Kingdom and Europe, with few exceptions. In the time of King Henry VIII, however, we read, according to Stow: "The first of September (1538) being a Sonday, one Cratwell, Hangman of London and two other, were hanged at the wrestling place by Clerkenwell, for robbing a booth in Bartholomew faire."

After the death of Henry VIII Sunday executions were abolished in England. In Catholic Europe they never obtained in civilised times, save during the French Revolution, when everything sacred was ridiculed and profaned, and people went to the guillotine just the same as on other days of the week.

When the jury bring in a verdict of "Guilty" in a trial for murder, the judge, if he thinks fit to do so because of any objection raised by the accused against his conviction, may respite judgment pending the determination of a point of law, and leave it to another judge to pass sentence in the event of the point being determined against the prisoner.

The words in which the death sentence is now pronounced are as follows, having been settled in the year 1903 after consultation among the judges:

"The sentence of the Court upon you is that you be taken from this place to a lawful prison and thence to the place of execution, and that you be there hanged by the neck until you be dead; and that your body be afterwards buried within the precincts of the prison in which you shall have been confined before your execution. And may the Lord have mercy on your soul."

The execution must take place within the prison walls and the body of the executed felon must be buried within the walls of the prison; but if the visiting justices of a prison consider there is not sufficient space within the prison, application may be made to one of H.M. Principal Secretaries, who may in writing appoint some other fit place.

The execution is usually not carried out until after the third Sunday from the passing of the sentence, and then generally at the hour of 8 a.m., and not on Sundays or Mondays.

In England when a woman was sentenced to death it was the duty of the Clerk of the Court to ask the woman whether she had anything to say in stay of execution of the sentence. If she then said that she was pregnant or if the Court later had reason to suppose that she was, a jury of twelve matrons was empanelled and sworn to determine whether she was pregnant. The jury of matrons, if they desired it, could have the assistance of a medical man. If the jury found that the woman was with child the Court stayed the execution until she was delivered of the child, and then she might or might not be executed. In 1931 a law was passed abolishing the sentence of death on any pregnant woman found guilty of murder. Under the old law there were a number of instances of women being hanged after they had given birth to a child in the condemned cell.

It is sometimes supposed that the King himself signs the order for the execution of a condemned criminal. This is not so. Till the close of the reign of George IV, the Recorder of London presented himself before the Privy Council, the monarch presiding, with a list of all those doomed to die. Whatever could be said in favour of the culprits was said, and orders for the execution of the worst of them were prepared by the Home Secretary, who forwarded them to the Recorder for signature. The Recorder of London informed the officers of Newgate of the decisions of Council, and it was the duty of the ordinary (chaplain) to tell each convict under sentence of death what the Council had decided for him. Generally the Recorder's report reached the prison late at night.

In a footnote to the trial of Corder for the murder of Maria Marten in 1828 it is stated:

"As the law formally stood, in regard to the execution of criminals, the usage was for the Judge to sign the printed calendar or list, containing the names of all the prisoners, with their separate judgments in the margin, which, having done, he signed his own name, and left it with the Sheriff. In cases of a capital felony, where the extreme sentence of the law was to be enforced, the Judge wrote opposite the prisoner's name—'Let him be hanged by the neck'—which was the only warrant the Sheriff had.

"In all cases (murder excepted) the Sheriff is ordered to do execution within a convenient time; but in *London* more exactness is used, both as to the warrant and the time of executing it.

"The statute 25 Geo. II, c. 37 is, however, unrepealed, and is observed throughout the kingdom; it enacts, 'That in case of *murder*, the Judge shall, in his sentence, direct execution to be performed on the next day but one after sentence is passed.

"When a Sunday intervenes, as in Corder's case, it is deemed '*dies non*'—no day."

It is interesting to give the actual warrant for the execution of Corder, as, in point of form, it differs materially from those issued before the revision of the Criminal Law.

Suffolk
to wit.   Friday, August 8th, 1828.

"William Corder, this day attainted of the wilful murder of Maria Marten.

"Let him be hanged by the neck until he be dead, on Monday next, the eleventh day of August, instant; and let his body be delivered to the Surgeons of the hospital of Bury St. Edmund's, to be dissected and anatomized pursuent to the Statute.

               "(Signed) W. ALEXANDER,
                "Harry Edgell, Clerk of the Assize.
"To Hart Logan, Esquire,
   and whom it may concern."

The following is the enactment of the statute 9 Geo. IV, c. 31, which deals with the dissection and anatomization of a murderer:

"And be it enacted,—That whenever dissection shall be ordered by such sentence, the body of the murderer, if executed in the county of Middlesex and city of London, shall be immediately conveyed by the sheriff or sheriffs, or his or their officers, to the Hall of the Surgeons' Company, or to such other place as the said Company shall appoint, or shall be delivered to such person as the said Company shall appoint, for the purpose of being dissected; and the body of the murderer, if executed elsewhere, shall, in like manner, be delivered to such surgeon as the Court or Judge shall direct, for the same purpose."

Under the Act of 1868 executions in public were abolished. The last man to be executed in public was Michael Barrett in 1868.

It was asserted, when Sir Roger Casement was sentenced to death in 1917 for treason, that he must be executed in public, as the Act abolishing public executions did not apply to treason. In any case, however, the Act of 1887 authorised Sheriffs to execute any death sentence in a prison under their jurisdiction.

An authority to hang a man is now given to the executioner by the Sheriff, who is responsible for seeing the hanging carried out. This authority is usually in the form:

"I, John Smith, of . . . . ., in the county of . . . ., sheriff of the said county of . . . . . do hereby authorise you to hang Tom Robinson, who now lies under sentence of death in His Majesty's prison at . . . . ."

It is dated and addressed to the executioner.

A postmortem examination is not now permitted on the executed criminal, the doctor in attendance judging the cause of death for the inquest from external appearances only.

Under the 1868 Act the Sheriff is responsible for an execution, and following it a coroner's inquest is held. A certificate has to be exhibited for twenty-four hours at least near the entrance to the prison where the execution has taken place. The Secretary of State is empowered to make rules to be observed at an execution. In August, 1868, the following rules were made:

(1) For the sake of uniformity it is recommended that executions should take place at the hour of 8 a.m. on the first Monday after the intervention of three Sundays from the day on which sentence is passed.

(2) The mode of execution, and the ceremonial attending it, to be the same as heretofore in use.

(3) A black flag to be hoisted at the moment of execution, upon a staff placed on an elevated and conspicuous part of the prison, and to remain displayed for one hour.

(4) The bell of the prison, or if arrangements can be made for that purpose, the bell of the parish or other neighbouring church, to be tolled for fifteen minutes before and fifteen minutes after the execution.

These rules have been modified considerably, notably the abolition of the tolling of the bell and the hoisting of the black flag.

CHAPTER II

IT is a remarkable commentary on human psychology that it should have been thought throughout the ages to be more honourable to have one's head cut off than to have one's neck broken. The axe and the sword were the instruments of capital punishment from the earliest times, and we find Xenophon, at the end of the second book of the Anabasis, stating that beheading was the most honourable form of death. The sword, too, was considered to be a less degrading instrument than the axe.

The Romans, like the Greeks, considered beheading honourable. An offender was tied to a stake previous to decapitation and whipped with rods. The actual decapitation was carried out with the axe or the sword, and the condemned placed his head upon a block placed in a pit dug for the purpose. Caligula, according to Suetonius, employed a soldier, who had a reputation for his skill as a headsman, specially to decapitate prisoners chosen at random from the gaols. The Roman magistrates were preceded by their lictors, carrying axes and rods, and decapitation was meted out to patrician and serf alike.

William the Conqueror is generally credited with having introduced beheading into England, and the first person to suffer was Waltheof, Earl of Northumberland, in 1076. The sergeants or bailiffs of the Earl of Chester had the power to behead any criminal, and this power was also granted to the Barony of Malpas. Beheading, indeed, is referred to in a roll of 3 Edward II as the "custom of Cheshire," and later the liberty of Hardwick, in Yorkshire, was given the privilege of beheading thieves.

Beheading was not usually resorted to in the case of common felons. The sword and the axe were reserved for offenders of high rank. "From the Fifteenth century onwards," says the *Encyclopedia Britannica* "the victims of the axe include some of the highest personages in the kingdom: Archbishop Scrope (1405); Duke of Buckingham (1483); Catherine Howard (1542); Earl of Surrey (1547); Duke of Somerset (1552); Duke of Northumberland (1553); Lady Jane Grey (1554); Lord Guildford Dudley (1554); Mary, Queen of Scots (1587); Earl of Essex (1601); Sir Walter Raleigh (1618); Earl of Stratford (1641); Charles I (1649); Lord William Russell (1683); Earl of Kenmur (1716); Earl of Kilmarnock and Lord Balmerino (1746); were all beheaded and the list closes with Simon, Lord Lovat, who (9th of April, 1747) was the last person beheaded in England. The execution of Anne Boleyn was carried out not with the axe but with the sword, and by a French headsman specially brought over from Calais. In 1644 Archbishop Laud was condemned to be hanged, and the only favour granted to him, and that reluctantly, was that his sentence should be changed to beheading. In the case of the fourth Earl Ferrers (1760) his petition was refused and he was hanged."

The common method of execution in Holland in the eighteenth and early nineteenth centuries used to be my means of a broadsword for unpremeditated murder. In Denmark it was considered more honourable to be beheaded by the sword than the axe. In Sweden the general mode of execution was by the axe. When women were beheaded the scaffold was set on fire at the four corners and the body cremated.

In London the place for executions was usually on Tower Hill, where there was a permanent scaffold during the fifteenth and sixteenth centuries. Some more than usually distinguished prisoners were executed on the green by St. Peter's Chapel within the Tower. Among those who suffered there were the unhappy Lady Jane Grey and the unfortunate Anne Boleyn. Charles I was beheaded before Whitehall. Traitors of the meaner sort were merely hanged and mutilated on the top of the acclivity called Hay Hill, Berkeley Square.

Stephen Perlin, a French physician, who was in Great Britain in the last two years of King Edward VI, in his Description of the Kingdoms of England and Scotland, published in Paris in 1558, was present at the execution of the Duke of Northumberland, and remarked on it.

"A lamentable thing to see a man beneath whom a whole kingdom trembled, to see him in the hands of the executioner. And the executioner was lame and he had a white apron like a butcher. This great lord made great lamentation and regrets at his death, weeping passionately, and after the execution you ought to have seen little children taking up the blood that had fallen through the chinks of the scaffold on which he had been decapitated. In this country they place the head on a pole of wood."

A little later the French physician adds: "In this country you will not meet with any great nobles whose relations have not had their heads cut off. Certes I should like better (with the reader's leave) to be a swineherd and preserve my head. For you will see these great lords in grand pomp and magnificence for a time; turn your head and you will see them in the hands of the executioner."

Beheading was part of the common law method of punishing traitors, and was usually accompanied by disembowelling. The Cato Street conspirators were hanged and afterwards beheaded. It was not until 1814 that the terrible words of the earlier Acts were done away with, and disembowelling and burning the bowels in front of the unhappy writhing wretch abolished. By the 1814 Act, too, hanging was substituted as the mode of death for traitors, though the king still had power under the Act to order beheading.

Nearly sixty years passed before the drawing and quartering part of a traitor's punishment was abolished by the Forfeiture Act of 1870. As in all ages, those who had influence were able to confine their punishment to beheading only, and only the unfortunate hirelings and the like suffered the full penalty of disembowelment.

In later years traitors were hanged first and decapitated afterwards. The method of decapitation was by means of an axe or a knife. In the case of the Cato Street Conspirators, for example, the head of each man was taken off with a knife, but in the case of Brandreth and his fellow conspirators an axe was used. In all cases a special block was used to facilitate the decapitation. In the report of the execution of Brandreth and his companions, published at the time at Nottingham, it is stated, "the two axes used were brought upon the scaffold, the bright shining heads of which formed a striking contrast to the black shafts fixed in them. The axes were as near as possible of the shape worn by pioneers; they were made by Mr. Bainford, of Derby, for the occasion. The axe heads measured at the foot eight inches and a half, and were about a foot long. The block was a long piece of timber, supported at each end by pieces of a foot high, and having a small cog of wood fixed across the upper end of it, on which the neck of the body was to be placed, for the purpose of decollation."

The sword was as frequently used as the axe, and usually without a block. The Calais executioner who decapitated Anne Boleyn used a long, heavy two-handed sword, such as was used for some centuries in many German towns for beheading. No block was used, the unhappy queen kneeling.

Both low blocks and high blocks were used for beheading with the axe. In the case of the low block a person would have to lie full length, and C. H. Frith and S. R. Gardiner state that they believe such a low block was used at the execution of Charles I. But the high block before which the headsman's victim knelt, was more usual, and such a block is to be seen in the armoury of the Tower of London. It is known that it was on this block that the last beheading, that of Lord Lovat, took place.

Many of the axes formerly used for beheading in Great Britain are still to be seen. In the Tower of London, beside the block on which Lord Lovat and other Jacobite lords suffered, stands the axe which was used at their execution. The headsman's axe, made in 1820, for the execution of Arthur Thistlewood and other Cato Street conspirators, can now be seen at the London Museum. Actually the conspirators were put to death by hanging, but were publicly decapitated after death.

On the ground floor of the King's House, at the Tower, is preserved the processional axe which figured in the journeys of State prisoners to and from their trials, the edge turned from them as they went, but almost always turned towards them as they returned to the Tower. The axe's head is peculiar in form, one foot eight inches high by ten inches wide, and is fastened into a wooden handle five feet four inches in length. The handle is ornamented by four rows of burnished brass nails.

The scaffold is the last place where one would expect to find any rules of etiquette. Yet there were many and those rigorously kept. Thus in cases where two or more peers have been beheaded, they were always brought to the block in order of precedence. Lord Capel, who tried to address the crowd with his hat on, was sharply reprimanded by the executioner; while in the case of Lords Balmerino and Kilmarnock, beheaded together in 1746, the latter offered his friend first place at the block, but etiquette would not allow Lord Balmerino to take advantage of his kindness.

Reference has just been made to the direction of the blade of the axe. In Lord Birkenhead's *Famous Trials of History*, in the trial of Lord Mohun by his Peers in 1693 for the murder of Will Mountford, an actor at Drury Lane Theatre, there occurs the following passage, " Lord Mohun came to the Bar of the Court accompanied by the Gentlemen Gaoler who bore the axe with its edge turned away from the prisoner. If the accused were convicted then its edge would be turned towards him."

The heads of traitors and others were often displayed for all to see, and to serve as a warning. London Bridge and Temple Bar and Aldgate were adorned with such heads, in London, and most large towns had the heads of traitors displayed at one time or another.

Fisher, Bishop of Rochester, was executed on St. Albans Day, the 22nd of June, 1535. It is recorded, " The next day after his burying, the head, being parboyled, was pricked upon a pole, and set on high upon London Bridge, among the rest of the holy Carthusians' heads that suffered death lately before him. And here I cannot omit to declare unto you the miraculous sight of this head, which, after it had stood up the space of fourteen dayes upon the bridge, could not be perceived to wast nor consume; neither for the weather which was then very hot, neither for the parboyling in hot water, but grew daily fresher and fresher, so that in his life-time he never looked so well; for his cheeks being beautified with a comely red, the face looked as though it had beholden the people passing by, and would have spoken to them; which many took for a miracle that Almighty God was pleased to shew above the course of nature in thus preserving the flesh and lively colour in his face, surpassing the colour he had being alive, whereby was noted to the world the innocence and holiness of this blessed father that thus innocently was content to lose his head in defence of his Mother the Holy Catholique Church of Christ. Wherefore the people coming daily to see this strange sight, the passage over the bridge was so stopped with their going and coming, that almost neither cart nor horse could passe; and therefore at the end of fourteen daies the executioner was commanded to throw down the head, in the night time, into the River of Thomes; and in the place thereof was set the head of the most blessed and constant martyr Sir Thomas More, his companion and fellow in all his troubles, who suffered his passion, on Tuesday the 6th of July next following, about nine o'clock in the morning."

The head of More, says his great-grandson, in his life printed in 1726, "Was putt upon London Bridge, where as traitor's heads are sett upon poles; and hauing remained some moneths there, being to be cast into the Thomes, because roome should be made for diverse others, who in plentiful sorte suffered martyrdome for the same supremacie; shortly after it was bought by his daughter Margarett, lest—as she stoutly affirmed before the councell, being called before them for the same matter,—it should be foode for fishes; which she buried where she thought fittest." The Chancellor's pious daughter is said to have preserved this relic in a leaden case, and to have ordered its interment with her own body, in the Roper vault, under a chapel adjoining St. Dunstan's, Canterbury, where the head, it is stated, was seen in the year 1715, and again subsequently.

After the remains of traitors ceased to be placed on London Bridge, when the right to dispose of the quartered remains of the subject devolved on the Crown, that right, as regards those who had suffered for high treason in London, was, with few exceptions, wholly or partially exercised in favour of Temple Bar. Thus the City Bar became the City Golgotha. The first person so exposed was Sir Thomas Armstrong, the last victim of the Rye House Plot. He was executed at Tyburn; his head was set up on Westminster Hall, and one of the quarters upon Temple Bar. Sir John Friend and Sir William Perkins, conspirators in the plot to carry off the king in 1695, on his return from Richmond to Kensington, were the next ornaments of the Bar; the head and limbs of Friend, and the headless trunk of Perkins, being placed upon its iron spikes. Evelyn refers to this melancholy scene " as a dismal sight, which many pitied. I think there never was such a Temple Bar till now, except once in the time of King Charles Second—viz., Sir Thomas Armstrong." The head of Sir John Friend was set up on Aldgate; on account, it is presumed, of that gate being in the proximity of his brewery.

The next head placed on its summit was that of Colonel Henry Oxburg, who suffered for his attachment to the cause of the Pretender. Next was the head of Christopher Layer, another of the Pretender's adherents, whose head frowned from the crown of the arch for a longer period than any other occupant. On the 17th of May, 1723, nearly seven months after his trial, he was conducted from the Tower to Tyburn and executed. " The day subsequent to his execution, his head was placed on Temple Bar; there it remained, blackened and weather-beaten with the storms of many successive years, until, as we have remarked, it became its oldest occupant. Infancy had advanced into matured manhood, and still that head regularly looked down from the summit of the arch. It seemed part of the arch itself."

THE RECORDER MAKING HIS REPORT
(*From an old print*)

The names of all those in London who were sentenced to death were sub-
mitted to the King in Council by the Recorder of London. The Recorder's
Report, giving a list of those reprieved and those not, usually reached
Newgate late at night.

[*Face page* 34.

AN EXECUTION IN RATISBON IN 1782
(*From an old German print*)

The heads of the victims of the fatal Rebellion of '45 were the last placed upon the Bar; those being Townly and Fletcher. Walpole writes to Montague, August 16th, 1746: " I have been this morning at the Tower, and passed under the new heads at Temple Bar, where people make a trade of letting spying-glasses at a half-penny a look." There is a scarce print in which the position of the heads is shown, and portraits cleverly engraved. For several weeks people flocked to this revolting exhibition, which yielded to some a savage pleasure.

Captain James Hind, a famous highwayman, who took a delight in robbing Roundheads, was executed September 24th, 1652. He was drawn, hanged and quartered. His head was set upon the Bridge Gate over the River Severn at Worcester. His quarters were put on other gates until they were destroyed by the weather. And there are many other similar records.

In Scotland the Maiden, described later, was used for beheading. The Maiden was an early form of guillotine as now used in France.

In Germany the instrument varies in different States, in the old provinces of Prussia the axe, in Saxony and Rhenish Prussia, the guillotine. Until 1851 executions were in public, but they now take place within the prison in the presence of certain specified officials.

Beheading was also the mode of capital punishment in Denmark and Sweden. The axe was used. In Sweden the execution took place on the order of the king within a prison in the presence of certain officials and, if desired, of twelve representatives of the Commune within which the prison was situate (Code 1864, Royal Ordinance, 1877). Capital punishment was abolished in Sweden in 1921.

In the Chinese empire decapitation was the usual mode of execution. An imperial edict (1905) suppressed certain barbarities as slicing and exhibiting the head of the criminal.

The disadvantage of the axe and the sword is that its humanity depends upon the skill of the executioner, a skill only acquired by long practice. As a result there are many examples in history of frightfulness on the scaffold. De

Thou's head was only removed after eleven blows had been struck, and many strokes were required by the bungling executioner before Madame Tiquet died.

Beheading always has taken a variety of forms. In Germany, which country has always had a partiality to this form of execution the condemned used to kneel on the ground with bent head, while the executioner standing behind swung a great two handed sword. Occasionally the sufferer sat in a chair. It is credibly recorded that one executioner in 1501 killed two malefactors with one blow. He placed them back to back a little distance apart and standing between them, swept his sword round in a circle and decapitated one after the other.

Another method of execution once fairly common in Germany took the form of a kind of primitive guillotine, a sharpened board being applied to the victim's neck and driven through by the blows of a mallet.

In the *Daily News*, for October 31st, 1893, appeared the following:

"To-day for the first time for many years, a woman named Zillman was beheaded in Germany. The prisoner had murdered her husband by poisoning him, after he had brutally ill-treated her and her children. She was yesterday taken to Plotzensee, where the execution took place. This morning she was quite apathetic while being prepared for the execution. Her dress was cut out at the neck down to the shoulders, and her hair fastened up in a knot, her shoulders being then covered with a shawl. At eight the inspector of the prison entered Zillman's cell, and found her completely prostrate, and not capable of putting one foot before the other. Two warders raised her up, and led her to the block. Without a sound she removed the shawl from her shoulders, and three minutes after eight the executioner had done his work."

Doctor Hermann Westphal, at Flensburg, in Schleswig-Holstein, who witnessed the execution of Franz Deppe in Germany in 1901 thus described the gruesome event:

"When the condemned man had heard read the affirmation of the sentence, and declared that he had nothing to confess, Herr Reindell, the executioner, wearing a frock coat and a silk hat, made a slight signal. The State Attorney exclaimed, 'Do your duty,' and on the instant two assistants seized the condemned and laid him prostrate on the block table. As his body fell into position, with his head on the block intended for it, one of the assistants fastened his hands in the condemned man's hair, and stretched his neck out on the block, holding it steady.

"Herr Reindell whisked off the white cloth which covered the axe on the table, lifted the implement of death, and with one preparatory swing to give his muscles full play brought it down upon the bared neck just above the shoulders.

"The act was so quickly, so skilfully accomplished that the murderer's head was cut off at one stroke, and the assistant, who had released his hold upon it, had laid it beside the block, while the other witnesses and myself were still straining to meet the climax. With a back swing of his axe the executioner laid it on the table, and turning to the First State's Attorney, said,

"'Mr. First State's Attorney, the sentence has been carried out.'

"There had been no struggle, nothing sensational, exactly 27 seconds elapsed between the time the State Attorney said 'Do your duty' and the time when Deppe's head was laid on the block. Instead of a horrible spectacle, such as I once witnessed when a man was executed by hanging, the decapitation was speedy, painless, I believe, and absolutely clean. It was conducted with calmness and decorum. There was no spurting blood. Of course, blood flowed, but the witnesses could not see it.

"On a table were spread the legal papers in the case and a small cabinet which contained two candles and a crucifix. Near one end of the table was the head block, separated from the body block by about $1\frac{1}{2}$ inches, the space being filled by a zinc receptacle, intended to catch the blood from the decapitated trunk.

"While I stood, somewhat aghast at the rapidity of it all, the executioner rinsed his fingers in a bowl of steaming water, and dried them upon a white napkin handed him by one of the assistants, bowed politely to the officials, and withdrew. Herr Reindell, I was told, receives 200 marks, or about £10, for an execution."

As late as 1914 two murderesses, Pauline Zimmer and Marie Kubatzka, were beheaded at Ratibor, in Germany. The official uniform of the public executioner was the usual black frock coat and silk hat. The axe used had a heavy blade, about twelve inches in length. The block was a high block before which, on a black cushion, the condemned women knelt in turn. The top of the block was higher on the side nearer the cushion, to throw into prominence the necks of the condemned. In both cases the manacled women had to be held into position so that the masked executioner could perform his task.

No history of beheading would be complete without mention of the Halifax Gibbet and the Scottish Maiden.

"From Hell, Hull and Halifax, good Lord deliver us," is a popular Yorkshire saying, and the Halifax referred to was the Halifax gibbet. The origin of the gibbet is uncertain but the following quotation from Holinshed's Chronicle, published in 1587, shows that the gibbet must have then been long established:

"There is, and has been, of ancient time, a law or rather custom, at Halifax, that whosoever doth commit any felony, and is taken with the same, or confesses the fact upon examination, if it be valued by four constables to amount to the sum of thirteenpence halfpenny, he is forthwith beheaded upon one of the next market days, or else upon the same day that he is convicted, if market be holden. The engine wherewith the execution is done is a square block of wood, of the length of four feet and a half, which doth ride up and down in a slot, rabet or regall, of five yards in height. In the nether end of a sliding block is an axe, keyed or fastened with an iron into the wood, which being drawn up to the top of the frame, is there fastened by a wooden pin (with a notch made in the same, after the manner of Samson's post), into the middest of which pin also there is a long rope fastened, that cometh down among the people, so that when the offender hath made his confession, and hath laid his neck over the nethermost block, every man there present doth either take hold of the rope (or putteth forth his arm so near to the same as he can get, in token that he is willing to see justice executed), and pulling out the pin in this manner, the head block wherein the axe is fastened doth fall down with such a violence, that if the neck of the transgressor were so big as that of a bull, it should be cut asunder at a stroke, and roll from the body by a huge distance. If it be so that the offender be apprehended for an ox, sheep, kine, horse or any such cattle, the self beast or other of its kind shall have the end of the rope tied somewhere unto them, so that they being driven, do draw out the pin, whereby the offender is executed."

The parish register at Halifax contains a list of forty-nine persons who suffered by the gibbet. The first entry is March 20th, 1541, and the last April 30th, 1650. The stone scaffold or pedestal on which the gibbet was erected was discovered in 1840 while Gibbet Hill was being reduced to the level of the neighbouring ground, and the gibbet axe is now preserved in the Rolls Office of Halifax. It weighs seven pounds and three-quarters; its length is $10\frac{1}{2}$ inches, its breadth 7 inches at the top and 9 at the bottom.

The efficiency of the Halifax gibbet so impressed the Earl of Morton, when he witnessed an execution by it, that he gave directions for a smiliar gibbet to be erected at Edinburgh, in 1565. It became known as the Maiden, and it is often stated that Morton was the first to suffer by it in 1581, but the statement is untrue. It was actually used for the first time to execute some of the lesser lights concerned in the assassination of Rizzio. Some one hundred and twenty people suffered death at the hands of the Maiden, including Sir John Gordon of Haddo; President Spottiswood and the Marquis and Earl of Argyle. The Earl of Morton suffered death at the hands of the Maiden on June 2nd, 1581, and for a year his head was exhibited on a pinnacle on the Tollsworth.

Its use was discontinued in 1710, and it is now in the museum of the Society of Antiquaries of Scotland, at Edinburgh.

In the case of the Maiden, a loaded blade or axe, moving in grooves, was fixed in a frame about ten feet in height. The blade was raised to the full height of the frame and then released, severing the victim's head from his body.

CHAPTER III

HANGING: THE SCAFFOLD AND THE ROPE

FROM time immemorial hanging has been considered a more disgraceful form of death than beheading or shooting. One of the earliest forms of execution, it has survived throughout the ages, and has gradually become more and more scientific and expeditious, until now it is looked upon by many authorities as the most merciful form of execution.

The most primitive gallows is provided by nature—the branch of a tree. A rope is passed over, one end formed into a slip knot and put round the neck of the condemned, who is hauled into the air and left to die of slow strangulation. Such a crude method of hanging is still, to-day, practised in the wilder parts of the world where Judge Lynch holds his courts. In America the struggling victim is often put out of his misery, as he is being hauled up, by a timely revolver shot.

Mr. Ralph Noel, writing in *Pearson's Magazine* in 1906 stated: "In the last twenty-two years the average number of lynchings in the United States per annum has been no fewer than one hundred and fifty—a monstrous figure."

Many of these lynchings were undoubtedly due to the fact that the law was not enforced.

The usual mode of inflicting death upon criminals in Anglo-Saxon times was by hanging, and the illustration on page 62 is a representation of an Anglo-Saxon gallows (gala) taken from the illuminations to Alfric's version of Genesis.

In Merrie England the ladder and rope were the methods of public execution. The condemned man climbed a ladder placed against the gallows beam and there, while the reigning Jack Ketch adjusted the noose, he stood on a rung and addressed the crowd, or listened to the ministrations of the parson or the jeers of those who had come to watch him die. Sometimes Jack Ketch would place a white nightcap over the condemned man's head, but the custom was not an invariable one until the nineteenth century.

"Every town, every abbey, and almost every large manorial lord," says Thomas Wright, speaking of the Middle Ages, "had the right of hanging, and a gallows or tree, with a man hanging upon it, was so frequent an object in the country that it seems to have been considered as almost a natural object of a landscape, and it is thus introduced, by no means uncommonly, in mediaeval manuscripts."

The gallows itself might consist of a simple cross bar or a triangular affair, with or without a platform. But till comparatively late the fatal ladder was the medium of the unhappy wretch's last climb.

Lacroix, in his *Mœurs, Usages, et Costumes au Moyen Age*, describing hanging in France, says:

"The executioner, in his rayed and party-coloured habit of red and yellow, mounted the ladder, placed opposite a convenient space, backwards, holding in his hand two slack ends of three cords placed round the culprit's neck; two of these cords 'les tortuses,' had slip knots. The wretch under treatment was encouraged to follow 'le Maître des haultes œuvres,' driven up after him—no doubt with blows and execrations, according to the Gallic fashion—and drawn forward by him by means of the third cord, 'le jet.' Arrived at the proper height, the operator, the mediaeval 'Monsieur de Paris,' rapidly attached the 'tortuses' to the gallows, or chain pendant from it, and, twisting the 'jet' firmly round his arm, by means of this, and the action of his knee, threw the culprit off the ladder into mid-air; the knots of the 'tortuses' ran home, and the man was strangled. The executioner then gripped the crossbeam, and, placing his feet in the loop formed by the bound hands of the patient, by dint of repeated vigorous shocking terminated his sufferings."

The scaffold from which Mary Blandy was hanged in

1752 consisted simply of a beam placed across the branches of two trees, from which dangled the rope. A ladder, draped with black cloth, was placed against the beam. It is erroneously shown in some prints, published a few years afterwards, as a triangular scaffold with a ladder on which she is standing addressing those who witnessed her execution.

The earliest mention of the triangular gallows occurs in an account of the execution of Dr. Story, in 1571, in which it is said that he was drawn "from the Tower of London unto Tiborn, wher was prepared from him a newe payre of Gallowes made in triangular maner." And it was this form of gallows, "Tyburn's triple tree," which was in use at Tyburn until 1759. In this year it was taken away and on the 3rd of October an execution took place upon the new moving gallows which, after the bodies were cut down, was carried off in a cart, according to a contemporary newspaper account.

Time wrought great changes in the methods of hanging, modes that were good enough for the Middle Ages being considered barbarous by those who succeeded them. The first alteration that was made was the substitution of a cart for the ladder. By humanitarians of the seventeenth century it was thought that the introduction of hanging by the cart marked an epoch, and was calculated to lessen the sufferings of the condemned.

The gallows were erected some distance away from the gaol, in most cases, and the vehicle in which the doomed man had ridden to the scene of execution served as a platform from which "to turn him off." Prisoners of distinction, however, were occasionally permitted to ride to their death in their own carriages, and a common cart was in waiting beneath the beam.

The condemned, on arriving at the spot where he was to suffer, addressed the assembled people, lamenting the misdeeds which had been the cause of his ruin, and generally giving utterance to the pious sentiments which were thought necessary in those days. The hangman, who had ridden with the condemned from the prison to the gallows, then ascended the cart, and placed the noose round the poor wretch's throat. That done, he attached the free end of the rope to the beam above. Where the cart was used the gallows were made much lower than when the ladder was in fashion. After drawing a cap over the head and face of the condemned, the hangman then whipped the horse, and the cart moved away, leaving the malefactor suspended by his neck. At the most a fall of a few inches was allowed and death resulted from slow strangulation. Sometimes the hangman and his assistants pulled on the legs of the dangling wretch to hasten his release from his sufferings, but in the majority of cases he was permitted to hang until death supervened.

Frightful scenes were witnessed at executions in those days, the crowd standing awestruck as it watched the convulsions of the strangling culprit. Every contortion of the limbs was hailed with a cheer or a groan, according as the sufferer was popular or not; appalling curses and execrations occasionally rent the air and rendered the last moments of the unfortunate criminal more odious; hawkers boldly sang the praises of their wares the while a fellow creature was being done to death. Rich and poor, thief and lord, gentle and simple, attended to see " the hanging," and cracked jokes at the sufferer's expense. It was noted that criminals took longer to die in those days than when the ladder was used for turning them off, but it was many years before anyone realized that the jump from the ladder often broke the neck of the condemned and quickly put him out of his misery.

Experiments were first tried with the noose to lessen the long agony of strangulation, and the situation of the knot was changed from the back of the neck to the right or left side, until at last it was decreed that, whenever possible, it should be placed beneath the ear and pulled fairly tight before the cart was driven off. This was done at the suggestion of a medical man, who declared that if the rope pressed on the great blood vessels in the neck death might ensue from apoplexy, which would be speedier than strangulation; while, if actual death did not take place very rapidly, at least the victim would lose consciousness from the pressure of blood on the brain—"effusion and concentration of tumours in the brain pan" were his words—and thus be spared much torment. Certainly the manner of adjusting the noose was an improvement on the old method, and, in spite of other great changes in the hangman's art, the "knot beneath the ear" was recognised as the correct practice for many a long day.

The next improvement was the introduction of the drop. Who was the actual inventor it is impossible to say. The earliest drops were simple enough in construction. They were small collapsible platforms, seldom more than a foot high, and placed on the top of the general scaffold. The mechanism by which they were operated was one of the crudest. The small square of planking on which the male-factor stood was supported by one or more beams of wood, to which ropes were tied. When all was ready the execu-tioner retired beneath the scaffold, and, on the word being given, pulled the ropes, which dragged away the props and the drop fell.

In an account of the execution of Earl Ferrers, on May 5th, 1760, quoted in *The Annals of Crime and the New Newgate Calendar* we read; "In the meantime a scaffold was erected under the gallows at Tyburn, and part of it, about a yard square, was raised about eighteen inches above the rest of the floor, with a contrivance to sink down upon a signal being given, and the whole was covered with black baize."

In another account it is stated, "The new moving scaffold consisted of a wide platform across which extended a stout beam, supported by tall posts. Beneath the cross-beam there was a little raised stage which could be lowered at will, leaving the criminal suspended. All was covered with black baize and there were black silk cushions to kneel upon during prayers. When the signal was given the raised stage sank a few inches, but the mechanism was faulty and it only went far enough for the toes of the hanging man to touch it, so that Ferrers was slowly strangled."

The amount of fall given to the condemned was at first very slight, six or eight inches being considered ample, the importance of a weight falling through a given distance not being recognised. Modifications of this primitive drop were used for some time, and in the life of Calcraft we read how the executioner used to go beneath the gallows to "draw the bolt." The bolt was a simple, sliding piece of wood, which supported the collapsible platform, and it was drawn by hand.

The New Drop set up at the Northampton County Gaol in 1818 was of such ample capacity that it was proudly described by the governor as efficient for the hanging of twelve persons "comfortably." (C. A. Markham, *Ancient Punishments in Northamptonshire.*)

The following description of the improved scaffold as used in 1828 at the execution of Thurtell for the murder of William Weare is taken from a contemporary account.

". . . The workmen laboured in erecting a scaffold and enclosure. This machine was constructed under the direction of Mr. Nicholson, the Under Sheriff, and had been commenced before the day appointed for the trial. Some objection was made by the magistrates to the use of it, upon the ground that it might be considered indelicate to commence such a work, as it were, in anticipation of the conviction of the prisoners. The fact, however, of there being no other fit machine of the sort in the county having being communicated to the High Sheriff, that gentleman, on his own responsibility, determined to adopt it, and it was by his direction finished, and used on the present occasion.

"The drop was ingeniously erected to the purpose for which it was intended and was calculated to terminate the existence of the unhappy culprit in the shortest possible period. There was a temporary platform with a falling leaf, supported by bolts, and upon this the prisoner was to be placed. The bolts were fixed in such a manner as to be removed in an instant, and as instantaneously the victim of his own crime would be launched into eternity. Above this platform was a cross-beam to which the fatal cord was to be affixed. The whole was solidly and compactly made, and capable of being taken asunder and removed in a very short time.

"The enclosure consisted of boards, seven feet in height, and dovetailed into each other, so as to close every crevice.

The extent of the space thus embraced was about thirty feet in length and fifteen feet in width. The platform was approached by a short flight of steps, which led directly from the door to the prison. The boards and all the other machinery, being painted black, presented a very gloomy appearance.''

Modifications of Thurtell's drop were largely employed in the United Kingdom till comparatively recent times. Several of the Scotch and Irish gaols were fitted with permanent gallows, constructed on this principle, the falling door being of iron, and the scaffold itself consisting of a balcony over the prison door, or in some other exposed place. Most of those who suffered outside the door of the Old Bailey prior to the passing of the Private Executions Act went to their deaths from a drop made on this plan.

When it was seen that public executions did not act as a deterrent to would-be murderers, and it was ordained that in future all malefactors should be hanged inside the prisons, more attention was given to the question of putting the condemned man out of his misery as speedily and humanely as possible. Medical men were invited to give their opinions as to the quickest method of hanging, and it was decided that the drop played an important part in the process. Calcraft worked by rule of thumb, and was notorious for his short drops, but it was during his tenure of office that the Government introduced the double flap drop. The pattern differed according to the gaol, and local engineers had a good deal to say in the matter of construction. Still, the double door, instead of the single flap, was generally adopted throughout the United Kingdom.

The Irish are more correctly credited with the invention of the '' long drop,'' with consequent fracture of the transverse processes of the second *cervical vertebra*, and instantaneous death by injury to the *medulla oblongata*.

The drops in Ireland ranged from 10 ft. to 17 ft. and death was instantaneous. Two cases occurred in which the weight of the criminals was the same, viz., 160 lb. and the long drop the same, 14 ft., but in one case the transverse processes of the *second vertebra* were broken across, and in the other case the head was cut off by the rope.

These cases led to a full discussion of the whole question, in which all the leading surgeons of Ireland took part, and particular attention was paid to the position of the knot, for which three positions were advocated, (1) the occipital position; (2) the subaural position; (3) the submental position.

The occipital knot had practice in its favour, handed down from the old times of the short drop; but experience showed that the long drop and occipital knot divided all the short tissues of the neck, except the skin, before the blow reached the second *cervical vertebra* and *medulla oblongata*, and that there was not sufficient margin of resistance left to prevent the head from coming off.

The subaural knot was merely a hangman's ignorant idea, and had no support from anatomy.

The submental knot and long drop delivers the first shock on the spine (like killing rabbits by a blow on the back of the neck) and causes immediate death, without dividing the soft parts of the neck, which remain to protect the head from coming off.

After a full discussion, the third method was unanimously adopted, and this decision of the Irish surgeons became known to Marwood, who introduced it into England, and claimed it to be his own. After the adoption of the submental knot, the long drop was reduced from twelve to fourteen feet to eight feet, and the results have proved that an eight-foot drop, with submental knot, will produce a greater destruction of the transverse processes of the *cervical vertebra*, than a fourteen-foot drop with the occipital knot. The transverse processes have been fractured as far down as the fourth *vertebra*, and death is, of course, instantaneous.

A man's physical build has as much to do with the length of drop now allowed as has his actual weight, and a drop of eight feet nowadays is rare. In the case of John Rose and Samuel Wilkinson, executed together at Nottingham by James Billington, different drops were given. Wilkinson stood 5 ft. 6 in. in height and weighed 148 lb.; while Rose, though only 5 ft. 4 in. in height, actually weighed 182 lb.

Wilkinson was given a drop of 7 ft. 6 in. as the lighter man, and Rose one of 7 ft. only.

In the case of Walter Millar, who murdered a bookseller named Moyse, in Liverpool, in the 'nineties, a drop of 7 ft. 2 in. only was given, though he weighed only 103 lb. and a much larger drop would have been expected. But Millar had such a thin, weak neck that it would have been risking tearing his head off to give him a longer drop. But Wright, who murdered four people at Mansfield, was given a drop of 7 ft. 10 in. by Billington, though he weighed the same as Millar. His neck, however, was normal.

It was in the days of Berry, who succeeded Marwood, that the Home Office had calculations made as to the proper length of drop to be given to convicts of different weights, and the principle of killing the murderer by strangulation was finally abolished. A regular scale of drops to be given was laid down, and though some latitude had to be allowed to the experienced hangman, when he gives a reason for his request, it is still in force.

James Berry, in his reminiscences, gives a list of the drops he allowed. For a man of 14 stone he allowed a drop of 8 ft., allowing a two inches longer drop for every half stone lighter in weight, so that a man of eight stone was given a drop of 10 ft. This table he did not adhere to rigidly. In the case of murderers of very fleshy build, who often have weak bones and muscles about the neck, the length of the drop was reduced by as much as a quarter or a half.

Even with the greatest care, unpleasant accidents happened. In the case of Robert Goodale, who was executed at Norwich Castle in 1885, the drop, according to the table, should have been 7 ft. 8 in. Berry reduced this to 5 ft. 9 in. because the muscles of Goodale's neck appeared weak. That they were weaker than was supposed was shown by the terrible sequel. Goodale's head was torn from his body. After that Berry worked out a fresh drop table, based on the striking force of given weights falling through given distances, and the drops he gave were, on the whole, considerably shorter.

Crippen, hanged by Ellis in 1910, was given a drop of 7 ft. 9 in. His weight was 136 lb. George Smith, the murderer of his three wives by drowning them in baths, weighed 161 lb. and was given a drop of 6 ft. 8 in. Sir Roger Casement, hanged in 1917 for treason, was a heavy man. He weighed 168 lb. and was given a drop of 6 ft. 1½ in. As a contrast in the length of drop given only two more instances need be cited. In 1916 James Hargreaves was hanged for the murder of a woman named M'Gee. He was a very heavy, short man, weighing 203 lb., and was given a drop of 5 ft. 4 in. Major Armstrong, who was executed in 1921 for the murder of his wife, was, on the other hand, a light man, weighing only 115 lb. and he received the unusually long drop, in these days, of 8 ft. 8 in.

Following the abolition of capital punishment in public, the executions at Newgate took place in the yard. In a contemporary account of an eye-witness of the execution of the four Lennie mutineers in 1876 it is stated:

"In the yard where the drop is placed there were assembled about forty persons, nearly all reporters of the Press. . . . From the cross-beam of the gallows were depending four large iron chains with eight circular links. To the end of each was affixed a very substantial rope, the noose of which worked through a metal ring. It was evident that some of these chains were new. The one generally hanging from the central beam had been shifted to one side so that all the chains were at an equal distance from one another. . . . The floor of the scaffold is remarkably ponderous, and appears unnecessarily so. The result is, the falling of the drop is attended with a good deal of noise. To remedy this, underneath the scaffold are suspended, on each side, three large bales of cotton, or some other similar substance, against which the sides of the drop strike. This, no doubt, deadens the sound considerably, but the noise, notwithstanding, is rather trying. One great improvement has, however, been effected over the old scaffold. The drop works by a handle on the upper surface of the platform, similar in form to the handles by which railway signals or switches are worked. This is

PEINE FORTE ET DURE
(*From an old print*)

The punishment of pressing to death was inflicted on those who refused
to plead to an indictment. By such refusal the accused were able to save
their property from being confiscated, and so leave it to their dependents.
The punishment was finally abolished in 1828.

[*Face page* 50

EXECUTION OF THE REBEL LORDS ON TOWER HILL
(From an old print)

On Tower Hill a permanent scaffold was erected during the fifteenth and sixteenth centuries, and here the less distinguished victims of the headman's axe were executed. The more distinguished were beheaded on Tower Green in the Tower of London.

close to the executioner's right hand as he stands in front of the prisoner, so that when the rope and cap are adjusted not one moment's delay takes place before the drop falls."

Another report added, " The penthouse containing the gallows is a permanent erection in the corner of the yard. Only the upper half of the front is open, a skirting of folding doors concealing the drop. The woodwork is painted a dull buff colour. On each side of the uprights there is a pulley used for raising the ponderous drop after the execution has taken place. At a quarter to eight the bell of St. Sepulchre's began to toll. At five minutes to, the execution bell, adding its harsh discordant notes to those of St. Sepulchre's, sounded the knell of the convicts."

It has already been stated that there were many different forms of scaffold in existence and it was not until the late 'eighties that a uniform type was established. Until then there were the double trap doors and the single trap and the side trap and the stage trap. At Manchester, for example, the side trap was used, and the whole platform moved vertically down beneath the condemned man's feet. Undoubtedly the double trap was the best, and this is the form now universally used. Even as late as the beginning of the twentieth century, however, complete uniformity had not been reached, especially in those prisons where executions were not common.

"In comparison with modern scaffolds," Ellis wrote after a visit to Glasgow, " as found in most parts of England, this affair was very antiquated. In the first instance the trap-doors were not flush with the surrounding floor as in modern scaffolds, but were raised four or five inches. More important still, the overhead beam was not constructed with a length of adjustable chain, as it ought to have been. Consequently the rope would have to be tied to it. Knots have a habit of slipping, and they also make it difficult to get the length of the drop measured off with the accuracy so absolutely necessary."

In the standardised form there is a heavy cross-beam into which bolts terminating in hooks are fixed. The trap doors on which the convict stands consist of two heavy oaken doors fixed in an oak framework on a level with the floor, and over a deep bricked pit. Underneath the doors are hinged bars which rest on an iron draw-bar that has openings in it. This draw-bar is attached to the lever pulled by the executioner. When the lever is pulled the draw-bar moves so that the openings in it come opposite the ends of the hinged bars supporting the trap-doors. The hinged bars immediately fall and with them the trap-doors, which are prevented from rebounding by spring catches.

The scaffold at Stafford, in the latter half of the nineteenth century, was a wooden enclosed structure, painted black, and was usually kept in a shed. It was fitted with wheels, and when required was run out into the middle of the prison courtyard. Some twelve broad steps led up to a platform, and these the culprit had to ascend with a warder at each arm. The prison chaplain and the executioner also mounted the platform. Below were the governor or his deputy, the under sheriff, the prison medical officer, some representatives of the Press, and perhaps half-a-dozen warders. When the bolt was drawn the executioner descended the steps and opened a door in the side of the scaffold. The doctor followed. Later a pit was dug in the floor of the coach-house, and the culprit was led on the drop, which was level with the floor. It was a similar scaffold which was drawn in front of the prison for the execution of William Palmer.

At Dorchester, in a contemporary report of the execution of Elizabeth Brown for the murder of her husband in 1856, it was stated "the scaffold was at some distance from the prison. The prison van was in readiness at the gaol door to convey the culprit to the place of execution but she preferred walking. . . . On arriving at the place of execution she walked with firmness up the first flight of eleven steps. The pinioning being completed, the culprit, in company with the executioner (Calcraft) then proceeded up the next flight of stairs, nineteen in number, to the platform, and, still walking with a firm step, crossed the platform to the next flight, which led to the gallows."

Now, however, there are no steps, and the scaffold is

within a very short distance of the condemned cell. That at Oxford is one of the farthest from the condemned cell, roughly about sixty yards.

The execution shed at Maidstone was a wooden shed at one end of the exercise yard, near which was the condemned cell. The platform, about eight feet by four feet, consisted of two trap-doors, hinged, and allowed to fall by means of a lever. The doors fell against the sides of a brick-lined pit. The platform was level with the ground outside the shed doors, and when the condemned man fell nothing could be seen but the taut rope.

The usual time of execution was in the morning between eight o'clock and noon. Where the gallows was erected before the prison the hour of execution was nearly always round about eight o'clock, but where it was some distance away the time was later. Where the authorities feared a riot or where there were other special circumstances the hour was made earlier. Gilham, in 1828, was hanged at Ilchester three hours before the usual time for fear of the dangers arising from a large crowd gathering near the banks of the river.

The hour now is nearly always eight o'clock in the morning.

The execution shed at Wandsworth stands apart from the prison, and is callously spoken of as the " cold meat shed." There are the usual double-flap trap doors. Close by is a strip of turf and in the wall bounding it are square stone slabs let in at intervals. Each denotes the burial of an executed man.

It is of interest to note that when Newgate was demolished the scaffold was removed to Pentonville. If necessary four men at a time can be executed on it, and it was used for the executions of such notorious criminals as Crippen, Seddon, and Sir Roger Casement.

In olden times the arms of the condemned man were bound with rope, either behind his back or in front of him. Calcraft introduced pinioning straps, and Marwood improved upon them. The pinioning straps were finally reduced to a belt which passed round the waist. To the belt were attached other straps which secured the elbows and wrists of the doomed man. Now a light double strap is used with which the wrists are fastened behind the murderer's back. As a result the process of pinioning, which once took several minutes, has been reduced to a few seconds. The murderer's ankles are also strapped together so that his body falls like a plummet. From the time of entering the condemned cell until the execution is over, is rarely a full minute nowadays. Everything is arranged to expedite the last scene as much as possible, and the condemned cell is usually situated close to the scaffold shed. A set of straps and ropes is not usually kept by each prison but is sent down specially for the execution from Pentonville or the Home Office.

The most important item in an execution is naturally the rope itself. The one used by Berry was always made of Italian hemp, ¾ in. in diameter, and consisted of five strands each capable of holding up a ton dead weight. Every rope was stretched before being used by hanging on its end a bag of cement. It is the usual practice now to leave a sandbag suspended all night at the end of the rope to take any stretch out of it, especially with a new rope. The rope used by Marwood was practically the same as that used by Berry, but that used by Binns was considerably thicker, being some 1¼ in. in diameter.

The ropes were often used for a number of executions and were supplied by the executioner himself until 1890 when a new rope was ordered to be supplied for every execution. Before an execution two or three ropes are nowadays sent from Pentonville to the prison authorities concerned. The ropes have a brass ring worked into one end, through which the other end of the rope is passed to form a noose. A leather or rubber washer, fitting the rope fairly tightly, is placed behind the brass ring to prevent the ring from slipping after being adjusted. The usual position for the ring is just behind the condemned man's left ear.

At one time the rope for the following morning's execution was left hanging so that it coiled itself upon the floor of the scaffold, but James Billington introduced the innovation by coiling the rope and attaching it to the beam by a

piece of thread, previous to the execution. Left to hang
and coil loosely on the floor as formerly meant that
there was a danger of the dazed criminal stumbling
over it at the last moment. It was Billington who introduced the leather or rubber washer behind the knot or ring
of the noose to prevent slipping. The noose itself is always
greased well with vaseline to make it more pliable.

For the morbid and curious several of these ropes have
been exhibited in the past, but now no ropes are allowed to
be sold for such purposes. Some are, however, preserved
in the Black Museum at New Scotland Yard. At one time
the executioner himself not only supplied the rope, but
made them for use in the Dominions and abroad. Marwood
is said to have netted quite a respectable sum in this way.

The rope has always been an object of superstition to
the ignorant. In *London in the Sixties* it is related that a
well-known function was the reception held after an execution by the hangman at the Great Dragon in Fleet Street,
where he took refreshment with his admirers, and sold
the fatal rope at the rate of sixpence per inch.

Old records of executions are full of accounts of the sale
of the rope. It fetched high prices in the case of notorious
malefactors and was one of the most greatly prized of the
hangman's perquisites.

In a contemporary account of the hanging of Corder for
the murder of Maria Marten, it is stated that immediately
after the corpse had been taken into prison there was a
considerable scuffle among the spectators; numbers of whom
wished to obtain a piece of the rope. Many exaggerated
reports appeared at the time with regard to the disposal
of this "relic," and some of the papers boldly asserted that
it was sold at the rate of a guinea an inch. That it made a
considerable sum there can be no doubt, for when Foxen,
the executioner, was questioned about his perquisites, he
replied, "What I got, I got, and that's all I shall say,
except that *that are* was a very good rope."

There was a good deal of swindling over the sale of the
rope, as might be expected, and much money was made
out of the morbid and superstitious. After the execution

of Governor Wall, in front of Newgate, the executioner sold the rope at a shilling an inch. At the north-east corner of Warwick Lane a woman, known as Rosy Emma, reported to be the hangman's wife, was selling what purported to be the same rope to the Epping Buttermen, who had come that morning to witness the execution. And in Newgate Street a third " identical " rope was being sold by another vendor at sixpence an inch.

There are many instances of the rope breaking, especially in earlier executions. The following is an extract from the *Historical Magazine*, February, 1789:

" At the beginning of this month were executed, at Heavetree Gallows, Exeter, William Snow, for house-breaking, and James Waybourn, for highway robbery. Snow declared that day to be the happiest of his life; and exhorted the spectators to avoid his errors. He had hung but a few seconds when the rope slipped from the gallows, and he fell to the ground. It is impossible to describe the feelings of the multitude at the thought of his being again suspended; yet was this painful interval less afflicting to the patient sufferer than to the spectators. Snow heard their sorrowful exclamations, and said, with an air of com-passion, " Good people, be not hurried; I am not hurried; I can wait a little." And the executioner wishing to lengthen the rope, Snow calmly waited till his companion was dead, when the rope was taken from the deceased's arms, in order to complete the execution of Snow; who was a second time launched from the cart, amidst the tears of thousands."

When the notorious Captain Kidd was hanged at Execu-tion Dock on May 23rd, 1701, the rope broke, and he was immediately raised from the ground again and hanged.

One of the most remarkable hangings Calcraft ever carried out occurred in his first year of office, when he went to Carmarthen to hang a man named David Evans for the murder of his sweetheart. The rope broke, and the unhappy man fell down beneath the gallows, unhurt but completely unnerved.

There were loud cries immediately from the crowd who were watching: " Shame! Let him go!"

The half-hanged man, staggering to his feet, exclaimed, "I claim my liberty. You have hanged me once, and you have no power or authority to hang me again."

He struggled to get away, and the gallows shook and threatened to collapse. It was discovered that the carpenter who had erected it had forgotten to fasten the cross-beam properly, and it nearly came crashing down on the executioner, officials and the struggling condemned man.

"It is against the law to hang me a second time!" cried Evans, half-crazed by the ordeal he had undergone.

"You are greatly mistaken," replied Calcraft firmly. "There is no such law as that—to let a man go if there is an accident and he is not properly hanged. My warrant and my order are to hang you by the neck until you are dead. So up you go, and hang you must until you are dead."

Evans was forced up the scaffold by Calcraft and two warders and duly hanged, with protests still on his lips.

Gibbeting or hanging in chains of the bodies of executed criminals, near the scene of their crimes, was a common practice. "It was frequently usual," says Blackstone in his Commentaries, "for the court to direct the murderer, after execution, to be hung upon a gibbet where the act was committed; but this was no part of the legal judgment; and the like is still sometimes practised in the case of notorious thieves."

Holinshed, in his Chronicle, asserts that in some cases "the criminal is either hanged alive in chains near the place where the act was committed, or else, upon compassion being taken, first strangled with a rope, and so continueth, until his bones come to nothing."

Henry Chettle, writing in the reign of Queen Elizabeth, also refers to hanging murderers alive in chains. It is certain, however, that the practice was not common, despite the many stories which were current.

In *The Antiquary* for November, 1890, the Rev. J. Charles Cox wrote with reference to the practice of gibbeting " It was usual to saturate the body with tar before it was in chains, in order that it might last longer. This was done with the bodies of three highwaymen about the middle of

the last century, gibbeted on the top of the Chevin, near
Belper, in Derbyshire. . . . After the bodies had been
hanging there a few weeks, one of the friends of the criminals set fire, at night time, to the big gibbet which bore
all three. . . . So thoroughly did the tar aid the cremation
that the next morning only the links of the iron chain
remained on the site of the gibbet."

These gibbets were expensive affairs, and it is recorded
that the gibbet for one Lingard cost over £85.

Hanging in chains was common in England for several
centuries. In Chauncey's History of Hertfordshire it is
stated :—

"Soon after the King came to Easthampstead, to recreate
himself with hunting, where he heard that the bodies which
were hanged here were taken down from the gallowes,
and removed a great way from the same; this so incensed
the King that he sent a writ, tested the 3rd of August,
Anno 1381, to the bailiffs of this burrough, commanding
them upon the sight thereof, to cause chains to be made,
and to hang the bodies in them upon the same gallowes,
there to remain so long as one piece might stick to another,
according to the judgment, but the townsmen, not daring
to disobey the King's command, hanged the dead bodies
of their neighbours again, to their great shame and reproach,
where they could not get any other for any wages to come
near the stinking carcasses, but they themselves were
compelled to do so vile an office."

During the second Northern Rising, in 1536, the bodies
of Sir Robert Constable and Ashe were hung in chains at
Hull and York respectively. The practice became a common
one in the seventeenth century. Lord Dreghorn, writing
in 1774, notes that the first instance of hanging in chains
in Scotland occurred in March, 1637. The delinquent was
one Macgregor, who suffered for theft, robbery and slaughter,
and he was ordered to stay on " the gallowlee till his corpse
rot."

Hanging in chains formed part of the sentence in Scotland,
but it was never the case in England, with the exception at
Easthampstead quoted above. By an Act of 25 George II,

however, gibbeting in chains was first legally recognised. By this statute it was enacted that the body should, after sentence delivered and execution done, be given to the surgeons to be dissected and anatomised, and that the judge may direct the body to be afterwards hung in chains, but in no wise to be buried without dissection. The post-mortem revengement was thought to be of great comfort to the relatives of the murdered person, and the Roman law, for a similar reason, also permitted the murderer's body to be gibbeted. In Howell's *State Trials* it appears that when the English Regency made an order, in 1742, to hang the body of the murderer of Mr. Penny in chains, they inserted therein that it was on the petition of the relatives of the deceased.

After the Act of 1752 the number of corpses exhibited in chains rapidly increased. At Newgate it was the custom, after execution, to convey the body into a place grimly called " The Kitchen." Here stood a cauldron of boiling pitch, and into this the carcase was thrown. It was shortly after withdrawn, placed in chains and there cold riveted in what was coarsely called " his last suit." Occasionally the bodies were put in sacks and hung up.

The numerous gibbets throughout the country often had the effect of terrorising the local inhabitants to such an extent that, at night at any rate, people would go several miles out of their way to avoid passing the creaking corpse. In the report of the trial of the Rev. Thomas Hunter, M.A., on the twenty-second of August, 1700, near Edinburgh, for the murder of two children named Gordon, it is stated that the sheriff passed the sentence that " on the succeeding day he should be executed on a gibbet, erected for that purpose on the spot where he had committed the murders; but that, previous to his execution, his right hand should be cut off with a hatchet, near the wrist, and then he should be drawn up to the gibbet by a rope, and when he was dead, hung in chains between Edinburgh and Leith, the knife with which he committed the murders being stuck through his hand, which should be advanced over his head and fixed therewith to the top of the gibbet."

Lady Haldane, the mother of Lord Haldane, writing in the St. Columba's Church Magazine on her ninety-eighth birthday, says in this connection:

"I can, remember driving fifteen miles to Cambo in an open dogcart to see a dentist from Newcastle at an inn. We had to drive over the bleak moors during a snowstorm, and not far from the roadside on a gibbet was hanging the effigy of a tramp named Winter who had murdered an old woman in a cottage in sight of the place. I can remember the clanking of chains to this day."

Alexander Gillam, was executed at Inverness on November 14th, 1810. Lord Justice Clerk, in pronouncing sentence, said:

"As there is no school of medicine here, where you can be publicly anatomised, and as the enormity of your sins cries for the severest punishment, I have resolved, by virtue of the powers committed to me by the laws of the realm, to make you a lasting and memorable example of the fate which awaits the commission of such crimes. . . . I have therefore determined that after your execution, you shall be hung in chains, until the fowls of the air pick the flesh off your body, and your bones bleach and whiten in the winds of heaven, thereby to afford a constant warning of the fatal consequences which almost invariably attend the indulgence of the passions."

In the windows of the waterside taverns at Blackwell "spy glasses" were affixed for people to obtain a close view of the bodies in their gibbets. Similarly, the Greenwich pensioners on the Hill used to exhibit the gibbeted pirates on the opposite side of the river, in the Isle of Dogs, through telescopes. When the bodies were removed by legislative enactment, some of the newspapers of the day made a great outcry that holiday-makers were being deprived of their amusement!

In 1742 John Breed, a butcher of Rye, murdered a Mr. Thomas Lamb of the same place. He was hung in chains, and for this purpose a gibbet was set up in a marsh at the west end of the town now called "Gibbet Marsh." The carcass of Breed swung for many years on the Morass, and when all but the upper part of the skull had dropped away the chains and frame were rescued by the Corporation of Rye.

In 1747 Christopher Holliday was beaten to death by Adam Graham, on Beck Moor, near Balenbush, on the English side of the Border. Graham was executed at Carlisle and the body hung in chains upon a gibbet twelve yards high, on Kingmoor, with twelve thousand nails driven into it to prevent it being swarmed, or cut down and the body carried off.

William Carter, smuggler and murderer, was executed and hung up in chains near Rake, on the Portsmouth Road, in 1749 (Sussex Archaeological Collections, Vol. XXIII, p. 215). This was in connection with the murder of Galley and Chater. William Jackson, also concerned, was so horror-struck when they measured him for his irons for the gibbet that he died of fright. His body was thrown into a hole near Carter's gibbet.

The last example of hanging in chains in England was that of a man named Cook who murdered a Mr. Paas, at Leicester, in 1834. His body was gibbeted in Saffron Lane, outside the town, and the disgraceful scene round the gibbet was like a fair, In the same year hanging in chains was abolished by Statute.

Gibbeting was common throughout Europe. In Spain, for example, the body of the executed criminal usually remained upon the gallows, which thus also served as a gibbet. In Holland the procedure was much the same as in France. In the latter country the gallows was a feudal right. Charles V granted leave to certain districts to have gallows *fourches patibulaires*—with two posts—and a curious question arose in consequence of the Count of Rhodes having placed his armorial bearings upon a gibbet of this kind against the prerogative of the king. It was an abuse of privilege, and implied the seizing of justice.

Such gibbets, of which the number of pillars (or, if of wood, of posts) varied from two to eight, according to the quality of the lord, were used to hang criminals from, and for the suspension, exposure or gibbeting of the bodies of men executed elsewhere upon temporary gallows.

At the end of the twelfth century there was a great monumental gibbet on the eminence of Montfaucon, between the faubourgs of St. Martin and the Temple, in Paris. In 1425 forty-eight old beams were replaced by new ones. In 1466 at the Great Justice of Paris were attached and nailed fifty-two iron chains to hang and strangle the malefactors "Who have been and shall be sent here by order of justice." Eight new ladders were subsequently added.

The only minor point in the favour of the humanity of the period with regard to gibbeting was the fact that the *post mortem* punishment was not applied to women, either in England or other countries, with very rare exceptions. For very grave offences women were burnt or drowned, and in France the punishment was that of "la fosse" or burying alive, usually in front of the gibbet.

ANGLO-SAXON GALLOWS

CHAPTER IV

ELECTROCUTION

It is a significant commentary on human emotions that with the progress of civilization there has been a corresponding demand for new methods of inflicting the death penalty. In the early days of civilization and during the Middle Ages, death at the hands of authority was hedged round with every conceivable form of physical and mental torture. The coming of the drop, the abolition of public executions and the extension of the time between sentence of death and its carrying out, have been hailed in England as evidences of our humane outlook. In France the advent of the guillotine was acclaimed as the final word in swift and easy death. In contrast with the British method, which informs the condemned man of the day and very hour of the execution, the Frenchman has no certainty of his impending fate until it is too late for him to brood upon it.

It was only natural, when electricity became controlled, that attention should be directed towards it by advocates of a more humane form of capital punishment. The many accidental deaths in the early days of the use of high voltage alternating electric current and the utter blasting of the human body by lightning added force to this advocacy. In the late 'seventies a patent was applied for in New York for "An improved device for executing criminals condemned to death." This patent application was no more nor less than the electric chair in crude form. In Germany, about the same time, a similar suggestion was put forward.

Electrocution was first adopted in the State of New York, the decree being signed by Governor David B. Hill on

June 4th, 1888, and became effective on January 1st, 1889. In that year a series of experiments was carried out on animals to test the efficacy of the new method, as animals had suffered under the guillotine before it was officially used. In these experiments varying voltage was passed through a calf and a horse. An alternating current of 50 volts was first tried, but though it rendered the calf unconscious the animal recovered some minutes later. The voltage was increased to 770 with, from the point of view of the experimenters, satisfactory results. There was great opposition by electrical companies to the use of electricity as a method of capital punishment, on the score that it would lead the public to believe that electricity was too dangerous for ordinary use. One company which made use of the innocuous direct current, as against the admittedly more risky alternating current, gave public demonstrations of killing animals to show the dangers of using any other system than their own. In this they overreached themselves, since several members of the legislature who happened to witness a bungled execution by hanging became convinced that the new system was far ahead of any other known method and pressed forward its legalisation.

Under the new law it was enacted that the warden of the prison, two doctors, twelve citizens and deputy sheriffs should witness the execution, and that the condemned man should have the services of a priest, if he wished, during his last moments. In the minds of the legislators there had remained a lingering doubt that, no matter how great was the voltage passed through the condemned man's body, it might not kill. The law further enacted, therefore, that a post-mortem should be held, and that the body, unless claimed by relatives, should be interred in the prison cemetery with a sufficient quantity of lime to consume it.

The first criminal to be executed by electricity was a man named Kemmler, who had killed his mistress in a fit of jealousy. He was condemned to death on June 24th, 1889. An appeal was entered on the ground that the new method of execution was against the Federal Constitution, which stipulated that executions should not be "cruel or unusual." As the new law had abolished hanging in New York, there was no method of executing Kemmler until the point which had been raised was settled. It was not until August 6th, 1890, over a year after he had been sentenced to death, that Kemmler was electrocuted in Auburn Prison.

The first electrocution was productive of a scene which very nearly caused the new method to be abolished. Kemmler, a man of about forty, offered no resistance to being strapped in the chair. The chair itself was a solidly built wooden affair fitted with pinioning straps. In the case of Kemmler one electrode of the apparatus was fitted in the form of a metal covering on his head and the other was applied to the back. When the signal was given to E. F. Davis to pull down the switch to allow the current to pass, a terrible scene ensued. To make sure that death would take place a far more powerful current than necessary was used, and the drying of one of the electrical conductors at the point of contact caused a burning of the flesh. The execution lasted five minutes, though there is not the slightest doubt that death was instantaneous and painless with the first shock. But the straining at the straps holding Kemmler, through the action of the electric current, gave a ghastly simulation of life which left a permanent impression on all those who watched.

One or two succeeding electrocutions passed off without incident, but on July 27th, 1893, the execution of William Taylor, at Auburn, once again caused an outcry against the new method of capital punishment. With the first passing of the current the chair broke and the unhappy man fell forward semi-conscious. He was removed to a bed and given chloroform and injections of morphia to keep him unconscious while the apparatus was being repaired. It was sixty-nine minutes before the current was restored and the execution completed.

By 1906, however, over one hundred murderers had been successfully electrocuted in New York State in the prisons of Sing Sing, Auborn and Dannemora. Electrocution has been adopted by, among other states, Ohio (1896),

Massachusetts (1898), New Jersey (1906) and Virginia (1908).

Since 1914 all electrocutions in New York State have taken place in Sing Sing, and the following description in taken in the main from *Life and Death in Sing Sing*, by L. E. Laws, Warden of the Prison.

The old execution chamber in Sing Sing was a small stone building attached to an annexe of the main prison. The small green door leading into the actual room where executions took place was in full view of the condemned prisoners who were awaiting execution. The final walk of the condemned took him past some of these cells, and those who watched him could, a few moments later, plainly hear the hum of the dynamo which signalled death at the hands of the State. So desperate became the state of those who watched and heard that some were driven insane and others made wild efforts to escape. Two men actually did escape, and were found drowned in the Hudson River, while a third, who killed a keeper and escaped, was re-captured and executed.

In 1922 a new execution building was finished, complete with its own hospital, exercise ground, visiting room and cells. There are twenty-four cells for men and three for women, and six cells in the pre-execution chamber to which the condemned are taken on the day of their execution. This section is callously called by the convicts "the dance hall," and is connected with the actual execution room by a corridor.

Under the New York State law a condemned man is kept in solitary confinement. The condemned cells are so arranged that no prisoner can see any other, though he is able to talk to prisoners on either side of him. Every pre-caution is taken to prevent a condemned man from com-mitting suicide and so cheating the law. He is provided with special clothing and, of course, knives and forks are not allowed. Even the wire stitching from magazines, which are allowed to be sent to a prisoner, is removed and regularly each convict has his nails trimmed to prevent his opening an artery. The law is very jealous of the life of the man it

EXECUTION OF JOHN THURTELL
(*From an old print*)

John Thurtell was found guilty of the murder of William Weare, and he had the distinction of being hanged on a new type of scaffold. Note the javelin men who were usually present at all public executions.

EXECUTION OF MARY BLANDY   [By courtesy of Messrs. Kegan Paul
(From an old print)

Mary Blandy is famous in criminal literature for her remarkable letters and apologia from the condemned cell. She was the victim of an unhappy love affair.

Miſs MARY BLANDY

Aged 33 and Executed at OXFORD
April 6, 1752. for poisoning her Father.

B. Cole Sculp.

Face page 67]

has decreed shall die by the law. In a number of cases there have been operations in the hospital of the prison to save the life of a man who has afterwards been electrocuted.

The average time which elapses between sentence of death and the carrying of it into effect is now about a year, though only a few years ago the period was two years. A remarkable commentary on this is that many of the condemned are illiterate when they enter the condemned cell, and have learnt to read and write by the time they are electrocuted. It is not to be wondered at that each prisoner is examined at intervals by three lunacy commissioners.

The actual date for an execution is fixed by the Warden of the prison, the law merely enacting that the condemned man shall be put to death "in the week beginning. . . ." The usual day chosen is a Thursday, a few minutes after eleven o'clock at night. The law prescribes that, among others, "Twelve reputable citizens of full age" shall be invited by the Warden to be present. In one case over a thousand applications were received, and in many instances relatives of the condemned asked to be allowed to witness his last moments. When a new executioner was appointed over seven hundred people applied for the post.

The technique of electrocution has been improved, much as has the technique of hanging. The condemned man is given one shock of single phase of 60 cycle alternating current at an average starting potential of 2,000 volts for 57 seconds. A second shock of the same voltage and period follows, giving a total application of the current of two minutes. Death is instantaneous with the first turning on of the current through paralysis and destruction of the brain, with such speed that it is most unlikely the nervous system can react quickly enough for any pain to be felt. During the application of the current the average body temperature rises to 140 F., which alone makes certain that there is no chance of resuscitation. Under the law a post-mortem is held immediately following the execution in a morgue attached to the execution room.

From the arrival of the condemned in the execution chamber until the application of the first shock not more than a minute usually elapses. Three keepers fasten the necessary straps while the executioner fits one electrode to the calf of the right leg and one to the crown of the head.

The behaviour of those who suffer death by law is much the same the world over. Some enter the execution chamber with a calmness which is almost unbelievable, others in a state of collapse, and others in a mood of religious exaltation.

The long delay between sentence and electrocution has either a hardening effect on the nerves of the waiting man or breaks him completely. One man who knew the executioner said quietly, "Make a good job of it, John." Another asked to be electrocuted in a white shirt—a request which was granted, and a third commented, as he was being strapped in the chair, "Everything happens for the best." Nearly all ate a hearty last meal, the New York law allowing any menu within reason.

Despite some terrible scenes when electrocution was first introduced, it is probably now the quickest, and certainly the least painful, of any mode of capital punishment.

CHAPTER V

THE GUILLOTINE

THE guillotine is thought by many to have originated shortly before the French Revolution, and many historians do not date it further back than the Halifax gibbet or the Scottish Maiden, described in Chapter II. But in Lucas Cranach's woodcuts of the Martyrdom of the Apostles, printed at Wittenberg in 1539, there is a representation of the death of St. Matthew by the guillotine with a description "it is said that his head was chopped off by a falling axe, after the manner of the Romans."

It is recorded that on one side of the walls of the Rathhaus of Nuremberg, painted about 1520, there was depicted a man being beheaded by the guillotine. Two copperplate engravings of the German school, of about the same date, one by George Pencz (died 1550) and the other by Henry Aldegraver, bearing the date 1553, both show the death of Titus Manlius by an instrument which was identical in principle with the modern guillotine. In the *Academy of Armoury*, by Randle Holme, dated 1678, he says of this method of beheading:

"This was the Jews' and Romans' way of beheading offenders, as some write, though others say that they used to cut off the heads of such with a sharp two-handed sword. However, this way of decollation was by laying the neck of the malefactor on the block, and then setting the axe upon it, which lay in a rigget (groove) on the two side posts or supporters. The executioner, with the violence of a blow on the head of the axe with his heavy maule (mallet), forced it through the man's neck into the block. I have seen a draught of the like heading instrument, where the weighty axe (made heavy for the purpose) was raised up, and fell down in such a riggeted frame, which being suddenly let to fall, the weight of it was sufficient to cut off a man's head at one blow."

There is little doubt that some form of guillotine was in use in quite early times. In Holinshed's *Chronicles of Ireland* it is stated "In the Yeere 1307, the first of April, Murcod Ballagh was beheaded near to Merton by Sir David Caunton, Knight." The description was accompanied by an illustration showing a guillotine not differing greatly from the modern one.

In the *Memoires de Puysegur* there is a reference to the execution of the Marshal de Montmorenci, at Toulouse, in 1632.

"In that province they make use of a kind of hatchet, which runs between two pieces of wood; and when the head is placed on the block below the cord is let go, and the hatchet descends and severs the head from the body."

These and many other references undoubtedly show that the guillotine was in common use on the Continent in the sixteenth and seventeenth centuries, and in the following century there are a number of other references which make it difficult to understand why the guillotine was hailed as something new at the end of the eighteenth century. Under the name of Mannaia it was common in Italy and was described very fully by Le Pere Labat in his *Voyage en Italie*, 1730. In an anonymous work, *Voyage historique et politique de Suisse, d'Italie, et d'Allemagne*, printed 1736–43, appears the following account of the execution at Milan, 1702, of Count Bozelli.

"A large scaffold was prepared in the great square, and covered with black. In the middle of it was placed a great block, of the height to allow the criminal, when kneeling, to lay his neck on it between a kind of gibbet which supported a hatchet one foot deep and one and a half wide, which was confined by a groove. The hatchet was loaded with a hundred pounds weight of lead, and was suspended by a rope made fast to the gibbet. After the criminal had confessed himself, the penitents, who are for the most part of noble families, led him up on the scaffold, and, making him kneel before the block, one of the penitents held the head under the hatchet; the priest then reading the prayers as usual on such occasions, the executioner had nothing to do but cut the cord that held up the hatchet, which, descending with violence, severed the head, which the penitent still held in his hands, so that the executioner never touched it. This mode of executing is so sure that the hatchet entered the block above two inches."

Among the early predecessors of the French guillotine were undoubtedly the Halifax gibbet and the Scottish Maiden, described in Chapter II.

It was on October 10th, 1789, that Dr. Guillotin, deputy for Paris, brought forward a motion in the Constituent Assembly which first proposed that there should be no penalty more severe than decapitation. The motion was adjourned and brought forward again in December, but it was not until May 3rd, 1791, that the Assembly decreed, "Every person condemned to death shall be beheaded."

On March 25th, 1792, there was issued the law relating to the death penalty and the method of execution "that will be employed in the future."

The law stated, *inter alia*, "The National Assembly, after having decreed urgency, decrees that Article 3 of Division 1 of the Penal Code shall be executed after the manner indicated, and the method sanctioned in the pronouncement signed by the life-secretary of the Academy of Surgery, which is appended to the present decree; and consequently authorises the executive power to incur the necessary expenses for the establishment of this mode of execution, in such a way that it shall be uniform throughout the kingdom."

The life-secretary of the Academy of Surgery, Dr. Louis, pointed out the defects of beheading by the sword. "To secure certainty in the proceedings they must necessarily depend on invariable mechanical means, of which the force and the effect can be determined. . . . The body of the criminal is laid face downwards between the posts joined by a cross-beam at the top, whence the convex hatchet is made to fall on the neck by means of a trigger. The beam of the instrument should be heavy enough and strong enough to act efficaciously, like the ram that is used for sinking piles. It is easy to have a machine of this kind constructed, and its effect is unfailing; the decapitation will be accomplished in an instant . . . experiments can be made on corpses or even on living sheep."

The pronouncement of the life-secretary ended with the words "This apparatus would not be felt and would hardly be perceptible."

Dr. Louis' report very nearly won for him eternal notoriety in that the new instrument was for some time called the Louisette, but ultimately the name guillotine prevailed. Guedon, a carpenter employed in the courts of justice, was ordered to supply an estimate for the guillotine, but his estimate was so high, that the contract was given to one Schmidt. Guedon's excuse for the great cost of his guillotine was that he had difficulty in obtaining workmen to carry out the actual construction. Those who agreed to do so only did so on the condition they were paid high wages and that their names should not be made known, so great was their repugnance of the work they were called upon to do. Schmidt had no such scruples and on the 15th of April, Sanson, the executioner, was told the machine was ready to be tested.

Two days later the guillotine was tested on a number of corpses in the great hospital of Bicetre.

The early guillotine was the most horrible of all guillotines. It had two huge uprights between which the knife was placed, and was erected on a platform reached by twenty-four steps. The whole apparatus was painted red, not a brilliant cheerful red, but the dark shade of blood when exposed to the air. The condemned was tied methodically to the plank. This form of guillotine was gradually reduced in size, the platform became lower and the primitive wooden grooves in which it slid—greased with tallow— were replaced by metal ones. In the modern guillotine there is no platform. It is erected on the ground itself, and is practically hidden by guards.

The first criminal to be executed was Nicholas Jacques Pelletier, who had been waiting some months the carrying out of the sentence on him. There was considerable doubt on the part of the authorities how the new method would be viewed by the populace, and orders were given that the execution in the Place de Greve should be attended by a sufficient gendarmes to keep the crowd in check. The execution passed off without a hitch, and Schmidt was commissioned to make guillotines for all the departments.

Though the novelty of the new form of execution attracted a large crowd, the *Chronique de Paris* stated, "The people, however, were not at all satisfied; they had seen nothing; the affair was too rapid; they dispersed disappointedly, and to console themselves for the disillusionment sang:

> Give me back my wooden gallows
> Give me back my gallows!"

On the 10th of August began the reign of terror, with the timely resuscitated guillotine as its main prop. It became *La Sainte* Guillotine, and became the model of ornaments for women, and of toys for children. Miniature guillotines were not only sold in the streets, but the vendors supplied living sparrows to be decapitated by them. One of these toys was presented to the son of Marie Antoinette, just before her trial, by the notorious Chaumette who, a few months later, was himself guillotined.

The Place de Greve saw the first use of the guillotine in France. Between the 22nd August, 1792, and the end of that year it was erected there for criminals and in the Place du Carrousel for political offenders. The Place de Carrousel was also called Place de la Reunion. On the 21st January, 1793, it was erected for the first time in the Place de la Revolution, formerly Place Louis XV. The change of scene for the king's execution was made with the definite object of preventing a rescue. He was imprisoned in the Temple, and if he had been executed either in the Place de Greve or the Place du Carrousel it would have involved a journey through narrow, winding streets where rescue would have been comparatively easy by a determined body of men. But the Rue de Temple, the boulevards and the Rue Royale formed a wide and easily guarded road from the prison to

the scene of the execution. It is stated on good authority
that over a hundred thousand soldiers were ranged in
impenetrable lines from the Boulevard du Temple to the
Pont de la Liberte, formerly Place de la Concorde. It was
here that Marie Antoinette was executed.

From the time of the installation of the Revolutionary
Tribunal the guillotine was not removed, as it first used to
be, after each execution, but was usually kept stationary
in the Carrousel. In the thirteen months ending June 8th,
1794, no fewer than 1,255 persons were guillotined in the
Place de la Revolution, to which the guillotine was removed
in May, 1793, "in consideration of the proximity of the
Carrousel to the Hall of the Convention." Here fell, besides
Marie Antoinette, Charlotte Corday, Madame Elizabeth,
Marie Phlipon, and Madame Roland. On June 7th, Robespierre made his famous declaration acknowledging a supreme
Being and arranged for a great fête in the Tuileries. The
guillotine was temporarily removed to the Place St. Antoine,
in front of the ruins of the Bastille. The local shopkeepers
protested so much that it was removed after five days,
during which short period ninety-six persons were executed.
It was then taken to the Barriere Renverse where it stood
until the fall of Robespierre. In less than two months
1,270 persons were guillotined on the new site, before it
returned to the Place de la Revolution to guillotine Robespierre and twenty-one of his followers on the 28th July.
The following day sixty-nine were guillotined. In all,
during the Reign of Terror many thousands of persons were
guillotined.

The guillotine was in as active use in the provincial towns
of France as in Paris. At Rennes blood flowed so freely
from the guillotine that it was erected over the sewer of
the Place de Palais, so that the blood could at once be carried
underground. In three days alone, December 24–26th,
1793, ninety persons fell to the guillotine at Rennes.

The falling knife did not fall quickly enough for those in
power, and hundreds were shot. At Arras, where Joseph
Lebon was in power, the guillotine was first set up opposite
the Town Hall in the Place de la Liberte, now the Petite

Place, and then nearer the centre of the town in the Place de la Revolution. Here, from the balcony of the theatre, Lebon and his wife could watch the executions. At Lyons the scaffold was known as the Altar of La Patrie, and on it the sanguinary sacrifices were as great as at Rennes. And so the story may be continued in its monotonous horror throughout France.

Of the executioners of France there are uncertain records. Few of the volumes of reminiscences by the headsmen of France were authentic. Most, indeed, were born in the vivid imaginations of the journalist.

Nor must it be thought that the Revolution was the hey-day of the headsman.

"On the contrary," says Lenotre, "no class of society suffered more from the great change that followed the establishment of the Parliamentary regime and the spreading of new ideas.

"Before 1789 there were in France, including Corsica, more than a hundred and sixty executioners; it is difficult to fix the precise figure, since the number of those employed in Alsace is not known. They held their Commissions, for the most part, from the king; only a very few had been commissioned by seigneurs or municipalities. The Sansons in Paris, Tours, and Rheims; the Desmorets at Étampes, Dourdan, Senlis, Noyon, Laon, Épernay, Châlons and Vitry-le-Francais; the Fereys at Rouen, Pont-Audemer, Provins, and Orléans; the Jouennes at Mélun, Évreux, Caen, Dieppe, and Caudebec,—these were the principal families in the North of France who handed down, from father to son, the functions of justice."

In the South of France executioners were fewer, a con-demned prisoner often being given the opportunity of saving his own neck at the expense of those whom he agreed to execute. Sanson, in a report (28th Thermidor, year 6) on the difficulty of obtaining executioners in the South of France, stated:

"In early days the executioners of the South were appointed to their posts by mere warrants. If a town possessed one, it paid him, and the highest salary was

350 livres. These executioners had no commission, and in consequence received no salary from the Government. These posts could only be filled by vagabonds, and very often were vacant. Then the magistrates in authority were generally obliged to appoint one of the condemned prisoners to execute the others. . . . Very often it became necessary to proceed against the man in question for fresh offences. These men, who were lodged outside the towns in abominable hovels, did not dare enter the towns except to perform an execution, and even then it was necessary to give them an escort.

"Since the Revolution and especially since the passing of the law of the 13th June, 1793, which gave them allowances amounting to 2,400 livres, many men have attempted to fill these posts, but several have been killed and others crippled, and the bakers would not let them enter their shops to buy bread, and indeed a shopkeeper who sold goods to them could never get any customers."

It is not surprising that only the very outcasts would serve in posts which in certain parts of France, at any rate, were looked upon with the greatest odium and horror. Where the office of executioner had been in the same family for generations the executioner was tolerated, largely because he was better known and also because he was, apart from his calling, an ordinary citizen who had not transgressed any of the laws. Following the Reign of Terror, the prejudice against the executioner became so powerful and articulate that the executioner often dared not show himself in public.

Little is known of these executioners, save here and there from a letter, a report, or a request filed in the National Archives. On the whole they were uncouth, often clumsy and untrained, evolving scenes of unspeakable horror on the scaffolds which revolted even the blood-loving spectators. By the decree of June 13th, 1793, each department of the Republic had attached to the criminal tribunals an executioner, who was paid 2,400 livres annually for towns with a population up to 50,000, 4,000 livres for towns of 50,000 to 100,000, and 6,000 livres for towns of 100,000 to 300,000.

In Paris the executioner received a salary of 10,000 livres. Allowances were given to the executioner when called upon to carry out an execution outside the town in which he lived. The decree abolished many of the privileges of the executioner, notably that of *havage*, *riflerie*, and other tolls paid in kind.

The decree brought forth a strong protest from the chief executioners, who addressed a petition to the National Assembly pointing out that under the new decree many would starve. The decree brought to light the fact that many who in the past had held the office of executioner, and had drawn all the perquisites, had never actually carried out an execution, and faced with the prospect of being called actively to office, hurriedly resigned. One actually wrote to say that when there had been an execution in the past he had employed the services of real executioners!

The fact is that the greater number of the so-called executioners before the decree were executioners in name only, and merely exercised the functions of a *rifleur*, whose part was to flog offenders against the law, and to skin dead beasts. The right of *riflerie* was the sale, for his own benefit, of the remains of these beasts. The so-called executioner was usually, in fact, the local knacker. The coming of the Revolution and the demand that they should actually practise the functions of their office sent most of them into a panic of resignation. But the loss of *riflerie*, and the certain prospects of starvation, forced others to accept.

Havage was the right to take toll of the corn and fruit exposed for sale in the markets.

The decree of 1793 was intended to appoint official executioners, to draw up a list of those who had been approved and appointed, but it was not until the Reign of Terror was over that the criminal tribunals received their *official* executioners. But there were many unofficial ones, many amateurs who did not wait for an official appointment, but took office in the hope that they would be later officially appointed.

The most famous executioners in France were the Sansons. In 1829 there was published in Paris a *Memoir relating to the history of the French Revolution,* by Sanson, and the following year another work, *Memoirs of the Chief Executioner, relating to the History of Paris during the Reign of Terror,* and finally in 1863 appeared six volumes entitled *Seven Generations of Executioners, 1688–1847. Memoirs of the Sansons, arranged, edited, and published by H. Sanson, formerly Chief Executioner to the Courts of Paris.*

None of these works is of the slightest historical value, and in fact the last one is pure fiction, Sanson being paid a fee for the use of his name. Actually he did not contribute a single word to the book nor a single authenticated story of any execution he undertook!

In the National Archives is preserved the Commission of 1688 by which Charles Sanson, called Longval, was appointed to succeed one Nicolas Lavasseur.

"Charles Sanson . . . office of executioner of judgments and criminal sentences . . . to have, hold, and henceforward employ, for the enjoyment and use of the said Sanson by the rights of *havage,* in the fairs and markets of our said town, provostship, and viscounty of Paris, all fruits, profits, revenues and emoluments belonging to it. . . ."

Charles Sanson was married to Marguerite Jouenne, daughter of the executioner of Caudebec-en-Caux, and this relationship was probably the cause of his applying for and being appointed the executioner for Paris. On her death he married, in 1699, Jeanne Dubut, and Charles retired from the office in fact, though not officially, and was succeeded by the son of his first marriage, also Charles.

The second Charles succeeded to the office officially in 1707 on the death of his father. He married his stepmother's sister and by her had three children, a daughter, and two sons, Charles Jean Baptiste and Nicolas Charles Gabriel. In 1726, when Charles Jean Baptiste was but seven years of age, his father formally transferred the office of executioner to him. He died the same year, so that the official executioner of Paris in 1726 was a boy of seven! There are other instances in the official records of children succeeding to their father, although they were specifically not called upon to act until they were of age, substitutes being appointed.

During Charles Jean Baptiste Sanson's minority François Prudhomme acted as executioner. Charles Jean took over his duties in 1740 and married his guardian's daughter by whom he had ten children, seven sons and three daughters. He was succeeded by Charles Henri, the eldest son, in 1778, on his father's death, although he had been carrying out executions on behalf of his father for some years previously. This Charles Henri was the Sanson of the Revolution, the executioner of Louis, by the Grace of God King of France and of Navarre.

All Charles Henri's six brothers became executioners, as well as his uncle, and it is related that the family used to meet and dine together at intervals, from which arose the custom of giving the executioners the names of the towns in which they practised, Charles Henri becoming Monsieur de Paris, another, Nicolas, Monsieur de Rheims, and so on, and Monsieur de Paris remains to this day.

When the Revolution began Charles Henri had been official executioner for twenty-one years. He retired in 1795, when the Terror was over. But of that time, of the flower of France who fell at his hand he left no note, spoke no word with one brief exception, a letter about the death of the king. The one man who could have told all—told nothing. During the Reign of Terror, Charles Henri was assisted by his son, Henri, who succeeded him officially in 1795 and died in 1840, being succeeded in turn by his son, Clement-Henri Sanson. In 1847 he was dismissed from his post for pawning the guillotine, and the long dynasty of the Sansons in Paris came to an end.

The last of the Sansons was succeeded by one Heindreich a descendant of executioners, who died in 1872, and was succeeded by Nicholas Roch, his chief assistant. Roch also came from a family of executioners. He took part in 173 executions, 82 of which took place during his term as chief executioner of France. He died in 1879 and was succeeded by one of his assistants, Louis Stanislas Deibler, in whose family the post of Monsieur de Paris still remains.

He died in 1904. He began as an assistant executioner in Brittany, and in 1862 was transferred to Algiers, where he found many opportunities of following his profession. He married the daughter of the celebrated executioner, Rassneuf, and was succeeded by his son, Anatole. Until the great prison was closed the Deiblers erected the guillotine outside the gates of La Roquette, where all Parisian executions took place.

Of the French Revolution and the Reign of Terror much has been written; of stories of the last moments of the victims of the guillotine there are many; of descriptions of the scenes round the scaffold, of the brutality of the mob much has been recorded. And of all these it can only be said that a great deal has been imagined.

There has come down no contemporary record by an experienced observer of the years of the Revolution. "Yet among all these people whom a horrible curiosity attracted to the spot," writes Lenotre, in his book *The Guillotine and its Servants*, "there was not one who thought of taking notes day by day of his impressions and recollections. Ah, if only we possessed—written by some obscure man with no prejudiced views and no thoughts of posing for posterity— the *Journal of a Parisian during the Terror !* But, incredible as it seems, that journal was never written."

And again, "Descriptions of the sad scenes are rare to a degree that no one could imagine." I am referring to descriptions that are sufficiently detailed to rise above ordinary insignificance, and sufficiently authenticated by the name of their authors to inspire complete confidence in the incidents they describe. I do not remember having read, in the journals of the time, a single one that is worthy of mention. . . . This absence of documents is one of the characteristics of the period. The number of onlookers surrounding the scaffold was great, especially in the early days.

Between July, 1789, and October, 1796, it is stated in one account that 3,000 persons in Paris alone were guillotined.

There was, during the Revolution, no such thing as the

freedom of the Press. Editors either wrote what they were told to write, or had their papers suppressed and their heads cut off. Some three hundred writers in Paris alone were guillotined. The files of the contemporary newspapers are unreliable, and where facts are recorded they are coloured with the opinions of the ruling faction. The silence of the contemporary Press about the guillotine itself is one of the most significant signs of the terror it inspired. But such silence has added greatly to the difficulties of the historian.

Sanson himself only revealed once what he and he alone could reveal. An account of the king's execution appeared in one of the papers, purporting to be an interview with Sanson. The latter wrote denying the account.

"Here is the exact truth of all that occurred at Louis Capet's execution," he wrote. "When he left the carriage to be executed he was told that he must take off his coat. He made difficulties about it, saying that he could be executed as he was. On its being represented to him that the thing was impossible he himself helped to remove his coat. He again made the same difficulty when the question of tying his hands arose, but held them out himself when the person who accompanied him told him it was a last sacrifice. He then asked if the drums would go on beating all the time. He was told that nothing was known about it and this was true. He mounted the scaffold and tried to press forward to the front, as though he wished to speak. But it was again pointed out to him that the thing was impossible. Then he allowed himself to be led to the place where he was to be bound, and there he cried out in a very loud voice:

" 'People, I die innocent!' Then turning, he said to us: 'Messieurs, I am innocent of all that I am accused of. I hope that my blood may cement the happiness of the French people!' Those were veritably his last words. The sort of little discussion which took place at the foot of the scaffold related to his thinking it unnecessary to remove his coat and to have his hands tied. He also suggested cutting off his own hair.

"And, to pay due respect to the truth, he went through all this with a degree of coolness and fortitude that astonished us. I am perfectly convinced that he derived his fortitude from the principles of religion, by which no man, it seemed, was more inspired or convinced than he,

SANSON

"Executioner of Criminal Sentences."

Under French law executions must take place in public. Nowadays the condemned man is guillotined at dawn, the place of execution is surrounded by troops and the watching crowd see little. The guillotine is erected but a short while before it is required, before the prison in which is the condemned man. The latter has no knowledge he is to die until he is awakened at dawn and told his hour has come. The following contemporary account of the execution of Landru, the notorious French bluebeard, in 1922, is typical of the modern procedure:

"The news that President Millerand had refused to accept an appeal for mercy was first known in Paris at 6 o'clock last night. Almost at once journalists and would-be sightseers started off to Versailles by train and by motor car.

"Large numbers of troops and police had been specially ordered for duty, and the magistrates had arranged for a system of tickets and inspection. At 3 o'clock in the morning, the streets which faces both the assize court and the adjacent low-lying wide walls of the prison, was cut off from traffic by a double line of infantry, while cavalry stood by their horses ready to mount at the order. In front of the court and prison stand the offices of the Versailles Préfecture, and the only private houses within view of the executioner are two cafés. One of these was closed at midnight and the other was kept discreetly open to provide a shelter for the journalists.

"Before the scaffold arrived the police magistrate in charge of the proceedings came up with an ample staff and all those without tickets and passes were ordered outside the police and military cordon. When the preparations were over and only those authorised were left facing the great dull-red archway set gloomily in the ghostly white wall

The "New Drop" at Newgate

The Newgate gallows was copied from a type used in Dublin, and had a collapsible platform. A dozen criminals at a time could be hanged from this scaffold, and the print shows ten sufferers being executed.

[*Face page* 82

THE DEATH CHAIR

The illustration shows the chair used for electrocutions in America.   The condemned man is strapped immovably in the chair as quickly as it takes to pinion a
man for hanging in England and a current of 2,000 volts is passed through his body,
causing instant death.

of the prison, a dull rumble arose in the distance. A low murmur from the crowd behind the cordon followed. The soldiers made way for a long, black van drawn by two horses which clattered along, and swerving in a wide circle drew up close to the prison gates.

"A frail black figure, clad in an ill-fitting frock coat and with a hard felt hat with a deep crêpe band, appeared as if from nowhere. It was Deibler—Monsieur de Paris.

"He conferred for a brief second with the two men who descended from the van, both clad in loose, ill-fitting overalls. With constant creaking and an occasional clatter the parts of the guillotine were brought out. It took an hour to erect. With its two arms stretched skywards, some twelve feet high, its plank facing the prison gates and some four paces from it, the guillotine looked strangely small and insignificant.

"The magistrates, the counsel for the defence, the Government prosecutor, the prefect of Versailles, the chaplain and the clerk of the court were assembled, meanwhile, in a waiting room in the prison. In Landru's cell there burned a solitary gas lamp. At 5.45 the procession of blackcoated officials halted at the door of the cell. A warder opened in response to a gentle tap. The Government prosecutor began his customary speech (to tell Landru his appeal for mercy had been refused), but Landru sat up and interrupted.

" 'I know, gentlemen, why you have come. There is no need to tell me. I am an innocent man, but I will die bravely. I know that this is not your fault and I forgive you.'

"With strange dignity Landru prepared for the executioner. He placed himself in position so that one of Deibler's assistants could cut away his shirt collar and trim his hair behind. The customary glass of rum and the last cigarette were waved politely aside. After being closeted alone a few minutes with the chaplain Landru announced that he was ready.

"The signing of the prison register for the last time and the final adjustment of the prisoner's hands behind his back took barely a minute more.

"Meanwhile Deibler had slipped out ahead. One last glance at the guillotine, and then he held on to the rope and pulled the weighty foot-deep triangular blade to the top of its course. It had a six-foot drop to reach the level of the block.

"Cavalry facing the prison gate were seated stiffly on their horses with drawn sabres. A hundred yards distant on the other side were mounted troops, and the infantry with fixed bayonets were standing to attention.

"The sun was not up, but a cold, clear grey light filled the sky. There was a creak, and the red double doors slowly swung back. Within was a small knot of officials—and the chaplain with uplifted crucifix. Then, framed against the opening—Landru. Erect, he kissed the Cross held to him by the priest and facing the guillotine just four paces from him, stepped forward, held on either side by the executioner's assistants. He was pushed forward on to the plank, which at once brought his head between the grooved uprights. The upper flap slid into place, and with a crash the knife fell. A minute later the baskets containing the body and head had been placed in the van which, followed by an escort of cavalry clattered away in the growing light to the cemetery."

The large crowd which had assembled saw practically nothing. And that is all that most French spectators see of an execution.

By the French code a parricide is executed under peculiarly impressive circumstances. The condemned man's head is muffled in a black veil, and he is barefoot. His sentence is read out to him as he stands facing the guillotine. Under the code a parricide shall also have his right hand cut off before he is executed, but this part of the sentence is always passed over, though the remainder of the ceremony is carried through.

"The connection of the guillotine with the horrors of the Revolution," says the *Encyclopædia Britannica*, "has hindered its introduction into other countries, but in 1853 it was adopted under the name of *Fallschwert*, or *Fallbeil*, by the Kingdom of Saxony."

In Germany the guillotine is used as well as the sword. I quote from an account of the execution of Kurt Tetzner, at Regensburg, in May, 1931.

"Kurt Tetzner was guillotined at Regensburg yesterday. As prescribed by law, twelve independent citizens witnessed the execution. Half a dozen representatives of the Press were also allowed to be present. The executioner, Reichhardt, is a man of 80. This was the sixtieth occasion on which he had exercised his office. There have been only two executions in Germany since 1928, when the Government began to contemplate the abolition of the death penalty in the new penal code."

There has, from time to time, been considerable controversy whether death by the guillotine is instantaneous. To settle the question it was carefully investigated by three doctors following the execution of a man named Prunier. Their report, given in the *British Medical Journal* for December, 1879, says, *inter alia*, "we have ascertained, as far as is humanely possible to do so, that the head of the criminal in question had no semblance whatever of the sense of feeling; that the eyes lost the power of vision; and, in fact, the head was perfectly dead to all intents and purposes."

CHAPTER VI

FAMOUS EXECUTIONERS

THE profession of headsman, hangman, remover, lord high executioner, or by whatever other title he may have been known, is very ancient. The predecessors of Tom Cheshire, Calcraft, Marwood, Binns, Ellis and Pierrepoint have been, through many generations, vile, despicable wretches, felons *in esse* or *in posse*, thieves and murderers who had barely escaped the gallows, who retained always an intimacy and fellow-feeling with criminals, and who not seldom relapsed into crime.

For example, in 1538 Cratwell, described as " the hangman of London," was executed at Clerkenwell for " robbing a youth in Barthemews Fayre," and a similar fate overtook John Price, who was hanged in 1718.

Roger Gray, who was the Exeter hangman in the seventeenth century, hanged, among others, his own brother, and he wrote to his nephew: " I am much afflicted to be the conveyancer of such news unto you as cannot be very welcome. Your father died eight days since, but the most generously I ever saw man. I will say this of him everywhere; for I myself trussed him up. He mounted the ladder with good grace; but spying one of the rounds broken, and being a lover of order, he turned to the sheriff and desired it might be mended for the next comer, who perhaps might be less active than himself."

Gray ultimately was drowned when on a drinking bout on board a ship at Topsham.

The following extract from the *Derby Mercury* for April 6th, 1738, is a striking commentary on the conduct of the public executioner of the time.

"Hereford, March 25th. This day Will Summers and Tipping were executed here for housebreaking. At the tree, the hangman was intoxicated with liquor, and supposing that there were three for execution, was going to put one of the ropes round the parson's neck, as they stood in the cart, and was with much difficulty prevented by the gaoler from so doing."

The hangman's functions under the old and ruthless penal code were those of a human butcher. The gallows were like shambles. The executioner not only slew; at times he dismembered. He performed ruthless barbarities, often with refined and sickening cruelty, on condemned traitors; carried their quarters and decapitated heads back to prison in a basket to be boiled previous to exposure.

It was inevitable that any man who discharged such loathsome duties should degenerate into a callous, cold-blooded ruffian. An executioner constantly and exclusively engaged in the taking of human life, under the conditions which formerly held, must, by the very nature of his avocation, become brutalised. Dr. Arnold, in 1854, relates how one executioner at Bamberg was present at 1,600 executions!

The hangman in Ireland wore a grotesque mask on his face, and was otherwise disguised in a most fantastic manner. On his back was an enormous hump, formed by a concealed wooden bowl, on which he received the shower of stones that poured on him the moment the cart drew away from under the culprit's feet. Tom Galvin, the hangman, was quite a noted character in his day. He is reported to have made a good deal of capital by the exhibition of the implements used in the execution of criminals. Persons used frequently to visit him in his old age to see the rope with which he had hanged many of his own nearest relatives.

On occasion he was asked to exhibit his system of placing the rope round the necks of those he was called upon to deal with professionally, and his favourite practical joke was to slip the noose suddenly round a visitor's neck, and give it a suddden jerk so as to nearly strangle him. If a criminal was ever respited, the old man would curse and grumble at anyone "taking the bread out of the mouth of a poor old man." He always exhibited the greatest impatience, and grumbled and swore if the criminal on the ladder took too long a time to say his last prayers.

"Long life to you!" he used to exclaim. "Make haste wid yer prayer; the people is getting tired under the swing-swong."

In early times in England the persons selected to inflict capital punishment were not voluntary servants. In many manors certain families were hereditary executioners, and though they held small plots of land as rewards for their services, they could not refuse to do the office to which they were born. Shakespeare (*Coriolanus*, Act I, sc. i) mentions hereditary hangmen, and it is noticeable that in the manor of Stonely, close to the poet's native village, there were four such hereditary officials. As a mark of distinction the " gallows men " had to wear red tippets on their shoulders. They had to do the menial work of the manor as well as hang the knaves.

Coke, in his *Commentary on Littleton*, also speaks of tenure for gallows services, and says that of all forms of socage, or tenure, that is the worst. France had the family of Sansons as headsmen from 1683 to 1847, but after seven generations the office fell into the hands of M. Deibler, through the direct Sanson line failing.

In Andrews' *Old-Time Punishments*, it is stated:

"The royal burgh of Wigtown had, in early days, a public executioner of its own, a privilege which was permitted it upon somewhat peculiar conditions, if the traditional accounts are to be credited. The law was that this functionary was himself to be a criminal under sentence of death, but whose doom was to be deferred until the advance of age prevented a continuance of his usefulness, and then he was hanged forthwith. If, it was said, the town permitted the executioner to die by the ordinary decay of nature, and not by the process of the cord, it would lose for ever the distinguished honour of possessing a public hangman."

It is said that Wigtown, made a royal borough in 1341, lost its hangman because he died a natural death.

Conventional pictures of old executioners, especially in

the case of the headsman, have usually shown him in a sort of uniform of black tights and wearing a black mask. It has not, however, been customary for the executioner to wear any definite uniform, although a certain conventional dress has been recognised from time to time. The executioners of the French Revolution often wore overalls, over their ordinary clothing, and a petition from one of Sanson's assistants appealing for an allowance for new clothing, reads "Our clothes are ruined in a very short time, in spite of the precautions we take to prevent, in some degree at all events, the terrible effect that executions have upon them."

In an old German pamphlet describing the execution of a man named Fetzer in 1803 by the guillotine there is a description of Hamel, the Cologne executioner. "On the day of an execution he appeared in a sort of official garb, a black tail coat, short silk knee breeches of the same colour, white silk stockings, shoes with silver buckles, a three-cornered hat with gold band and tassels, and a sword with silver hilt and white metal sheath."

A top hat is part of the present day conventional dress of the German executioner.

The executioners of Spain were for a time compelled to have their houses painted red, and were not allowed to walk in the streets except in a garment which had a gallows embroidered on it.

The literature of Great Britain on the hangman is very varied. Of one of these worthies it is related that in order to escape punishment for stealing chickens John High or Heich, accepted the office of Edinburgh executioner in the year 1784. It was one of the customs of " Auld Reekie " to confine in jail the executioner for eight days previous to an execution, so as to have the official there in good flesh, sober and to a certainty.

The public executioner of Dumfries had a curious privilege. The remuneration for his services, for some centuries, was largely in kind, and was levied by the executioner himself. He would walk through the market place, where farmers and others had set out their wares, and dip a large iron ladle into the sacks, putting the result of each dip into his own sack. This levy was strongly resented by the farmers, but it was not until 1781 that any serious attempt was made to stop it. The levy was all the more onerous, as it was made weekly and not on the occasion of an execution. But despite protests the tax continued to be levied until 1796, when the hangman was given the sum of £2 yearly as compensation for its abolition, an amount which was far from compensating him. He, however, was paid a regular salary and allowed to live rent free.

The London executioner came latterly to be a great character, for one by one the provinces lost their professional hangman by death, and their places were not filled but the London man sent for. Calcraft made large sums officiating in this way.

Bleackley, in his *Hangmen of England*, quotes a remarkable list of perquisites of Donald Ross, of Inverness, at the beginning of the nineteenth century. Ross was in office for over twenty years and during that period had hanged only three men. The following were his privileges:

"First, he had been provided with a house and bedding.

"Second, he was allowed 36 peats for the tacksman of petty customers.

"Third, he had a bushel of coals out of every cargo of English coals imported into the town.

"Fourth, he was allowed a piece of coal, as large as he could carry, out of every cargo of Scotch coals.

"Fifth, he had a peck of oatmeal out of every hundred bolls landed on the shore.

"Sixth, he had a fish out of every creel or basket of fish brought to the market.

"Seventh, he had a penny for every sack of oatmeal sold in the market.

"Eighth, he had a peck of salt out of every cargo.

"Ninth, he was allowed every year a suit of clothes, two shirts, two pairs of stockings, a hat, and two pairs of shoes.

"Finally, he had levied extensive blackmail in the shape of Christmas boxes."

The city of Glasgow, in the early nineteenth century, contracted with one Young to act as executioner for £1 a week, a free house with coal and candles, a pair of shoes and stockings once a year, and a fee of a guinea for each execution.

The following account shows that hanging was an expensive matter:

"To the Right Honourable the Lord Commissioners of His Majesty's Treasury.

"The humble petition of Ralph Griffin, Esq., High Sheriff of the County of Flint, for the present year, 1769, concerning the execution of Edward Edwards, for burglary:

"SHEWETH

"That your petitioner was at a great difficulty and expense by himself, his clerks, and other messengers and agents he employed in journeys to Liverpool and Shrewsbury, to hire an executioner, the convict being of Wales it was almost impossible to procure any of that country to undertake the execution.

	£	s.	d.
Travelling and other expenses on that occasion .	15	10	0
A man at Salop engaged to do this business, gave him in part	5	5	0
Two men for conducting him, and for their search of him on his deserting from them on the road, and charges on inquiring for another executioner .	4	10	0
After much trouble and expense, John Babington, a convict in the same prison with Edwards was by means of his wife persuaded on to execute his fellow prisoner. Gave his wife . . .	6	6	0
And to Babington	6	6	0
Paid for erection of gallows, materials and labour: a business very difficult to be done in this country	4	12	0
For a hire of a cart to convey the body, a coffin, and for burial	2	10	0
And for other expenses, trouble and petty expenses on the occasion at least	49	19	0

Which humbly hope your lordships will please to allow for petitioner who, etc. . . . .

In Scotland, up to the end of the eighteenth century, civic feasts were often held before or after an execution. Thomas Potts, who was hanged at Paisley in 1797, cost the town £33 5s. 3½d., out of which £13 8s. 10d. was expended on a civic feast and £1 14s. 3d on the entertainment of the executioner and his assistants. At Edinburgh, the evening before an execution, the magistrates met at Paxton's Tavern, in the Exchange, and made the final arrangements over their drinks. These gatherings were appropriately known as "splicing the rope."

Jane Jameson, who murdered her mother near Newcastle, was executed on the Town Moor. She was taken to the Moor in a cart, which was also occupied by a turnkey. In the cart was her coffin, upon which she sat. By the side of the cart walked the five porters with javelins and twenty constables with staves.

Afterwards a statement of accounts was published of the cost of the execution. These showed that the executioner was paid £3 3s.; the cart which the unhappy woman occupied along with the driver cost 15s.; mourning coach 15s. 6d.; joiner's bill for the erection of the scaffold, £8 5s. 3d.; and special allowance to joiners, 6s. Altogether it cost the county £28 13s. 3d. to execute Jane Jameson.

It will be noticed how heavy the joiner's bill for the erection of the scaffold. The supplying of the material for such purpose and the erection of the scaffold were not any man's work, and often great difficulties were experienced in finding the men to do the work. As late as 1912, for example, when two men lay under sentence of death at Lewes, in Sussex, the local tradesmen refused to supply any of the materials necessary.

It is interesting here to see how the art of hanging has contributed to the language. Every sailor, builder and the public generally know what a derrick is. Early in the seventeenth century a man named Derrick served under the Earl of Essex. For a serious crime he was condemned to death but pardoned, and employed to hang twenty-three others. He did it with gallows in the form of a little derrick.

In a number of European countries grandees, nobles and other distinguished people have as coats of arms such suggestive articles as ladders, gibbets, wheels, racks, axes, blocks and similar symbols of the scaffold to indicate their ancestry.

The origin of the name Jack Ketch as applied to the public executioner is thus explained in Lloyd's "MS. Collection of English Pedigrees" in the British Museum. "The Manor of Tyburn, where felons for a long time were executed, was formerly held by Richard Jacquet, whence we have the name Jack Ketch as a corruption."

The earliest hangman whose name has descended to us, if we may trust the authority of that accomplished anti-quary, Dr. Rimbault, is one Bull, who is mentioned in his public capacity in Gabriel Harvey's tract against Nash, called "Pierce's Supererogation" (1593). Bull was succeeded by the more celebrated Derrick, already mentioned. In Dekker's *Bellman of London*, printed in 1608, under the article "Prigging Law," are the following notices of this worthy.

"For he rides his circuit with the devil, and Derrick must be his host, and Tiburne, the land at which he will light. . . . At the gallows, where I leave them, as to the haven at which they must cast anchor, if Derrick's cables do but hold." . . . Derrick held his unenviable post for nearly half a century.

The next hangman was the notorious Gregory Brandon, who, as the story goes, by a ruse played upon Garter King at Arms, had a grant of arms conferred on him, and was thereby "made a gentleman"; which the mob in a joke soon elevated into esquire, "a title by which he transferred to his successors in office." The coat of arms was granted in December, 1616 (Register of the Garter, ii. 399). He had frequently acted as a substitute for Derrick, and had become so popular that the gallows was sometimes called by his Christian name, as may be seen by the following lines:

" This trembles under the Black Rod, and he
   Doth fear his fate from the Gregorian tree."

Gregory Brandon, who died about the year 1640, was succeeded by his son, Richard, who claimed the gallows by inheritance. He had the credit of being the executioner of Charles I, and of being honoured by an account in the *Dictionary of National Biography*, from which some of the following notes are taken. The son was usually known as "Young Gregory," and he is said to have prepared for his calling at an early age by decapitating cats and dogs. He succeeded his father shortly before 1640. In 1641 he was a prisoner in Newgate on a charge of bigamy, from he seems to have cleared himself. He was the executioner of Stafford (12th May, 1641) and of Laud (10th January, 1644–5). Brandon asserted, after judgment had been passed on Charles I (27th January, 1648–9) that he would not carry out the sentence. On 30th January, however, it is said he was "fetched out of bed by a troop of horse" and decapitated the king. He "received 30 pounds for his pains, all paid in half crowns, within an hour after the blow was given," and obtained an orange "stuck full of cloves" and a handkerchief out of the king's pocket; he ultimately sold the orange for 10s. in Rosemary Lane where he lived. The evidence for Brandon being the executioner of Charles I, however, is not strong. The question is discussed at length in the *Trial of Charles I*, by G. J. Muddiman. Brandon executed the Earl of Holland, the Duke of Hamilton, and Lord Capel in the following March, with the same axe used on the king, suffered much from remorse, died on June 20th, 1649, and was buried the next day in Whitechapel churchyard.

On October 15th, 1660, William Hulett, or Howlett, was condemned to death for having been Charles' executioner; but three witnesses asserted positively that Brandon was the guilty person, and their statement is corroborated by three tracts, published at the time of Brandon's death. "The Last Will and Testament of Richard Brandon, Esquire, headsman and hangman to the Pretended Parliament," 1649; "The confession of Richard Brandon, the Hangman," 1649; "A Dialogue, or a Dispute between the Late Hangman and Death," 1649.

Other persons who have been credited with executing Charles I are the Earl of Stair (Hone, *Sixty Curious Narra-*

tives), Lieutenant-Colonel Joyce (Lilly, *Life and Times*), and
Henry Porter (Cal. *State Papers* Dom, 29th April, 1663;
Lord's Journal, XI, 104). Very many references to Brandon
and his father are met with in contemporary dramatic and
popular literature.[1]

An old print of the day says of Richard Brandon:

> " Who do you think lies buried here?
> One that did help to make hemp dear.
> The poorest subject did abhor him,
> And yet his king did kneel before him;
> He would his master not betray,
> Yet he his master did destroy.
> And yet, as Judas—in records 'tis found—
> Judas had thirty pence, he thirty pound."

"Squire Dun" was the next common hangman after a
very short reign by a man named Lowen, of whom nothing
is known. He is mentioned in Butler's "Ghost."

> " For you yourself to act Squire Dun,
> Such ignomy ne'er paid the sun!"

The addition of "Squire" with which Mr. Dun is here
dignified is a mark that he had beheaded some State criminal
for high treason.

Charles Cotton, the famous angler and adopted son of
Izaak Walton, refers to Dun in his *Virgil Travestie*, published
in 1670:

> " Away, therefore, my lass does trot,
> And presently an halter got,
> Made of the best strin hempen teer,
> And ere a cat could lick her ear,
> Had tied it up, with as much art
> As Dun himself could do for his heart."

Little is known about Dun, however, and he was succeeded
by the notorious John Ketch.

The first printed notice of Ketch occurs on December
2nd, 1678, when a broadside appeared called "The Plotters
Ballad," being Jack Ketch's incomparable "Receipt for the
Cure of Traytorous Recusants, or Wholesome Physicke for

[1] Cat. of Satirical Prints in Brit. Mus., Div. I; Ellis's Orig. Letters, 1st
ser. ii, v, xx, vi; 2nd ser. ix, xi; 3rd ser. iii; 5th ser. v.

a Popish Contagion." At the top of this sheet was a woodcut,
in which was shown Edward Coleman being drawn in a
sledge to the place of execution, exclaiming "I am sick of
a traytorous disease," while Jack Ketch, with a hatchet in
one hand and a rope in the other, is saying, "Here's your
cure, sir." Of the remarkable quality of the ballad below
the woodcut, the following verse is a very flattering specimen :

> " You are sick, I am told, even sick unto death,
>   And of a rebellious disease ;
>   A hempen cravat to stop up your breath
>   Will give you abundance of ease."

It may safely be assumed that there is nothing in the
whole range of English literature to equal these lines in
the boldness of the sentiment and the lucidity of the
expression.

In 1679, it appears from another pamphlet purporting
to be written by Ketch himself and entitled "The Man of
Destiny's Hard Fortune," that the hangman was confined
for a time in the Marshalsea prison. "whereby his hopeful
harvest was like to have been blasted." A short entry
in the autobiography of Anthony à Wood for 31st August,
1681, tells how Stephen College was hanged in the Castle
Yard, Oxford, and "when he had hanged about half an
hour, was cut down by Catch or Ketch, and quartered
under the gallows" (cf. Hist. MSS. Comm. 12th Rep. App.
vii, 183). In a pamphlet probably written by Ketch himself
and entitled "The Apologie of John Ketch, Esquire" (the
title of esquire being still claimed by the hangman in confirmation of the arms granted to Richard Brandon), "vin-
dication of himself as to the execution of the late Lord
Russell, 21 July, 1683," Ketch repudiated the charge that
he had been given "twenty guennies the night before that
after the first blow my lord should say, 'You dog, did I
give you the guennies to use me so inhumanly?'" He
attributed the bungling of the execution (described by
Evelyn as done in a "butcherly fashion") to the fact that
Lord Russell "did not dispose himself for receiving the fatal

stroke in such a position as was most suitable" and that he moved his body, while Ketch himself "received some interruption as he was taking aim."

Ketch successfully struck for higher wages in 1682—a fact to which allusion is made in D'Urfey's popular Butler's "Ghost" (1682). In the "Supplement to the Last Will and Testament of Anthony, Earl of Shaftesbury" (1683 fol. p. 3) Ketch is referred to under the name of Catch as a person of established reputation, and in the epilogue to Dryden's "Duke of Guise" he is termed an "excellent physician." From the fact that the manor of Tyburn "where felons are now, and for time out of mind," have been executed, "was leased for a considerable time during the seventeenth century to the family of Jacquet, Arthur Collins, in his *Memoirs of the Sidneys*, assumed that the "name of the executioner has corruptly been called Jack Ketch", a suggestion already noted on page 93.

At Monmouth's execution, 15th July, 1685, Ketch played a prominent part. Monmouth, in his address to him on the scaffold, alluded to his treatment of Russell, and this appears to have totally unnerved the hangman. After three ineffectual blows, he threw down the axe with the words, "I can't do it!" and was only induced to complete his task by the threats of the sheriffs. Sir John Branston (Autobiog. p. 192) and others confirm the fact that Ketch dealt at least five strokes, and even then, according to Macaulay, he had recourse to a knife completely to sever the head from the trunk.

In January, 1686, Ketch, for affronting the sheriff, was turned out of his place and committed to Bridewell, one Pascha Rose, a butcher, taking his job. But on the 28th May, following, Rose himself was hanged at Tyburn and Ketch was reinstated.

His behaviour at the execution of Russell and Monmouth, combined with the prominent position he occupied in carrying out the barbarous sentences passed on Titus Oates and his fellows, greatly increased Ketch's notoriety. He died towards the close of 1686.

Any bungler might put men to death, it was stated of Ketch by his wife, but only her husband knew how to *Make them die sweetly*. Ketch is mentioned in Butler's " Ghost" in the following lines:—

> " Till Ketch observing—he was chous'd,
> And in his profits much abused,
> In open hall the tribute dinn'd
> To do his office or refund."

Another well-known executioner of the time was Crosland. In the days of Charles II the father and his two sons were tried at Derby Assizes for horse-stealing. All were found guilty, and the bench of judges, in a cruel whim, said they would pardon any one of the criminals who would consent to hang the other two. This barbarous offer was first made to the father, who indignantly refused it.

"What!" said he, "a father hang his two sons? Can I consent to take away the life I gave? Shall I put to a cruel death the boys I have cherished, and who to me have been dearer than life itself? No, no! Let me suffer a hundred deaths first!"

The elder son was then asked if he would put to death his father and younger brother, and so save his own life.

"No!" said he. "Life is the most valued of all possessions, but even life may be purchased too dear. I cannot keep my own life by taking that of him to whom I owe my existence. How could I have the world? How could I endure *myself*, the only one left of a family I had destroyed?"

The offer was then made to John, the younger son, who accepted it.

He proved expert enough to be appointed to the post of hangman for Derby and two or three neighbouring counties. This office he held to an extreme old age. He was heartless and cruel, and long after he died, in 1705, mothers frightened naughty boys into quietness with the detested name, "John Crosland."

John Price, an ex-seaman of the Royal Navy, was appointed public hangman for the City of London and the

*Traîtres regardez et tremblez, elle ne perdra son
activité que quand vous aurés tous perdu la vie*

THE GUILLOTINE

The guillotine is associated with France more than any other
country, but in a similar form it was used in Germany and Italy many
years before its terrible falling blade cut off the flower of France in
the Reign of Terror..

[*Face page* 98

Scottish Maiden

The Scottish Maiden, a form of guillotine, was introduced into Scotland by the Earl of Morton who was beheaded by it in 1581. Its use was discontinued in 1710.

Halifax Gibbet
(*From an old print*)

"From Hell, Hull and Halifax, good Lord deliver us," is a popular Yorkshire saying. The Halifax referred to the Halifax gibbet, a form of guillotine which flourished in the sixteenth century The last known execution by the gibbet was in April, 1650.

County of Middlesex in 1714. Price was too fond of women, wine and song to last for long. While returning from an execution at Tyburn he was arrested for non-payment of a debt of 7s. 6d. This was followed by other summonses, and Price was confined in the Marshalsea, and William Marvell appointed temporary hangman in his place.

The hangman was paid partly by "piece work," partly by a small fixed salary, and partly by the receipts from perquisites. These latter included the clothes of the malefactors he hanged and payments for their corpses from the Company of Barber-Surgeons by which they were "anatomised" under the law. At the time of Price, the hangman's post was worth about £40 a year, equivalent to about ten times that amount in present day money.

Robbed of his salary and perquisites, Price found no opportunity to pay his debts. In 1718 he escaped from prison, attempted to ravish an old stall-keeper, named Elizabeth White, and so severely assaulted her that she died. He was hanged at Bunhill Fields on May 3rd, 1718, the crowds cheering as they lined the route from Newgate where he had been confined.

William Marvell, who took Price's place, was the executioner of the Jacobite rebel lords who were beheaded in 1716, Lord Derwentwater and Lord Kenmure on Tower Hill among them. Marvell received a fee of £3 for each such execution, apart from the presents from the peers themselves. But Marvel, like Price, could not resist women and drink, and getting into debt was served with a writ on the way to Tyburn in November, 1717, following which he was dismissed from his post. The following appeared in the columns of John Applebee's *Journal* for November 16th, 1717.

"On Tuesday last (November 12th, 1717) Ketch Esqre, was removed from the office of Executioner-General of Great Britain; and one Banks, a Bailiff's follower, is appionted to succeed him."

Marvell was convicted of stealing in 1719 and sentenced to transportation.

Little is known about Banks, who succeeded him. In Applebee's *Journal* for November 30th, 1717, it is stated,

"This week a new hangman was presented to the Collegians at Newgate, who, we hear, highly approved of the choice, and 'tis expected he will this day at the Old Bailey perform some part of the operation of his office."

Banks hanged the Marquis de Paleotti, the brother-in-law of the Duke of Shrewsbury, who had murdered his servant. Banks also hanged John Price, his predecessor but one in office.

When Banks ceased to be executioner and was succeeded by Richard Arnet is not known. Arnet died in 1728. During the years when Banks and Arnet were executioners Jack Sheppard was hanged at Tyburn and Catherine Hayes burnt alive for the murder of her husband. It seems certain that Arnet was the executioner in the latter case.

Arnet was succeded by one John Hooper, who held office for seven years, 1728-1735. He was assistant turnkey at Newgate when his application for the part of hangman was acceded to. Reed's *Journal* of the time, recording the appointment, referred to Hooper as a man "Of an unspotted character." Hooper hanged Sarah Malcolm, in Fleet Street, for the murder of her mistress and two fellow servants in 1733. Two years later the post of hangman was being held by John Thrift, but there is no record of Hooper's death or dismissal. Thrift held his post for seventeen years, and on the day of his appointment he had to execute no fewer than thirteen criminals.

Thrift beheaded the Jacobite rebels of 1745, including Lord Kilmarnock and Lord Balmerino, but he was a bad headsman, and bungled many of the executions so terribly taking two or three blows of the axe to decapitate his victims, that he became one of the best hated of all executioners. He was followed by hooting crowds, and in March, 1750, he was forced to defend himself with a drawn cutlass. In the riot which followed, a man named Ferris was cut down and killed, and Thrift was tried for his murder and sentenced to death. He was, however, reprieved and carried on as the hangman, though broken in health, and he died on May 5th, 1752, after having been public executioner for nearly eighteen years.

Thrift was succeeded by Thomas Turlis, who held office for twenty years. Like other hangmen before him, and his own immediate predecessor in fact, he narrowly escaped the gallows, his offences being stealing coals. Turlis reigned during the Wilkes agitation and riots, and during 1768–1769 he was on peril of his life on more than one occasion. He was a man of great personal courage, however, and never lost his presence of mind.

Turlis hanged Earl Ferrers, whose procession from Tower Hill to Tyburn was particularly impressive. He drove to the gallows in his own carriage drawn by six horses, followed by a hearse and six to convey his body afterwards to the Surgeons' Hall. Turlis died suddenly in 1771 on his return from a hanging at Kingston.

Edward Dennis, who succeeded Turlis, was hangman for fifteen years from 1771–1786, and had the unique distinction, among hangmen, of carrying on his trade first at Tyburn for twelve years and then at Debtors' Door outside Newgate Prison. He also saw the pulling down of old Newgate Prison and the erection of a huge new prison in its place.

Dennis was a rather stupid and unimaginative man, an industrious plodder, with no claims to brilliance.

During his reign Dennis hanged the well-known highwayman John Rann, nicknamed Sixteen-string Jack, because he used eight strings to tie each of his breeches.

The first well-known criminals hanged by Dennis were twin brothers, Robert and Daniel Perreau, hanged at Tyburn in 1776. They were forgers, and their case became a *cause célèbre*, largely owing to the implication of Margaret Caroline Rudd, the mistress of Daniel, a lovely and clever woman with great personality. She was, however, acquitted.

It was January, and London was frost-bound and under deep snow. The brothers went to Tyburn in a mourning coach, preceded by a black-draped open cart containing a boy highwayman, gaudily dressed, and two ragged Jews, housebreakers, who were also to suffer. On a hurdle behind were two coiners. An unprecedentedly large crowd filled the streets.

A double gallows had been erected, with a cross-beam on the left for the Jews and another on the right for the Christians.

Dennis hanged in June, 1777, a clergyman, the Rev. William Dodd, D.D., a popular preacher and a man of good life, who fell into debt owing to extravagance and committed forgery to clear himself. He was a fop nicknamed the "Macaroni Parson." Owing to the good he had done, there was great agitation for a reprieve, but it was not granted. While in the condemned cell Dr. Dodd wrote *Thoughts in Prison*, a work which long survived him.

His friends planned to save him at the last by having him cut down and hurried to the house of an undertaker in Goodge Street, where a famous surgeon would be waiting to revive him. It was reported that Dennis would make a specially loose noose, also that a silver tube would be placed in Dodd's throat. The consequence was that a crowd even surpassing that at the Perreaus' execution turned out to see Dr. Dodd hanged.

For fear of a rescue Hyde Park was filled with two thousand soldiers. Dodd journeyed to Tyburn in a mourning coach, accompanied by a friend and the famous Ordinary, the Rev. John Villette (1773–1799). The crowd sympathised entirely with Dodd, and most of them were in tears as he passed.

A third famous criminal whom Dennis hanged was the Rev. James Hackman, author of a *crime passionel* which aroused widespread interest. He was infatuated with an actress, Miss Martha Ray, who was the mistress of Lord Sandwich, First Lord of the Admiralty, and shot her in a portico of Covent Garden Theatre as she was leaving after a performance. He was hanged at Tyburn on 19th April, 1779, and was accompanied to the scaffold by James Boswell, the biographer of Dr. Johnson.

Edward Dennis figured prominently in Dickens' *Barnaby Rudge*, but the picture given of him there, a ringleader in the attack on Newgate Prison, is not historically true, nor did he die on the gallows as Dickens portrayed.

His part in the riots was only a small one, and came about accidentally. Going home one evening along Holborn, he saw a crowd looting a Catholic chandler's shop at New Turnstile, and out of excitement got drawn into the work of destruction. The authorities were informed and he was arrested. He pleaded that the mob had forced him to take a hand in the looting, under threat of burning him. He was brought in guilty and sentenced to death.

He cried and knelt for mercy.

"My will was innocent, but my body was compelled," he pleaded.

At the Tothill Fields bridewell he was placed in a separate room, as the keeper was afraid his fellow rioters would kill him if he were housed with them. He begged that if he were hanged his son might succeed to his post; however, a few days later he received a free pardon, "so that he could hang his fellow rioters."

For some weeks afterwards there was a series of bungled executions, but it is not known if Dennis had resumed his executions or whether some inefficient person was still acting as substitute.

So thoroughly did Dennis regain favour that in 1785 the Sheriffs of London presented him with a most gorgeous official robe "as a testimony to his excellent mode of performing business." Dennis found this robe not only inconvenient when at work, but rather conspicuous at other times, so he sold it to Old Cain, a well-known charlatan of the day. Decked in the hangman's robe and a pasteboard crown, the fortune-teller cut a most imposing figure.

At this time, according to a contemporary newspaper, the hangman's salary was £30 a year. Fees of 6s. 8d. for each execution and 5s. for each whipping brought the total up to about double this sum.

The following from contemporary prison records throws a vivid light on the cost of the average "common" execution:

"Paid for halters, 5s. Cart and horse to attend execution, 10s. Paid executioner, £1 1s. 0d. Wine for Sacrament, 1s." and another, from a record of the following year (1780),

"For executing William Childs and Thomas Chitwynd, £1 1s. 0d. For halters, 2s. Wine for the Sacrament, 1s. 3d. Cart and horses to attend the execution, 10s."

The last of Dennis' four famous criminals was William Wynne Ryland, hanged for forgery in August, 1783. Ryland met death very bravely, though a thunderstorm delayed execution for thirty minutes. The execution of John Austin, in November of that year, was the last to take place at Tyburn. The march through the town had become an obstruction and waste of time, collecting unsavoury crowds. Tyburn was now a fashionable residential district and the inhabitants objected to a gallows there.

Henceforth City of London or County of Middlesex felons were hanged in front of Newgate. Dr. Johnson objected strenuously to the change, on the ground that an execution ought to draw spectators. "The public was gratified by a procession; the criminal was supported by it. Why is all this to be swept away?"

The first execution here, of ten criminals, was performed by Dennis and Brunskill on December 9th, 1783.

Dennis died on November 21st, 1786, at his home in the Old Bailey. He was buried at St. Giles'-in-the-Fields on November 26th.

William Brunskill succeeded Edward Dennis, immediately, for on the very day after Dennis' death he had to execute seven criminals single-handed. In spite of a large and critical crowd watching, Brunskill, though very nervous, managed everything admirably.

As the bodies swung side by side in their white caps, Brunskill, in an access of nervousness, stepped forward and bowed deeply to the crowd as though to ask their commendation. This had never been done before, and was typical of the man's deprecatory nature, always humble and intensely anxious to be approved. He was a careful but not a particularly skilled hangman, and sometimes bungled things.

Hitherto the punishment for women for husband murder, coining and debasing the coinage had been to be burnt at the stake (after first being strangled). This barbarous custom was abolished during Brunskill's hangmanship, and the last sentence of this kind was carried out in 1789, when Christian Murphy, convicted of coining, suffered at the Old Bailey. The law was abolished in 1790.

At the execution of Governor Wall, Brunskill bungled badly. The hostility of the crowd to the felon apparently made him nervous, and he was further worried by having had to give a promise that the condemned man's leg should not be pulled, as was now the invariable custom. He arranged the noose twice, and even then, on the fall of the drop, the knot slipped behind Wall's neck, and he took fifteen minutes to die in agony, with both hangmen pulling his legs to shorten the pain.

Brunskill also hanged Colonel Despard, sentenced to death for high treason in 1803. This execution took place on the roof of Horsemonger Lane Gaol—called the New Gaol—in the Borough. He and six associates were condemned, for plotting to assassinate the king, to be hanged, drawn and quartered, but actually they were beheaded after death—a farcically horrible proceeding. As each head was severed by a masked man, said to be a surgeon, Brunskill held it up to the crowd, crying, "This is the head of a traitor."

At the execution of two criminals in February, 1807, when the mob sympathised with the condemned, the huge crowd was packed very tightly. Suddenly an unexplained panic broke out, and for a long time there was fighting, scrambling and trampling. The bodies were finally cut down, still to the accompaniment of shouts of fury and groans of pain. Thirty people were killed that day, and many others badly injured. Criminals condemned for crimes at sea were not executed outside Newgate, but at Execution Dock, at the riverside between Wapping New Stairs and Wapping Dock Stairs. A primitive gallows was erected as required on the foreshore when the tide was low. Brunskill hanged here Captain John Sutherland, for the drunken murder of his negro servant, after an imposing procession from Newgate, which included the Deputy Marshal bearing the Silver Oar. This marked the authority of the Civil Court over those afloat. The execution was watched by a huge crowd gathered on the foreshore, in small boats at the water's edge and up in the riggings of ships.

The last notable criminal hanged by Brunskill was John Bellingham, the murderer of Spencer Perceval, then Prime

Minister. The murder was committed in the lobby of the House of Commons, and the slayer was a homicidal maniac. But in those days there was no Broadmoor, and so on May 18th, 1812, Bellingham paid the penalty. As the Government was unpopular, the murderer had much sympathy from the populace gathered to see him hang. Many were the cries of "God bless you", many the hoots directed at the hangman.

Brunskill had now held his post as chief executioner for twenty-six years and was an old man of sixty-nine in poor health.

In 1814 he had a stroke and John Langley, his assistant, actually succeeded him as hangman, though Brunskill did not formally resign until the following year, when Langley, who evidently felt secure as to the permanence of his post, had engaged James Botting as his assistant. Owing to his long service, the Court of Aldermen granted Brunskill the generous pension (in those days) of fifteen shillings a week.

John Langley was appointed, on account of his service of nearly twenty-five years as Brunskill's assistant. Very little is known about his character or personal life, beyond the fact that he was forty-eight when appointed as hangman, a married man with three children.

John Langley hanged Eliza Fenning, a famous murderess of only twenty-one, who at the time was widely believed to be innocent. Efforts for a reprieve failed and she was hanged at the Old Bailey in July, 1815, dressed all in white except for lilac-coloured boots.

Langley and Botting passed through an ordeal in March, 1817, when they hanged John Cashman, in Skinner Street, Snow Hill. Cashman had been condemned to death for participation in the Spafields Riots, and as these were a popular outbreak and he was the sole sufferer, the crowd sympathised entirely with him, and persistently hooted the hangmen, who were guarded by police and soldiers.

Shortly afterwards Langley, who had been out of health for some time, was taken to the London Hospital, where he died on the 27th of April, 1817, at the age of fifty-one, "of mortification."

James Botting, who succeeded Langley as chief hangman, was one of the least attractive of the long line of "Jack Ketches." He had a surly and callous nature, and was only too fond of asserting himself, as is evidenced by the fact that in the first few months of his tenure of office as assistant he asked the court of Aldermen for a rise in salary. He received 10s. 6d. a week, which does not seem exorbitant, but the records do not state if his request, which was referred to the sheriffs, was granted.

After being appointed to be chief hangman, Botting tried again, this time making the usual request to be allowed to employ an assistant. For some reason this request was refused, the Court declaring that an assistant was unnecessary.

Much arggieved, in 1818 Botting compiled a third petition bristling with grievances.

"Your Petitioner, James Botting, succeeded to the office of executioner on the demise of the John Langley, the late executioner who as his predecessors had always received small fees from the undertakers and friends of the criminals executed, also the privilege of rubbing persons afflicted with wens, for which it was usual to receive 2s. 6d. for each person. That the late John Langley at the time of the Sessions received 2s. 6d. per day for his attendance, whereas your Petitioner has the duty of two persons, there being no assistant executioner as was always before, and your Petitioner has only 1s. a day.

"That your Petitioner from the demise of John Langley until within a few weeks received the usual fees and payments with his weekly pay. He was fully satisfied, and always endeavoured to discharge his duty with diligence and attention.

"That your Petitioner understands he no longer receives the fees and emoluments due to him.

"That you Petitioner prays your consideration as regards the loss of his fees, for his small salary is insufficient to support him."

This was signed with a mark, "Jemmy" Botting being illiterate.

Apparently this petition had some effect, for at about this time the post of hangman improved both socially and pecuniarily. He became a salaried official of the Old Bailey, receiving from this establishment a settled wage of £1 a week. He was better protected from the mob at executions, which must have been a satisfaction to Botting, who in his petition had complained of the "great personal danger" of the office of executioner.

Of all hangmen, Botting was perhaps the most hardened and the least amiable. He seemed thoroughly to enjoy his unpleasant work, and never showed the criminals he hanged any of the little courtesies possible in his office. He was dirty and ill-groomed in his person. In general he had no humour, but when he showed it it was always in connection with his grim work.

Thus on one occasion, in the days when he was still assistant to Langley, some loafers gibed at him relentlessly about his work, and a listener asked him if he did not answer back.

Jemmy frowned. "Nay, I never quarrel with my customers," he said.

That there was truth in his words is shown by the fact that one of his foremost persecutors on this occasion, Falkener by name, did, a short time afterwards, become one of his "customers," being hanged for rape.

"Jack Ketch" did not confine his work to London, for many local authorities found it hardly worth the expense of keeping their own hangmen, and would send to London for Botting when occasion required. Better transport made it possible for the hangman to travel almost as long distances as he does in modern days, and Botting went all over the Home Counties, and often to the West or Midlands of England on jobs. In Scotland, Lancashire and Yorkshire, however, local hangmen were employed. At this time York, Lancaster, Edinburgh, Glasgow, Perth and Inverness each had its own Jack Ketch.

Botting's most notable execution was that of the five ringleaders of the Cato Street conspiracy on May 1st, 1820. Thistlewood, who had also been concerned in the Spafields riot, but had got off then on a legal technicality, was the moving spirit. All five were decapitated after being hanged.

Soon afterwards, for some reason not known, Botting's tenure of the hangman's post came to an end, and it is recorded that in February, 1824, James Botting, "late hangman," was resident in the London and Middlesex debtors' prison. The Corporation procured his release and granted him a pension of 5s. a week, in 1826 increasing this by the same amount. Jemmy went to live at his birthplace, Brighton. He was now crippled after a paralytic stroke, but used to get about by pushing a chair in front of him and sitting on it whenever he felt fatigued. He was well hated and shunned by his neighbours.

Botting died on 1st October, 1837, seventeen years after his retirement.

John Foxton, or Foxen, who became Botting's assistant in 1818 held office until 1829. His first famous criminal was Henry Fauntleroy, the banker, and it was Foxen who executed William Corder, the author of the murder of Maria Marten in the Red Barn. Corder fainted on the scaffold and Foxen hanged him before the signal was given by the governor of the prison. He considered that he had been interfered with in the execution, and said indignantly afterwards, "I never like to be meddled with, because I always study the *subjects* which come under my hands, and according as they are tall or short, heavy or light, *I accommodate them with the fall.* No man in England has had so much experience as me, or knows how to do his duty better."

In the later part of the day of execution he visited the corpse in the Shire Hall, for the purpose of claiming Corder's trousers. On this occasion he pointed to his handiwork upon the neck of the criminal, and asked exultingly if he had not "done the job in a masterly manner." A city contractor, who was in the habit of showing Foxen some favours, said to him one day, "Suppose I were to have the misfortune to be condemned to death, could you have the heart to hang me?"

Foxen replied, scratching his head, "You know, master, somebody must do it, and why not me, because I know how to do it more comfortably for you than anybody else."

William Calcraft, who succeeded Foxen, held office as public executioner for a longer period than any other man, being hangman from 1829 to 1874, forty-five years. He beat by the substantial margin of five years his predecessor, John Foxen.

Calcraft is said to have been born at Baddow, near Chelmsford, in 1800, one of a family of twelve children, and he followed various precarious occupations before he became a hangman. He was in turn a shoemaker, a watchman at a brewery in Clerkenwell, butler to a gentleman at Greenwich, and finally a hawker earning his living from hand to mouth. It was while hawking that he accidentally made the acquaintance of Foxen.

"You're a fine strapping fellow," said Foxen. "I want a fellow like you to help me at Newgate with the floggings. A reg'lar job's better than hawking any day."

Calcraft accepted the offer of ten shillings a week which was made to him to flog youngsters who had been sentenced by the magistrates. While in the prison Calcraft watched Foxen carrying out his executions in front of Newgate, and soon learnt all there was to know in those days of crude executions. At that time most capital offenders were tried on a Friday and executed in rows of from three to six the following Monday. On one occasion when Foxen was engaged in London, Calcraft was sent up to Lincoln to execute two men there. He did it so successfully that on Foxen's death, in 1829, he was appointed public executioner. Practically all the most notorious murderers during his period of office passed through his hands, including James Greenacre, who murdered and horribly mutilated a woman named Hannah Brown; Courvoisier, who murdered Lord William Russell; John Tawell, the Quaker murderer of Sarah Hart; Rush, the Stanfield Hall murderer; the Flowery Land pirates; Catherine Wilson, one of the most notorious poisoners who ever lived; Margaret Walters, the baby-farmer; and a host of others.

Calcraft's first execution after his appointment was that

of a woman, Esther Hibber, condemned to death for the murder of a workhouse child. She had had charge of a number of these poor children and the story of her cruelty had so inflamed everyone that when Calcraft appeared on the scaffold to hang her he was cheered again and again, and there were loud cries of: "Good old Calcraft! Three cheers for the hangman!" It must surely have been almost unprecedented for the hangman to be greeted in that way. Another remarkable thing connected with Hibber's execution was that she was hanged in a strait waistcoat. She had been extremely violent ever since her arrest and it was impossible to control her in any other way.

For his services Calcraft was paid a guinea a week by the City of London, and a guinea for every execution. He still continued to carry out the floggings ordered, each flogging netting him half a crown.

But there were many other perquisites of his office. He was also appointed executioner to Horsemonger Lane Gaol in Surrey, for which he received a guinea for each execution and a yearly retaining fee of five guineas, and here he hanged the Mannings. As he became better known his services were in great demand in different parts of the country, and he was able to command a fee of £10 to £15 every time he went out of London. In one way and another, indeed, Calcraft earned a very good income.

Another way in which he made money was by the sale of the perquisites of his office. For years it was the custom for the executioner to have the *criminals'* clothing and all the property found on *them* at the time of their execution, and these Calcraft usually sold to exhibitions, such as Madame Tussaud's and others. He also had the rope with which he hanged a culprit, and this he would sell to morbid relic-hunters at anything up to five shillings an inch, according to the notoriety of the offender.

All accounts go to show that normally Calcraft was a kind-hearted man enough, though he betrayed no signs of emotion on the scaffold. He was very fond of his children and grandchildren, and kept a number of pet animals, to which he was devoted. On the scaffold he invariably dressed in dead black, and he rarely allowed himself to be hurried or to betray any emotion. He was a rather remarkable-looking man, with a beard which turned white before he retired. In the streets he might easily have been mistaken for a prosperous grocer or other tradesman. He was a man, too, of great physical strength, a very necessary thing at times in those days of public executions, when a lesser man might have gone in fear of his life from the mob.

Calcraft, during his long term of office, became very well known, and his many friends used to chaff him about his work. One day he came into his club, and a man cried out, "When I come to London the hangman is always the first person I see."

"You may be sure," retorted Calcraft good-temperedly, "that he will also be the last."

As might only be expected in the days of public executions, when ignorance and superstition were rife, Calcraft was the recipient of more than one curious request. There were many superstitions about hanged men, such as that a piece of the rope with which they were hanged warded off the evil eye and insured its owners freedom from danger of hanging.

It was in connection with one such superstition, extremely widespread in the last century, that Calcraft was the object of an angry demonstration from the mob. It was at the hanging of John Holloway, in December, 1831, for the murder of his wife. At the execution was a man who all his life had suffered from an unsightly wen on his neck, and he persuaded Calcraft to allow him to come on the scaffold to try the old superstitious method of attempting to cure the wen by stroking it with the hand of a hanged man.

As soon as Holloway had ceased to struggle Calcraft unpinioned his arms, and, taking one of the dead man's hands, began stroking the man's wen with it. The mob at once started to groan and hiss, thinking Calcraft and his companion were playing some terrible joke. The performance was hurriedly stopped by the sheriffs, and Calcraft very nearly lost his position for agreeing to the extraordinary request.

This year was the year of the great Reform Bill riots all over the country. The gaols in Bristol and Gloucester were attacked and set on fire, and hundreds of prisoners were set free. There were riots in nearly every big town, and many of the rioters were sentenced to death, Calcraft being kept very busy travelling all over the country executing offenders. Many of these were absolutely indifferent to their fate. One man, George Hearson, at Nottingham, for example, did a dance on the scaffold, and called out to various friends in the crowd, while Calcraft adjusted the ropes round the necks of two of his companions who were being hanged with him.

There is a well-known rule that the executioner must sleep in the prison the night before an execution, though this rule was not in force when Calcraft was first appointed. But in his later years he had to observe it, and once very nearly failed to carry out an execution on that account. He had to go to Scotland and he was met at the station by some practical jokers who carried him off and kept him till late at night. Meanwhile the sheriff had been sending all over the place for the missing executioner, and was almost in a state of collapse when Calcraft at last managed to get away and appear at the prison. His anxiety can be understood when it is realized that the law lays it down that the sheriff himself must carry out an execution in the absence of a properly appointed deputy.

One of the most remarkable men Calcraft hanged was William Godfrey Youngman, who murdered his sweetheart in the Walworth Road, London, and was executed before Horsemonger Lane Gaol in 1860. Youngman's crime was an extremely callous one and was carried out for a paltry amount of insurance. When Calcraft appeared Youngman greeted him quite coolly.

"Strap my legs tight and be sure to shake hands with me before I go," he said calmly.

This request of the condemned for one last handshake was very commonly made to the famous hangman, and was one which he never refused.

Calcraft carried out the last public execution in England, that of Michael Barrett, the author of the Clerkenwell

Explosion in 1868. Barrett was executed in front of Newgate, and as it was well known that this would be the last public hanging a large crowd assembled to witness it. Barrett's body was left to hang the usual hour, and when Calcraft came out to take it down he was greeted with loud cries of "Come on, body snatcher! Take away the man you've killed." But he went on with his grim task as though there was not a soul present.

The last criminal whom Calcraft hanged was John Goodwin, executed at Newgate on the 25th of May, 1874. He resigned his appointment and was given a pension of twenty-five shillings a week, by the City of London. He died in Hoxton in December, 1879.

William Marwood, who succeeded Calcraft, was famous as the inventor of the "long drop," which was certainly the forerunner of the much more humane method of execution now employed. Before Marwood's time the process of hanging was, in the great majority of cases, only a form of slow strangulation and a very slow one at that.

Marwood was born at Horncastle, in Lincolnshire, in 1820, and there he lived all his life, following the trade of a cobbler when not engaged at an execution. He early took a great interest in executions, though until he was appointed hangman he had never actually seen a man hanged. But he had read everything he could on the subject, and he was always very eloquent on the way in which Calcraft used to choke his subjects to death.

Marwood worked out his long drop method, by which a man's neck was scientifically broken by the sudden jerk on the rope, and when he was called to London to answer to his application for the post of executioner on the death of Calcraft, he was so eloquent and convincing in his arguments that he was appointed out of a large number of applicants.

It is very extraordinary, by the way, how many people are eager to occupy the post of public hangman. On Marwood's own death nearly a hundred candidates applied for the vacant position. These included men from all ranks of society, among them being clerks, doctors, ex-army and navy men and a butcher.

ARREST OF JACK KETCH
(*From an old print*)

The early executioners were sorry ruffians and more than one suffered on the scaffold and went through the agonies which he had inflicted on others. Cratwell, in 1538, the hangman of London, was executed for robbery, and a similar fate overtook John Price, the hangman, in 1718.

[*Face page* 114

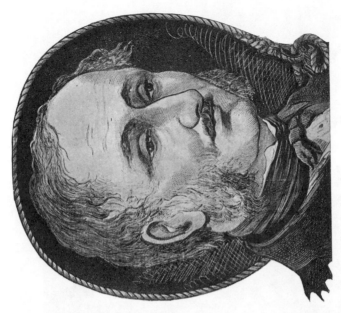

WILLIAM MARWOOD

William Marwood was appointed executioner in 1879. He was famous as the inventor of the "long drop" and for being the man who executed the notorious Charles Peace. He was executioner for only four years, but during that period he introduced many reforms

[*By courtesy of Messrs. Chapman & Hall*]

WILLIAM CALCRAFT

William Calcraft held the post of hangman longer than any other man, from 1829 to 1874. He carried out the last public execution in England, that of Michael Barrett in 1868.

Face page 115]

It is a curious fact that, although the applicants hail from all parts of the country, the greatest numbers write from Lancashire, with Yorkshire next, and other counties a long way behind.

Marwood's first execution was at Lincoln, where he hanged a man named Harry so successfully by his new method that he was soon in demand by various prison authorities throughout the country.

When he was appointed to the post he was successful for some time in keeping his new position from the knowledge of his neighbours. But when it became known in Horncastle he was continually being hooted at and hissed for some months afterwards. He was actually very proud of his position and had cards printed:

WILLIAM MARWOOD,
Public Executioner,
Horncastle, Lincolnshire.

He strongly disliked the word hangman, and never referred to himself as anything but the public executioner. Over the door of his little cobbler's shop in Horncastle he had printed in large letters, "Marwood, Crown Office." The shop was a small, one-storeyed place close to the church, and in addition to the implements of his trade which filled the place, there were hung from the roof the coils of rope with which he had carried out many of his executions. He was very proud of them and was always prepared to talk about them and the famous criminals whom they had hanged. One such rope had hanged four well-known criminals, Charles Peace, Dr. Lamson, Lefroy and Kate Webster.

Marwood had a very high view, in fact, of the office he held.

"I am doing God's work," he said, "according to the Divine command and the law of the British Crown. I do it simply as a matter of duty and as a Christian. I sleep as soundly as a child and am never disturbed by phantoms.

Where there is guilt there is bad sleeping, but I am conscious that I live a blameless life. Detesting idleness, I pass my vacant time in business. It would have been better for those I executed if they had preferred industry to idleness."

Charles Peace used frequently to tell a story about himself and Marwood. He related that when he was living at Nottingham he took a journey to London and travelled in the same compartment as Marwood, who was going to officiate at an execution. Marwood, as was his wont, talked freely of his past executions, and when the train arrived in London Peace shook hands with his fellow-traveller and said jokingly, "If you ever have to do the job for me, be sure you grease the rope well, to let me slip."

"All right, I will!" laughed Marwood.

Even on the morning of his execution Peace could not refrain from joking. He had been worried by a very bad cough for some days.

"I wonder," he said to one of the warders, after a fit of coughing, "if Marwood can cure this cough of mine."

He asked to see the executioner a few minutes before he was officially due to appear.

"Do your work quickly," he begged Marwood.

"You shall not suffer pain from my hand," was the answer.

"God bless you!" returned Peace. "I hope to meet you all in Heaven!"

He allowed himself to be pinioned with no show of fear, and walked to the scaffold with a steady step. After he had taken his place on the trap-door and his feet had been strapped together, Marwood prepared to adjust the white cap, when Peace cried out, "Stop a minute!"

For several minutes then he made a farewell speech to the newspaper reporters and others present. Marwood then drew the white cap over his head.

While waiting for the appointed hour to hang Lefroy, who murdered Mr. Gold on the Brighton railway, Marwood actually gave a lecture to the reporters who were allowed to be present, and showed the greatest pride in all his preparations.

"That rope you see there," he said, pointing to the rope hanging from the scaffold, "is two and a half inches round. I have hanged nine with it."

The lecture went on for ten minutes, until a warder came up and signified to Marwood that the time had come for him to pinion Lefroy. "Death is proverbially swift," wrote a reporter, describing the scene. "In the guise of Marwood it moved with appalling celerity."

In Marwood's day the condemned man or woman was not always pinioned in the condemned cell. Kate Webster, for example, was pinioned on the scaffold, as were Lamson and others. Dr. Lamson, who murdered his nephew, was in a completely dazed state, and seemed utterly oblivious of what was happening, having to be supported all the time by two warders. From first to last he never spoke.

Another notorious medical man whom Marwood hanged was Dr. Chantrelle, who poisoned his wife and was sentenced in Edinburgh after a most sensational trial. Chantrelle was very self-possessed on the morning of his execution. He made a good breakfast of coffee, bread and butter and eggs, and asked to be allowed to have a last smoke, a wish that was naturally granted. Just before Marwood pinioned him he was given a glass of whisky. He gave every assistance he could to the hangman, remaining stoically calm. When he came in sight of the scaffold he seemed to eye it with an air of sheer curiosity. He did not say anything or show any fear at all, but stepped quickly on the drop and went to his death apparently the calmest person present.

Wainwright, the Whitechapel murderer, who was executed in Newgate, was another whom Marwood hanged and who appeared fearless on the scaffold. He walked rapidly and coolly from the condemned cell, and did not speak.

"Aren't you sometimes nervous of the work you have to do?" Marwood was once asked.

"Nervous?" he echoed. "England does not send nervous men out on a job of this kind, and why should I be nervous, I'd like to know?"

Marwood always carried his own straps and ropes with him, and he often made his hotel expenses by pinioning a number of people and showing them how he would hang them if he were officially called upon to do so!

Yet Marwood was a pious man, and, like Berry, he used to kneel down and pray to God for the man whose life he was about to take. He was a very mild man, who delighted in the company of others. His life was threatened on more than one occasion, and particularly after he had hanged Joe Brady, for the Phœnix Park assassinations of Lord Cavendish and Burke. He was offered an escort by the Home Office, but he pooh-poohed the idea.

"No! Do you think I am afraid?" he wrote. "I have had too many years at my trade to be afraid now."

Before he carried out the execution of Brady in Ireland for the Phœnix Park murder he received the following letter from the notorious Invincibles:

"Dublin, 19th May, 1882.

"Marwood. It was decided last night at a meeting of the Secret Association here to forward this communication to you to the effect that no doubt you are longing intensely for the job to murder us here by your rope for the wilful murder of Burke and Cavendish. Well, don't be in a hurry, for although we are all in Dublin we are not caught yet and not likely to be for this paltry £10,000 (the reward offered). Should we be arrested and convicted, on the peril of your life you must not set foot on the soil of this city or any part of this country of Ireland. If you do you will never get out of it alive. You very narrowly escaped from Armagh the last time you were there, but you will not escape the next time you come over here. Even if you have an escort we shall manage the whole lot of you about right. We know you. There can be no mistake in the carrying out of this resolution, so now you are warned. Your movements will be telegraphed here from the time you leave Horncastle until you get here, if you get so far under a false name and false business. We want no hangmen in this country to carry out English law."

Marwood merely forwarded the letter to the Home Office, with the brief comment that he was taking no notice of it.

Not long before he died he created quite a sensation by visiting the House of Commons during a sitting. He was at once surrounded by the members of Parliament and asked innumerable questions, and before he left he had presented one of his cards to all who spoke to him, with the joke on his lips that he would always be willing to oblige any member if called upon!

He was an inveterate joker, except when actually carrying out an execution. At Kirkdale Gaol there were some steps leading up to the execution shed, and, going up them to prepare the rope and so on, Marwood slipped.

"Somebody will be killed coming up these steps, if they don't mind," he remarked.

When Sir Robert Meade was at the Colonial Office he was shocked at the way in which executions were carried out in Malta. He summoned Marwood to advise him on a change, and the executioner advocated the long drop.

"Why," he said to Sir Robert, "Charles Peace was a little man, and I gave him the long drop, and 'e passed hoff like a summer's heve."

Marwood received £10 for each execution, in addition to his expenses. Like Calcraft, he had a retaining fee from the City of London, of £20 a year. Calcraft, however, was a recognised official, whereas Marwood had no official status.

He died at Horncastle in 1883, and an inquest was held on his body because wild rumours were flying about that he had been poisoned by the Irish Invincibles in revenge for his executions. The *post mortem* showed, however, that he had died of inflammation of the lungs.

"I can see him now," wrote Major Arthur Griffiths, in his *Fifty Years of Public Service*, "as he stood talking to us, and found it difficult to reconcile his external appearance with his dreadful calling. He looked what he had been, not what he actually was; he was once a local preacher and leading light in one of the little known sects, and had achieved success in the line of pulpit oratory. Be this as it may, he still dressed the part, and in his plain pepper-and-salt overcoat, dark trousers, and his wisp of white neckcloth round his short throat, he seemed capable of still engaging the attention of his audience. His face was hard, shrewd, but not unkindly. It was strongly marked, rugged almost in its deep lines and furrows; the eyes were quiet, resolute, and penetrating; the mouth grim, firm, and set as one of his own nooses."

James Berry was the public hangman from 1884 to 1892, and though executioner for only eight years, he hanged two hundred persons, and had some very remarkable experiences during those years. Few men have had such a strange career as the Yorkshire ex-policeman who also in his time was a shopkeeper, a showman, lecturer, auctioneer, lay preacher and farmer.

Berry was born in the little town of Heckmondwike, in Yorkshire, on February 6th, 1852. His father was a wool stapler, and he was rather better educated than most boys of his station. When he was old enough he became a policeman in the Bradford and West Riding police, and while in the force he was introduced to Marwood, with whom he soon became great friends.

Marwood explained to Berry all the details of hanging, and, though Berry had no intention at that time of changing his job, what he learnt from the hangman was later to come in extremely useful. But a bad wound he received on the head during a fight with some ruffians in a public-house in Bradford incapacitated him from further police work and he was compelled to resign. For a little while he tried his hand at salemanship, without much success, and shortly afterwards he saw the announcement of the death of Marwood.

In 1884 two poachers, Vickers and Innes, were sentenced to death at Edinburgh for the murder of two gamekeepers, and Berry learnt that the magistrates of Edinburgh were looking round for a hangman. He wrote:

"I was very intimate with the late Mr. Marwood, and he made me thoroughly acquainted with his system of carrying out his work, and also with the information he learnt from the doctors of different prisons which he had to visit to carry out the last sentence of the law.

"I have now one rope of his which I bought from him at Horncastle, and have had two made from it. I have also two pinioning straps made from his, also two leg straps.

"I have seen Mr. Calcraft execute three convicts at Manchester thirteen years ago, and should you think fit to give me the appointment I would endeavour to merit your approval."

Berry was accepted on the strength of this letter; but when he reached the prison he began to have qualms as to whether he could carry out his task properly, despite what he had learnt from Marwood. But his natural Yorkshire obstinacy made him determined to see the thing through.

He was a deeply religious man—he turned preacher after he resigned from his post—and that night he knelt down and prayed for the souls of the men he was to hang. He made it a constant practice to pray for the condemned on the night before their death at his hands.

He admitted, afterwards, that he was in a terrible state of nerves over this first execution. He hoped against hope for a last-minute reprieve. He related that on the night before he carried out his dread duty he tried to read, but the word "gallows" seemed perpetually to be jumping out of the page at him. He was up at five on the execution morning. He had provided himself with an assistant named Chester, and in actual fact the execution not only passed off without the slightest hitch, but the new hangman was complimented on the quickness and skill he had displayed.

After this he was called upon to carry out many executions. He was the first hangman to work out a series of graduated drops according to the weight of the man he was executing.

The drop does not always break a man's neck. In the 'eighties a Royal Commission took evidence in some forty cases of hanging, and found that in nine instances the neck was neither broken nor dislocated. During that period Berry was called upon to hang a man named Henry Devlin who brutally murdered his wife. At the last Devlin proved to be an utter coward and had great difficulty in walking to the scaffold, having to be supported on each side by warders.

When Berry pulled the lever the condemned man disappeared from sight in the execution pit, but to the horror of everyone present the rope still continued to quiver, and there seemed to be sounds coming from the pit. Berry instantly knew that the drop had failed to break Devlin's neck and he was strangled to death. The fact was not allowed to leak out at the time, however. All executions at the time are without incident.

John Withey, who murdered his wife, was thought by the prison officials at Horfield Gaol, Cumberland, to be an innocent man until the very last minute. Steadfastly he had protested his innocence to the warders, the governor of the prison and the chaplain. When Berry entered the condemned cell, he said quietly to the prisoner, "Are you ready?"

"Yes," replied Withey. And then, suddenly, "I am not going to confess to you."

"Will you confess to the chaplain?" asked Berry.

"Yes, I will," answered Withey, white-faced.

Berry immediately went out of the condemned cell to where the officials were waiting. They were astonished to see the executioner coming from the condemned cell alone, and his words astonished them still more.

"The prisoner wishes to confess, sir," he said to the waiting clergyman.

And for a few minutes all stood there except the chaplain, who entered the condemned cell and learnt the truth at last from the man who had so steadfastly protested his innocence. Afterwards the unhappy man broke down and wept on his way to the scaffold.

One of the most nerve-racking ordeals Berry underwent was when he was called upon to hang Walter Wood, at Strangeways Gaol. Wood had been sentenced for the murder of his wife, but the remarkable thing was that Berry and Wood had been to school together. Berry was very distressed over this execution.

Berry was a leading figure in one of the most extraordinary scenes which ever took place on the scaffold. That was the attempt to hang Lee, the Babbacombe murderer. The story has often been told.

Three times Berry placed Lee on the drop and pulled the lever, and three times the trap doors refused the fall. Yet the scaffold worked perfectly when Lee was not on it, as Berry tested for himself. Altogether the unnerved officials spent half an hour trying to carry out the sentence of the law, and at the end of that time the governor was so overwhelmed that he took on himself the responsibility of ordering the execution to be postponed until he had received further instructions from the Home Office. In consideration of the ordeal Lee had undergone, he was afterwards reprieved. It was suggested that the wood work of the scaffold had expanded with the wet and that it jammed every time a weight was placed on it.

Mr. Bowen-Rowlands, in his book *In the Light of the Law*, gives a prosaic explanation of the failure to hang Lee.

"An old lag in the gaol confessed that he was responsible for the failure of the drop to work. It appears that in those days it was the practice to have the scaffold erected by some carpenter from among the prisoners.

"The man inserted a wedge which prevented the drop from working and when called in as an expert he removed the wedge and demonstrated the smooth working of the drop, only to reinsert it before he (Lee) was again placed on the trap."

This experience with Lee had a very bad effect on Berry, and he began to think that it was the hand of Providence which had prevented him from hanging an innocent man. In after years he publicly announced that he felt convinced he had hanged several innocent persons, though it is extremely doubtful if this was the case. The plain fact was that he was suffering from nerves.

On several occasions he went to Ireland to carry out an execution, but it was always a nerve-racking ordeal.

"How I hated those executions in Ireland, and how I trembled for my own safety!" he exclaimed once.

The Irish hated the hangman, whoever he was, and Berry, while in Ireland, habitually carried a loaded revolver. Crowds always assembled outside any prison in which an execution was taking place, and blood-curdling threats were uttered as to what would happen to the hangman if they caught him. Berry left the prison as soon as possible after his task was done on these occasions, and by some back way. After he had executed Arthur M'Kevan, for instance, for the murder of his sweetheart, a huge crowd gathered on the quayside at Belfast by the boat on which it was expected that Berry would return to England. It was only with the greatest difficulty that he arrived on board safely.

When Berry hanged James Kirby, in Ireland, a large crowd gathered outside the prison in Tralee, kneeling in the road to pray for the soul of the man about to die. In the midst of them was Mrs. Kirby.

"You are hanging an innocent man!" cried Kirby, when Berry entered the condemned cell. "I never did it. I want you all to take notice of what I say."

"I am convinced," said Berry in his reminiscences, "that on that day I hanged an innocent man, but I was the servant of the Government, so what could I do?"

Berry was taken away from the prison in a carriage protected by a mounted escort. The large crowd which had assembled hooted and jeered and shook their fists at him as he was driven away. This execution produced in the hangman a serious nervous breakdown, from which he did not recover for some weeks.

The last execution at which Berry officiated was that of Conway in Liverpool. The condemned man had tried to commit suicide by cutting his throat, and there ensued a ghastly scene when he was hanged, all the large blood-vessels of the neck being lacerated. This execution so sickened Berry that he sent in his resignation.

Afterwards the ex-hangman became a lay preacher, and was strongly opposed to capital punishment. He always expressed the hope that he would live to see the day when hanging would be abolished in England.

He was paid £10 for each execution, plus second-class travelling expenses. If the condemned man, for whose execution he was retained, was reprieved, Berry was paid a fee of £5. Berry died in 1913.

James Billington succeeded Berry. He had been an executioner for some seven years, but had only carried out executions in Yorkshire, for which county he was the official hangman.

Billington was a hairdresser in Farnworth when he carried out his first execution in 1884 at Armley Gaol, the gaol in which Charles Peace was hanged. From the very first Billington had no feelings of nervousness, and the execution of Laycock passed off without any incident at all. Billington was a man who early made up his mind that an execution could not be too quickly accomplished, and he made a number of improvements which resulted in the cutting down of the time to a minimum. He discarded the belt and straps which had been used, and substituted a double buckled strap which was much quicker. The old form of pinioning before his time usually took a minute and a half. The new hangman reduced this to half a minute.

Among the notorious criminals James Billington hanged were Neil Cream, Louise Massett, who murdered her illegitimate son at Dalston railway station, Patrick M'Kenna, the Bolton murderer, and James Canham Read, the Southend murderer.

Cream poisoned a number of unfortunates, and it was in connection with this form of crime, made notorious by Jack the Ripper, that a remarkable scene occurred on the scaffold at his execution. Jack the Ripper, whose murders of women of this class had terrorised London, was never identified. After the rope had been placed round Cream's neck and the white cap drawn over his face, he called out sharply,

"I am Jack——"

He never finished the sentence, for Billington had pulled the lever.

"If I had only known he was going to speak I should have waited for the end of the sentence," declared Billington afterwards. "I am certain that Neil Cream and Jack the Ripper were the same man."

It will never be known for a certainty, however, though there is little doubt that Jack the Ripper must have been a man with good surgical knowledge, and the highest authorities held that he was a doctor. That he was Neil Cream, however, is doubtful, for certain known dates in the latter's career make it appear impossible for him to have carried out some of the Ripper murders.

Canham Read, who murdered Florence Dennis at Southend, was very afraid of death. On the morning of his execution he asked particularly to see the surgeon of the prison.

"Are you sure it won't hurt me?" he asked.

Although assured that it would be absolutely painless, he was in a state of collapse when Billington entered the condemned cell, and he had to be given a strong dose of brandy to enable him to walk to the scaffold.

In the fortnight which included the hanging of Canham Read, Billington was called upon to carry out no fewer than seven executions in different parts of the country. One of these was that of George Emery, hanged at Newcastle on December 14th, 1894, who appeared completely indifferent to his fate. The following morning Billington hanged two men at Winchester. One, a sailor named Rogers, kicked off his shoes on the way to the scaffold.

"That's better," he said with a smile. "I'll not die in those. It was them that brought me here."

Very few men make any resistance when the executioner enters the condemned cell. An exception was Walter Horsford, who poisoned his cousin, Annie Holmes, with strychnine. He was executed at Cambridge on June 28th, 1898.

When Billington entered the condemned cell, Horsford refused to have his arms pinioned, and when the hangman caught hold of him he resisted violently, and for a few moments there was an unpleasant scene. But Billington was very powerful, and he forced the murderer's behind his back and fastened the straps on his wrists.

After that Horsford was helpless and he ceased to give any further trouble.

Horsford's struggles were in great contrast to the last minute of the life of Joseph Canning, who was hanged in June, 1895, for the murder of his sweetheart. All the time he was being pinioned by Billington he kept on saying, "I wish to die. I am perfectly prepared to die. I want to join the girl I love better than my life."

He walked quickly to the scaffold and seemed anxious to get it all over.

In July, 1896, Billington, with an assistant, was called upon to carry out a triple execution at Winchester. The three condemned men were named Burden, Matthews and Smith. Burden had murdered his paramour, Angelina Faithfull, Matthews his child, and Smith a man named Payne.

A special new scaffold had to be erected in Winchester for this triple execution. The three ropes, coiled on the top of the beam, were all new ropes, which had been stretched by hanging bags of earth from them during the night.

Billington was a very human man and dearly loved a practical joke, and he used to delight in telling stories of the practical jokes he played. Once, for example, he wandered into a waxwork show in Bolton, and found one room devoted to life-sized effigies of famous criminals. The room was empty when he entered it, and Billington immediately took his place among the row of wax models and stood perfectly still.

A few minutes later a number of people entered and a woman stopped in front of Billington and vainly searched her catalogue for a description of the famous criminal! While she was looking steadfastly at the supposed effigy Billington solemnly winked one eye. Scared, she cried out to her companion. "Jack, come here. This one's alive!"

Her companion laughed at her and poked Billington in the ribs with his stick.

"Nay, lass——" he began, when Billington held up his arm and, pointing to the man, let out a loud yell. In less time than it takes to tell it the Chamber of Horrors was empty, and half a dozen terrified visitors were incoherently telling the proprietor of their experience. But when the proprietor hurried into the room a quiet-looking man was interestedly examining a wax model and reading a description of it from his catalogue as though he had never noticed anything unusual!

Billington was responsible for the execution of Milsom and Fowler, the Muswell Hill murderers, who were hanged with a man named Seaman.

Milsom made a full confession, and Fowler would have killed him for this if he had had the chance. It was anticipated that there might be trouble on the scaffold, and Seaman was placed between the other two condemned. On the scaffold Fowler called out:

"Is Milsom there?"

He looked round, saw his fellow murderer and added:

"Very well, you can go on."

Billington's last execution was that of Pat M'Kenna, on December 3rd, 1901, at Manchester. The hanging passed off without a hitch, but on the way home the executioner caught a bad cold, which rapidly developed into pneumonia. He was engaged to execute two men named Miller, at Newcastle, on the 8th of December, and he became very anxious as to whether he would be able to officiate. But he never recovered and died a few days later.

Billington was succeeded by his two sons, William and John. Both learnt their work from their father, whom they frequently assisted before they became the chief hangmen themselves. Among the famous murderers the brothers hanged were Edgar Edwards, author of the Leyton horrors; Chapman, who murdered a barmaid; Woolfe, the Tottenham murderer, the last man hanged in old Newgate; Dougal, the Moat Farm murderer; Sachs and Walters, the baby farmers; and Wade and Donovan, the murderers of a Mrs. Farmer at Stepney.

William Billington was actually the chief executioner, and was assisted by his younger brother John.

John Ellis was one of the mildest-natured men who ever

became public executioner. He was passionately fond of animals, and had been known to refuse to kill one of his own chickens because he was so attached to it. There was nothing which made him more angry than to hear of anyone who had been cruel to an animal. Very fond of dogs, especially whippets and bulldogs, he won quite a reputation for breeding the latter.

Ellis was born in Rochdale in 1874. He was the son of a hairdresser, and eventually became one himself, though he never liked the occupation. For some years he earned his living in a spinning mill, and afterwards in a big textile machine maker's before he set up as a barber on his own account, owing to an accident which prevented his carrying on with heavy work.

He was appointed assistant to William Billington in 1901, and from that time until his retirement in 1923, he was present at many famous executions, including those of Seddon, Casement, Crippen, George Smith, Armstrong and Mrs. Thompson.

It is not generally known that nowadays hangmen have to pass a kind of examination and preliminary training before they are allowed to take part in an execution. They must be men of the highest character, too, and men who, during their official life at any rate, must be capable of the most discreet silence, whatever temptations may be offered them to describe hangings in which they have taken part.

The preliminary training which they have to undergo consists in pinioning a dummy figure of a man in the condemned cell, conveying it to the scaffold, and there at a given signal "executing" it by pulling the lever. Many applicants for the post of executioner finds this ordeal quite enough for their nerves, and never get to the stage where they officiate at a real execution.

It was early in May, 1901, that Ellis was informed that he had passed the test successfully and that he had been put on the official list of executioners, but it was not until six months later that he was called upon to act as assistant to William Billington.

Ellis' first function was an ordeal even for an experienced hangman, for it was the comparatively rare double execution. The condemned men were named Miller, uncle and nephew, and they had been sentenced to death for the murder of the uncle's brother. There was no doubt that the older man was the real instigator of the crime, though he left most of the carrying out of it to his nephew, whom he plied with a drink. The result was that the nephew had nothing but feelings of animosity against his uncle, and as it was feared that there would be a scene on the scaffold it was decided to hang the nephew at eight o'clock and the uncle at nine-thirty. The long interval between was necessary, as the body of an executed man has to hang a full hour by law before it is taken down.

That night Ellis slept in a room close to where young Miller was confined. The latter was not in the condemned cell, since the only cell for that purpose at Newcastle, where the sentence was being carried out, was occupied by his uncle. All night Ellis had hardly any sleep, partly because this was his first execution, but more on account of the cries of the condemned man, who spent most of the night railing against the uncle who had ruined him.

A little less than fourteen years afterwards Ellis attended the execution of the one man who, he considered, more richly deserved his fate than any other man he had hanged. This was George Joseph Smith, of "Brides in the Bath" notoriety.

From the doctor in Maidstone Prison, the night before the execution, Ellis learnt that Smith has a diseased heart, and the doctor though it quite likely that Smith would collapse on the scaffold under the strain. It was decided to give the murderer a stiff dose of brandy a few minutes before his excution.

"I do not require that," cried Smith, when the glass of brandy was brought to him.

He walked steadily enough to his doom. Just before he reached the trap-door he called out wildly, " I am innocent of this crime!" and while Ellis was fixing the rope round his neck he again called out, "I am innocent." Those were

THE CONDEMNED SERMON

The Condemned Sermon was preached on the Sunday preceding an execution, and was attended by the rank and fashion of the day who came to look at the condemned and to hear the reading of the Burial Service.

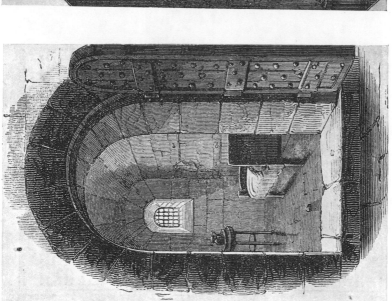

CONDEMNED CELL AT NEWGATE

The condemned cells at Newgate were ill-lighted, narrow, cold and cheerless until reforms were introduced making a condemned man's last hours comparatively comfortable.

SCAFFOLD AT WANDSWORTH

The execution shed at Wandsworth stands apart from the prison, and is callously called by convicts the "cold meat shed." The photograph shows clearly the executioner's lever and the drop.

Face page 131]

the last words he spoke. There is no doubt of his guilt, however.

Major Armstrong was a very different class of prisoner. He hardly ever spoke (unlike Smith, who spent a great deal of his time chatting with the warders), and spent nearly every waking hour reading. He was executed, in 1922, for the poisoning of his wife. Armstrong spent most of the time on his last night tossing about on his bed, and often getting up and pacing about his cell.

"It's hard to wait to die!" he cried once, on being told by one of his guards what the time was.

Armstrong was courageous at the last, one of the most courageous men who ever died on the scaffold.

"Please look straight at me when you get to the scaffold and it will soon be over," said Ellis to him, when the pinioning was taking place in the condemned cell.

"I will," replied Armstrong.

Ellis left his assistant to walk with the condemned man, while he went to the scaffold to be ready to pull the lever. As Armstrong walked along he kept his eyes firmly fixed on the executioner until the white cap was pulled over his head. As Ellis pulled the lever the condemned man called out, "I am coming, Katie!"

Katie was the Christian name of his wife.

Sergeant O'Donnell, who murdered Lieutenant Watterton, at Aldershot, on New Year's Day, 1917, was exceptional in that he was hanged in prison clothes. A condemned man always wears prison garb until the morning of his execution, when he is given his own clothing. But O'Donnell's clothes were those of a sergeant in the R.A.M.C., and it was considered a disgrace to the King's uniform that he should be hanged in it. Private Thomas Clinton, who was executed in 1917 at Manchester, was also hanged in prison dress for the same reason.

O'Donnell was in a state of collapse on the scaffold, and as Ellis stood at the lever watching his assistant strapping the condemned man's ankles he suddenly realized that the murderer was about to faint.

"Get out of the way!" he cried sharply to his assistant,

and pulled the bolt immediately. If he had not done so O'Donnell would have pitched forward in a swoon and the execution might have had to be postponed.

During his long career Ellis hanged only three women, and he always had a great and very natural repugnance from doing so. The women were Edith Thompson, Mrs. Swann, and Mrs. Newell, the Coatbridge murderess.

As is well known, Mrs. Thompson collapsed pitifully in the condemned cell, and was carried to the scaffold unconscious. The harrowing experience which Ellis underwent then was so great that he never really got over it. Susan Newell, who murdered a boy named Johnson, was actually the last woman Ellis hanged, and she created a scene on the scaffold by refusing to allow the executioner to put the white cap over her head.

Mrs. Emily Swann was the first of the three women he hanged, and as in the case of the other two, the carrying out of the sentence brought trying scenes. Mrs. Swann had been condemned to death with her lover, a man named Gallagher, for killing her husband, in 1903 at Wombwell, in Yorkshire.

When Ellis entered the condemned cell he found the prisoner on the floor, half unconscious and moaning pitifully, the two wardresses with her trying to console her and to get her to face death bravely. Ellis procured some brandy for her, and made her gulp half a glassful. It had a remarkable effect, for in a few moments she had regained control over herself.

On the scaffold she saw her lover waiting, and there ensued a strange and nerve-racking scene. Mrs. Swann seemed to be completely calmed and she said:

"Good morning, John!"

Gallagher could hardly speak for a moment, and then he replied huskily, " Good morning, love."

As the rope was placed round her neck Mrs. Swann cried out, "Good-bye. God bless you!"

If he had never hanged anyone else, Ellis would be remembered as the executioner of Dr. Crippen. It was one of three hangings in three successive days. On November 22nd, 1910, Ellis hanged Henry Thompson at Liverpool, on November

23rd Crippen at Pentonville and on November 24th William Broome at Reading.

Crippen had counted all along on a reprieve at the last moment, and when he realised that there was no hope for him he collapsed in the condemned cell, and afterwards tried to take his life by opening an artery with a piece of broken glass from his spectacles. But on the last morning he was outwardly calm, though his inward agitation was shown when he waved away the breakfast which had been prepared for him. Despite the many stories current at the time, it can be stated definitely that Crippen made no confession.

At the last he allowed himself to be pinioned without resistance, and he walked to the scaffold with a smile. From the moment Ellis entered the condemned cell Crippen never spoke. So great was the excitement over the condemned man, and so great was the public curiosity as to the last scene, that Ellis was actually offered £1,000 to give a series of lectures with Crippen as his subject.

This was not the only time Ellis was called upon to carry out three executions in as many days. In three successive days in December, 1905, he carried out executions at Stafford, Leeds and Derby. At Stafford he hanged a young man, named Edge, who had been condemned to death for killing the child of his landlady in revenge for being told to give up his rooms.

George Smith, whom Ellis hanged the next day at Armley Gaol, Leeds, was a man of great violence, and he was sentenced for the particularly callous murder of his wife. In the condemned cell he was very violent and abusive, swearing that it would be a bad day for Ellis when he entered the condemned cell. So continued were Smith's threats that the governor of the prison provided assistance outside the condemned cell on the execution morning, in case of trouble. But to the astonishment of everybody, Smith calmly and silently allowed himself to be pinioned, and never spoke at all after Ellis had started to strap his wrists together.

The day previous to executing Crippen, Ellis hanged Henry Thompson at Liverpool. Thompson brutally strangled his wife and from the first showed a callous indifference to his fate. He knew that Crippen was to be hanged the day after himself and he remarked to a warder on the night before his own execution, " Well, I shall be senior to Crippen in the other shop!"

Nor was his attitude mere bravado. He allowed himself to be pinioned with a smile, and walked to the scaffold with a smile, outwardly the coolest man present.

The day following the execution of Crippen, Ellis hanged William Broome at Reading. Broome had murdered an old woman at Slough for her money, a paltry £20. He was in such a state of nerves when Ellis entered the cell that he was given a stiff dose of brandy. The effect was extraordinary, for he pulled himself together and walked firmly to the scaffold. There he suddenly exclaimed, as the rope was being put round his neck, " I am innocent!" The next moment he was dead. Ellis always had certain doubts as to the guilt of Broome.

Occasionally the man whose official duty it is to take criminals' lives finds his own threatened. Once Ellis was apprised that he might be called upon to execute some Irish rebels, and the detectives at Scotland Yard learnt that sympathisers of the condemned men would leave no stone unturned to prevent their being sent to the scaffold. Ellis was threatened by Sinn Feiners and detectives were specially sent to Rochdale to guard him.

They were not a day too soon. It was reported to them that several strange men had been seen lurking round Ellis' house, and the evening before the Scotland Yard detectives arrived four of these mysterious men had called and frightened Ellis' wife by demanding to see him. Luckily the executioner was out.

The detectives, who were fully armed, remained hidden in Ellis' house for several weeks after that, and it was only the reprieve of the condemned men which allowed the protection to be removed.

In 1915 Ellis officiated at a double execution, though the two men concerned were unconnected with one another in regard to the crimes they had committed. One was a man named Thornly who killed his sweetheart, and the other

Hill, a negro who had murdered a companion on one of the Atlantic liners. When Thornly was in the condemned cell he remarked, "I know Ellis, the executioner. I saw him in Manchester once. I expect he will be the one to do me in."

There ensued a terrible scene on the scaffold. Thornly had taken the pinioning quietly, had walked firmly to the drop, and allowed the rope to be placed round his neck without showing any sign of fear. The negro Hill, however, was in a state of collapse, despite the dose of brandy which had been given to him in the condemned cell. He watched Ellis with terror-stricken eyes pull the white cap over Thornly's face, and he shook with fear when the executioner stepped to his side. His knees were beginning to give under him, and Ellis instructed one of the warders to hold him up while the noose was being adjusted.

Then Hill gave vent to a blood-curdling yell of despair which unnerved everyone present except Thornly, who stood immovable on the drop. Ellis pulled the lever as the terrified negro was falling over. It is a remarkable coincidence that on the previous occasion when Ellis had officiated at a double execution one of the condemned men had also been named Hill, and he also had fainted on the scaffold.

Ellis, like all executioners, was called upon to carry out hangings in all parts of the country. One of his visits was to Glasgow, in 1917, the first time he had been called upon to visit the Scottish city. The condemned man, Thomas M'Guinness, had murdered a little boy of five.

There were misgivings that M'Guinness would collapse at the last moment, and, as is usual in such cases, he was offered brandy just before he was pinioned, but he waved it away.

"I have been a teetotaller all my days, and I'll manage without it now," he said firmly.

On the scaffold itself there was very nearly a serious accident. The executioner's assistant was still fastening the straps on the legs of the condemned man when Ellis pulled the lever. He gave a sharp cry of warning, and the assistant jumped clear as the trap-doors began to give under his feet.

Ellis was always exceedingly quick in carrying out any execution once he had the condemned man on the scaffold.

Many people will recall the murder by Louis Voisin, in November, 1918. Voisin dismembered his victim, a Madame Gerard, and left her remains in a parcel in Russell Square, London. Those were the days of food rationing, and the governor of Pentonville Prison, in which Voisin was hanged, wrote to Ellis:

"I beg to inform you that it will be necessary for you either to bring your own meat, bacon, sugar, butter or margarine, for which you will receive the money equivalent, or bring your food cards and the articles will be purchased here for you. If you have no difficulty in obtaining supplies I would advise you to adopt the former course."

Accordingly Ellis took his own rationed supplies with him.

John Ellis retired in 1923, after being assistant executioner for seven years and chief executioner for sixteen years. A gentleminded man, with an intensely human outlook on life, he executed some hundred and fifty criminals. His usual fee for attending an execution in England and Scotland was £10 10s. 0d. plus expenses, or £15 and expenses in the case of a double execution. His assistants received £2 2s. 0d. plus expenses.

H. A. Pierrepoint, who died in 1922, was public executioner for eleven years and carried out a hundred executions in the period he was in office. He hanged, or assisted at the hanging of, among other notorious murderers, Brinkley, the Croydon poisoner, Wade and Donovan, who murdered a Miss Farmer in the East End of London, Dhingra, who killed Sir Curzon Wylie at the Imperial Institute, and Mrs. Walters and Mrs. Sachs, the London baby farmers.

Major O. Mytton Davies, one time governor of Pentonville, in his reminiscences, states that Pierrepoint and Ellis were both trained by him. "They were trained under the supervision of the medical officer and myself assisted by the chief warder of Brixton. A dummy figure was used for instructional purposes, and it was not until we were satisfied that they were competent that the Home Office placed their names on the list. They were quiet men and well-behaved."

Pierrepoint was a butcher by trade when he first applied for the post of executioner, and he believed that his knowledge of anatomy would make him a very suitable person for the post. He made several applications before he was accepted by the Home Office, and he was appointed first as assistant to Ellis and the Billingtons.

In 1907 Pierrepoint was asked to go to Jersey to hang a man named Thomas Connor. There had been no execution in the Channel Islands for many years, and no one there could recollect having ever seen the public hangman, or what was the correct procedure at an execution. In fact no execution had taken place in Jersey for over thirty years.

Pierrepoint was received in state, and banqueted and fêted as though he were some national hero. He was taken drives in what served for the State coach throughout the island, and after the execution it was intimated to him that the officials intended giving him a farewell dinner. At that function he was publicly congratulated on the expeditious way in which he had carried out the execution, and all present afterwards joined in signing, "For he's a jolly good fellow.

Few executioners, one imagines, could boast of such a reception!

It has been mentioned that Pierrepoint helped to execute the two baby farmers, Walters and Sachs. The executioner kept a diary in which he made notes of all his executions.

"These two women were baby farmers of the worst kind," he wrote in his diary, " and they were both repulsive in type. One was two pounds less than the other, and there was a difference of two inches in the drop which I allowed. One had a long, thick neck and the other a short neck, points which I was bound to observe in the arrangement of the rope. They had literally to be carried to the scaffold and protested to the end against their sentences."

It was Pierrepoint who executed Mrs. James, at Cardiff, on August 1st, 1907. The sun was shining with extreme brilliance and Pierrepoint recorded in his diary, " She was a woman of 5 ft. 2½ in. in height, and weighed about 145 lb. But I was attracted and fascinated by the blaze of her yellow hair, and as she left her cell and walked in the procession to the scaffold the sunlight caused her hair to gleam like molten gold. For the first time in my career as a public executioner I felt ashamed. I had hanged women before, but never one so beautiful or so appealing to a man who, after all, had sentimental leanings. But it had to be, and the procession moved on to the scaffold, where a beautiful fiend met the death she certainly merited."

Pierrepoint hanged two coloured men, one Dhingra, and the other Pasha Liffey, a young Basuto boxer who murdered a woman named Walsh under particularly brutal circumstances, near Glasgow, in 1905. When he entered the condemned cell Pierrepoint was greeted with a broad smile, and Liffey almost ran to the scaffold, hurrying so fast that the executioner had to hold him back with the pinioning strap. All the time he continued to smile, even when the hangman was adjusting the rope and putting on the white cap.

Dhingra, executed at Pentonville in 1909, was the lightest man Pierrepoint ever hanged, weighing only just over 100 pounds. He was, in consequence, given the exceedingly long drop of eight feet three inches. At the last, the murderer of Sir Curzon Wylie lost his nerve, and he was trembling violently when Pierrepoint pulled the lever.

Pierrepoint carried out several double executions. One was of the brothers Reubens, Marks and Morris, who were hanged in 1909 for the murder of William Sproul in Whitechapel. After their sentence the brothers did not see one another until they met on the scaffold. They utterly ignored each other until the last minute. When Pierrepoint was fixing the rope round the neck of Marks, the latter called out, " Good-bye, Morris. I am sorry."

The most callous man Pierrepoint ever hanged was Edmunds, who killed a woman named Harris on a farm near Abersychan. He smiled on his way to the scaffold and stepped on the platform with a jaunty air as though completely indifferent to his fate.

When Pierrepoint retired, the Home Office received applications from clergymen, lawyers, undertakers and doctors, among others, to be appointed to the post of hangman. Pierrepoint himself received some remarkable requests to be allowed to be his assistant. A publican wrote and offered him £100 if he could be allowed to help at an execution, and he had a similar offer from a woman who wished to witness a hanging.

Pierrepoint, even more than Marwood and Berry, tried to make the business of hangman into a science. He most carefully calculated a series of drops for various weights, and he never bungled a single execution. But he was a nervy man, and there is no doubt that his trying calling preyed on his mind, for he died at the early age of forty-eight.

CHAPTER VII

IN THE CONDEMNED CELL

UNTIL comparatively recent times the state of prisoners, whether under sentence of death or not, can only be described as desperate. The remains of old prisons, castles and the like, reveal horrifying dungeons, often underground, shut off from every ray of light or at the best with but a tiny slit of a window far up. In many of these cells there was no door, the prisoner being lowered into his place of confinement, and what meagre food was allowed flung down to him. Damp, noisome, indescribable in the their filth, unventilated, many a prisoner in them died before the day fixed for his execution.

Even in such regular prisons as existed the prisoners were entirely at the mercy of their keepers, and the scandal of their treatment was allowed to continue despite constant protests. What reforms were carried out were of the crudest. The following is a description, written in 1831, of the cells in Newgate, by E. G. Wakefield. The cells were constructed in 1728.

"The cells consist of a number of chambers, placed in three rows, one above the other, in a stone building, which fronts one side of the press yard, at the north-east corner of the prison, adjoining the residence of the ordinary or chaplain. Each cell is eight feet long by six wide, and generally contains three, sometimes four prisoners. The only furniture of the cells consists of a rope mat and a common stable rug for each prisoner, with an iron candlestick for the use of the party. The walls, floors, and roofs of the cells are of stone. The only communication of the cells with the outward air is by a hole through the front wall, which is three feet thick;

and the hole is all but stopped by two frames of close iron bars, crossed.

"The time during which the prisoners are strictly confined to their cells is from dusk until daylight during winter, and from dusk till eight o'clock next day in the summer. In winter, and in the neighbourhood of St. Paul's, dusk begins at three o'clock in the afternoon, and daylight at nine in the morning, leaving convicts under sentence of death six hours of the twenty-four for washing, eating, exercise, intercourse with their friends, the chapel service, which they attend every day, and lastly, exertions to propitiate the King in Council, on whose opinion of their cases depends the question of life or death.

"During the few hours that remain to a murderer after sentence he is confined in a solitary cell, set apart for that purpose. If visited at all, it is only by a clergyman, and that by stealth, as it were, since it is understood that the offices of religion are denied the murderer. In the same unostentatious way he is taken to the scaffold, and is put to death without any religious ceremonies or other formal observances —a mode of treatment widely different from that pursued towards most of the persons under sentence of death.

"It must not be supposed, however, that the keeper of Newgate, or his servants, treat prisoners under sentence of death with peculiar harshness. . . . Before sentence, a prisoner has only to observe the regulations of the jail in order to remain neglected and unnoticed. Once ordered to the cells, friends of all classes suddenly rise up; his fellow prisoners, the turnkeys, the chaplain, the keepers, and the sheriffs, all seem interested in his fate; and he can make no reasonable request that is not at once granted by whomsoever he may address."

It will be noticed that Wakefield points out the distinction of treatment between the condemned murderer and those condemned to death for other offences. Under the statute of 9 Geo. IV, c. 31 it was enacted:

"That every person convicted of murder shall, after judgment, be confined in some place safe within the prison apart from all other prisoners, and shall be fed with bread and water only, and with no other food or liquor, except in case of receiving the sacrament, or in case of any sickness or wound, in which case the surgeon of the prison may order necessaries to be administered. And no person but the gaoler and his servants, and the chaplain and surgeon of the prison, shall have access to any such convict without the permission, in writing, of the Court or Judge before whom such convict shall have been tried, or the Sheriff or his Deputy. Provided always that, in case the Court or Judge shall think fit to respite the execution of such convict, such Court or Judge may, by a license in writing, relax, during the period of the respite, all or any of the restraints or regulations hereinbefore directed to be observed."

The attitude towards the condemned slowly improved, however.

In the case of Thurtell, as reported fully in a contemporary account of his trial and execution for the murder of William Weare, we read, "the room in which Mr. Wilson placed Thurtell little corresponded with the idea generally formed of a condemned cell. It was large, spacious and airy, lighted by a lamp and candle, and warmed by a comfortable fire. Three or four persons were ordered to attend him constantly."

The Times of April 1st, 1856, reporting the execution of William Bousfield, for the murder of his wife, stated, "The public is aware that the condemned cell which was formerly the receptacle for prisoners condemned to death during the short period allowed them by the law after sentence, is no longer made use of; but the prisoner is placed in a sufficiently comfortable room, with a good fire, and watched night and day by one of the officers of the gaol."

Now, when a prisoner is sentenced to death, he goes straight to the condemned cell. He is a marked man, isolated in every respect from his fellow prisoners.

In 1902 Newgate Prison was closed and condemned prisoners were sent to Pentonville for execution. A shed was built for that purpose and the beam was brought from Newgate. Pentonville was a model prison built to furnish an example of the way prisons should be constructed.

In Pentonville there are two condemned cells, each formed of a pair of ordinary cells converted into one large one. They are well warmed and have two large windows which, though not permitting anyone from outside to see the condemned man, allow the sunlight to enter and the closely guarded prisoner to see the sky.

There are the usual items of furniture, tables, chairs and a comfortable bed. On the wall facing the bed hangs a great picture of Christ on the Cross. Among those who have occupied the condemned cell at Pentonville are Devereux, who murdered his wife and children at Kensal Rise in 1905, Dhingra, the Indian student, who shot Sir Curzon Wylie at the Imperial Institute in 1909, Seddon, who poisoned Miss Barrow at Tollington Park in 1911, and Voisin, the murderer of Mme. Gerard in 1917.

When Field and Gray were awaiting execution in 1921 for the murder of Irene Munro on the dismal wastes of the Crumbles at Eastbourne, they occupied the condemned cells in Wandsworth Prison—large rooms with cheerful fires and bright pictures. Their beds were of the hospital pattern, with soft pillows, clean white sheets and warm blankets.

The food provided for the condemned is considerably better than that allowed to ordinary prisoners. It is based on the usual prison hospital diet, but the medical officer is given a perfectly free hand and the diet is usually augmented with fish or eggs and bacon for breakfast or supper. It is often stated that the condemned may choose what food they like, but this is not true, though there is a greater consideration shown than with ordinary prisoners, and in America the greatest latitude is allowed. But the stories which usually appear in the British newspapers regarding some notorious prisoner, of his life in the condemned cell, are sheer imagination and nothing else.

When Rouse, executed in 1931 for the murder of an unknown man in a blazing car, was awaiting death, there were vivid accounts of his daily life and of the "fact" that he was allowed a gramophone in his cell. None of these stories was true.

Contrary to popular belief, most murderers eat and sleep
well up to the end, most of them even making a good breakfast on the last morning.   Many murderers, when they
know that death is certain, appear to adopt as their motto,
"Let us eat and drink, for to-morrow we die."

A young Chinaman named Lee Doon, who was hanged
in Armley Gaol, Leeds, in 1923, for the murder of a fellow
countryman, had, as an Oriental, special tastes in food.
While he occupied the condemned cell the prison authorities
made every effort to meet his needs in respect of diet.   He
did not care for potatoes, for instance, so other vegetables
were served to him instead.   He was also allowed two
half pints of beer daily.

One of the most trying features of life in the condemned
cell is that the doomed man is never alone.   Two warders
sit in the cell day and night.   They are usually on duty for
eight hour periods, and the only times when the prisoner
is not with them, until the day of his execution, are during
the visits of the chaplain and in the brief intervals when
the guards are relieved for meals.   Formerly only one
warder sat in the condemned cell, but following the violent
conduct of a man named Spicer, who murdered his two
sons at Brighton in 1889, warders now always watch in
pairs.

The governor, chaplain and medical officer pay daily
visits and the condemned are allowed to receive visits
from their relations and friends.   During the first week
after conviction nearly all prisoners spend a great deal of
their time writing to the Home Secretary to protest their
innocence, pointing out grounds for a reprieve or preparing
an appeal.

Exercise is allowed twice daily, and is the only time,
except for chapel on Sundays, when the condemned man
issues from his cell.   There is no fixed period laid down by
the prison authorities for this exercise, and the murderer is
allowed his temporary freedom from his cell as reasonably
long as he may wish.   Smoking is permitted during exercise time, but as a rule only cigarettes are allowed.

Exercise is taken in the prison yard; if there is more than

one condemned man in a prison at any time, they are separated from one another, and take their walks in distant parts of the yard.   As under no circumstances may a condemned man be seen by other prisoners, these latter are kept under lock and key during the whole period when the murderer is out of his cell.

A prisoner in the condemned cell is allowed to read as much as he wishes, a privilege which is often eagerly made use of to pass the slow hours of waiting.   Romances and magazines are by far the most popular, for the man naturally seeks distraction from his thoughts, and seldom welcomes the tracts and religious works often sent to the governor of the prison by well-meaning but misguided persons for the use of the condemned.   Of course the governor exercises a strict supervision over such outside books.

They are not invariably sent, however, for the edification of the condemned.   When Crippen was in the condemned cell at Pentonville in 1910, a man in South Wales sent him a Testament which the governor allowed him to use.   After Crippen had been executed the donor wrote and asked to have his Testament returned.   His request was not granted.   Instead, he was sent a new copy, for it was perfectly evident that his motive was merely to acquire a valuable relic.

Crippen, like other condemned men, read many popular novels in his cell.   But he also asked for scientific works from the prison library, and both his medical training and the cast of his mind which led him to poison his wife came out in one request of his—which was refused—to be allowed to read a work on subtle poisons.

Some occupants of the condemned cell do their best to cheat the gallows by simulating insanity in the hope of getting a reprieve.   In the past many who were undoubtedly insane were hanged, but nowadays if there is the slightest doubt of a condemned man's sanity he is reprieved.

Prisoners often kill time, while waiting execution, in the most unlooked-for ways.   It is not unusual for them to write verses and stories, sometimes with themselves figuring as chief characters or giving full descriptions of their crimes.

Sherwood, who was sentenced to death for the murder of an old woman in a house in Holborn, London, shortly after the war of 1914–1918, seemed to have little idea of the seriousness of his position. While in the cell at Bow Street during his trial he spent most of his time singing popular songs with great spirit.

The same manner of occupying himself was employed by Thomas Cowdrey, who, with his accomplice William Brown, murdered a woman named Esther Atkins, near Aldershot, in 1903. While waiting execution Cowdrey became absolutely hilarious, and passed the greater part of his days singing comic songs—when he was not vigorously protesting his innocence. He had a curious kink in his nature, too, which made him think that no human being would go to the length of hanging him.

"Think," he said once, "what a terrible sight it will be for the governor and chaplain to have to stand by while the lever is pulled and my body disappears."

Brown, Cowdrey's confederate, was a complete contrast, for he was sullen and morose and spoke very little to the warders in charge of him.

Some fourteen years later there occurred another murder at Aldershot. Sergeant Lee O'Donnell, a Canadian serving with the R.A.M.C., was found guilty of killing the father of his sweetheart in January, 1917.

He showed an extraordinary interest in the actual method of execution, and his one fear was that there would be some hitch at the last moment.

"Tell me all about it," he demanded of the warders guarding him. "I don't want to make a mistake. I should like to rehearse it all beforehand."

Hardly a day passed without his asking further questions as to exactly what would happen on the execution morning.

"I hope there will be no squinting people present," he remarked, on one occasion. "Squinting men have always proved unlucky to me, and if I see one when I am hanged I shall know that something is going to go wrong. I met a man who squinted on the night of the murder. He made me feel so queer that I was not accountable for my actions."

EXECUTION OF WEBB AND RUSSEL
(*From an old print*)

George Webb and Richard Russel were executed on Shooter's Hill, August 19, 1809, for burglary.

EXECUTION OF REBELS ON KENNINGTON COMMON
(*From an old print*)

Kennington Common was at one time a regular place of execution. Here suffered the Scottish rebels in 1746. The gallows for the county of Surrey was erected on Kennington Common, which is now a playground for children.

It has always remained a matter of doubt whether O'Donnell was normal. It is needless to say that none of his forebodings as to a hitch on the morning of his death came true. In fact, his last words, as he waited for the rope to be adjusted, admitted that his fears had been groundless.

"It is all simple enough," he observed.

It is recorded that during the Reign of Terror in France one of the chief amusements of the prisoners in the Conciergerie Prison, while awaiting their turn for the guillotine, was to stage a parody of capital punishment; they called such parodies their "rehearsals."

Alfred William Hancock, who murdered his daughters at Birkenhead in 1905, occupied his time in the condemned cell catching and killing all the flies within reach.

While some murderers view the prospect of death with exaggerated anxiety about details, others are remarkable for their apparent complete indifference to their fate.

At the Surrey Assizes in March, 1738, a man named Gill Smith, an apothecary, of Dartford, was tried for the murder of his wife, found guilty and condemned to be executed. It appears that Smith was in good circumstances, kept a pack of hounds and lived as expensively as any country squire. He insured his wife for £200, with a view to gaining that sum by murdering her, which he did in an exceedingly brutal manner.

After his condemnation he was brought back from Guildford and, in the manner of the eighteenth century, chained to the floor of his cell. He said he wanted his supper and hoped they would not leave him with a hungry inside. He was closely watched and carefully searched for any concealed weapon with which he might possible commit suicide.

"You need not give yourself so much trouble," he said with an ironical smile to the warder who searched him. "I have no knife about me. And if I had, I would rather kill all the world than hurt myself."

Smith showed no sign of the terror of death; his appetite was huge, his jokes perpetual.

"I am to be hanged in chains," he remarked to a warder one day, "but if I am to be crows' meat, I'll live accordingly." And he ate and drank more inordinately than ever.

Some days after this a Mr. Hardy, who was noted for his skill in playing the French horn, came to visit him and told him how sorry he was to see him in such an unhappy plight.

"Oh," replied Gill Smith. "I am well enough. Don't be sorry for me. I am to be hanged in a few days, and if you'll come and blow the "Death of the Stag" as I go to the gallows I shall take it as a great favour."

Two days before his execution, when he learnt that he was to be hanged with two other criminals, this incorrigible jester could not refrain from one last grim joke.

"If that be so," he remarked, "then there will be room to let here."

Dr. Arthur Warren Waite, a New York dentist, who was convicted for killing his parents-in-law in 1916, showed an amazing disregard for his fate. For days before his execution he was in communication with a woman spiritualist, and he promised her that after he was dead he would return and give her some message to prove the existence of the world beyond. But so far as we know he never fulfilled this pledge.

A somewhat similar but more gruesome idea ran in the mind of Lieutenant Anastay, a French murderer who was executed at the Roquette Prison, in Paris, in 1892. While in the condemned cell he demanded that doctors should be present at his execution, as he wished to communicate with them after death as to his subsequent experiences. This he had a firm faith that he would be able to do. His plan was that the doctors should ask questions of his decapitated head, to which he would reply by turning his eyes to the right for yes and to the left for no.

Of course no such experiment was tried, though he asked on the scaffold if a doctor was present. "I should be very glad to have the tests made," were his last words on earth.

"Did he confess?"

This is always the first question asked by the public on the day an execution takes place. Perhaps everyone, despite the care taken in administering justice, secretly fears, when a capital sentence is in question, that a fatal error may have taken place. And this doubt lingers subconsciously whenever a doomed man meets his death in silence.

Many warders and prison officials, in close contact with condemned criminals, have this feeling even more acutely than the outside public, and have admitted on various occasions that their minds are eased when the prisoner admits guilt, sometimes on the scaffold itself.

Although at the time of the execution it is rarely that anything is allowed to leak out, sooner or later it becomes definitely known whether or not a prisoner has confessed.

Charles Peace owed much of his long series of successes to the fact that he was extremely thorough. This trait he took with him to the condemned cell, where he repented of his crimes as whole-heartedly as he had committed them and drew much consolation from religion.

That this penitence was genuine, and not the outcome of fear or hypocrisy, seems evident from the fact that he not only confessed to Mr. Littlewood, a clergyman for whom he had a great respect, that he had murdered Arthur Dyson (the crime for which he was condemned to death) but he also quite unexpectedly divulged that he was the slayer of P.C. Cook for the murder of whom a man named William Habron had been wrongfully convicted.

The Seddon poisoning case, which caused so much public interest in 1912, is still fresh in many people's minds. Frederick Henry Seddon persistently protested his innocence during his trial and after, for he cherished the greatest hopes of a reprieve at least, if not a free pardon. It was only when his appeal had been dismissed that the poisoner seemed at last to realize that he must die. He then fully admitted his crime, giving a long account of the poisoning of Miss Barrow to one of the warders in the condemned cell.

"I never had any luck," he stated. "I had a big family and many expenses and money seemed to be always short."

In point of fact the trial amply proved that Seddon was well off but extremely avaricious and miserly.

Seddon mentioned that he became nervous when the doctor seemed suspicious and asked a number of questions; but on thinking it over he came to the conclusion that if he stuck to one story nothing could be proved against him. His trial, of course, proved otherwise.

Seddon, however, made no official confession, and it has often been stated that he never did confess; but this is not true. After his execution Mrs. Seddon published an account in which she practically admitted that she knew of his guilt but was terrified into silence.

Dubious or bogus confessions in the condemned cell are fairly common. Criminal psychology is a queer and often startling thing, and there is little doubt that many convicted wretches seek to relieve the long weeks of waiting for the end, or to make themselves more interesting to their friends, warders or the public, by confessions more remarkable for imagination than truth.

Samuel Herbert Dougal, the Moat Farm murderer of Miss Camille Holland, in 1899, spent the last three days of his life in Chelmsford Gaol writing a long and most artistic account of how his crime was committed, and sold the document to a London evening paper. Money, not truth, was his motive, for the police were able to prove that the "confession" was a mass of false statements.

His second acknowledgement that he murdered Miss Holland was much more dramatic, and it cannot strictly be called a voluntary confession. In this case the chaplain of the prison overstepped the unwritten law that no pressure shall be put on a condemned man to confess. On the very scaffold, when the rope was actually in position round Dougal's neck, the clergyman stepped forward and excitedly asked:

"Dougal, are you guilty or not guilty?"

His outstretched hand, pointing to the criminal, gave additional force to his totally unexpected question. Dismay shook the group around the scaffold; but Dougal remained silent.

"Guilty or not guilty?" the over-zealous clergyman persisted.

Then Dougal spoke. The white cap was already over his head, so that he could not see his questioner. But turning in the direction of the voice, he said clearly and firmly, "Guilty!" one second before he was launched into eternity.

George Smith, the "Brides in the Bath" murderer, made a voluminous confession in writing which was true as far as it went, but omitted any explanation of how he drowned his victims without leaving any marks of violence on their bodies. This has always been the one puzzling thing connected with the case.

The Reading baby farmer, Mrs. Dyer, who was executed in 1896 for drowning a number of babies, wrote so long a "last true and only confession" that it filled five exercise books with a rigmarole which contained little truth and a great deal of fiction.

"Have you nothing to confess?" asked the chaplain, disregarding this obviously manufactured document, when he visited her on the last night.

"Surely this is enough?" she replied, tendering her little pile of copybooks.

Such instances of bogus accounts of crime do not mean that authentic last minute confessions are unknown. There have been many at different times. In the days of public executions any eleventh-hour confessions were sure of a much greater audience than in these times. George Manley, who was hanged in 1738 for murder, took full advantage of this opportunity to deliver an harangue and confession in one as he was on the scaffold.

"Marlborough killed his thousands and Alexander his millions. Many others who have done the like are famous in history as great men. I am a little murderer and must be hanged. Marlborough and Alexander plundered countries; they are great men. I ran into debt with the ale-wife; I must be hanged. I killed a solitary man—I'm a little fellow. What is the difference between running into a poor man's debt, and, by the power of gold or any other privilege, preventing him from obtaining his right and clapping a pistol to a man's breast and taking his purse? Yet one shall thereby obtain a coach and honours and titles; the other a cart and rope."

A confession wrung from the very jaws of death was that made by Joseph Fee in 1903. The hangman was stooping to tie his legs when the condemned man cried, "Executioner!" Pierrepoint, the hangman, took no notice, but silently adjusted the noose. Suddenly from under the white cap came four disjointed words:

"Guilty, executioner, guilty, guilty."

Pierrepoint afterwards admitted the enormous relief this confession had brought to him, for in common with many other people he had believed in the innocence of Fee, and had felt himself to be the instrument of a fatal miscarriage of justice.

"The sentence is just, but the evidence was false," were the last words of Mrs. Pearcey, who killed Mrs. Hogg and her baby in 1890. Almost the same last sentence was spoken by Palmer, the Rugeley poisoner, when he was executed at Stafford in 1856.

Few crimes made a greater sensation at the time than the murder of Mr. Briggs, in a North London railway carriage in 1864, by a German, Franz Muller. The man persistently maintained his innocence, even when questioned on the scaffold by the chaplain.

But just before he was hanged he whispered, "Ja, ich habe es gethan (Yes, I have done it)."

A noticeable fact is that the hopeless prisoner always has a craving for self-expression by means of writing. In *A Tale of Two Cities*, Charles Dickens tells of some poor wretch who, long ago, was confined in one of the dungeons of the Tower of London. After his execution initials were found on the wall of his cell which puzzled everyone— D.I.C., they seemed, but they were roughly and unsteadily scrawled. Then someone suggested "Dig," a command, not initials, and they found under a paving stone in the floor the charred ashes of sheets of writing.

What it was no one knows. Perhaps a confession of crime —perhaps outpourings desperately penned by the lonely man and then thought too intimate to be left behind for others to read.

That was long ago. But to-day the modern light, well-furnished condemned cell is filled, as was that dark dungeon, with the scratching, sometimes hour after hour, of pen on paper. Warders have recorded that educated criminals, especially, seldom speak, but write almost incessantly. And many a man of little education, who has always found letter writing a work of difficulty, during his last few weeks seeks consolation in committing his thoughts to paper.

Letters, confessions, diaries, fiction of various kinds— these are the records handed to last visitors, or left in the condemned cell when its occupant has quitted it for ever. It is strange—and yet it must be infinitely consoling to the relatives—how eloquently an ordinarily inarticulate person will become when he is writing to his loved ones from the brink of the grave.

"Well, Lizzie, by the time you get my letter I shall have gone to my Maker," wrote Edward O'Connor, hanged in Birmingham in 1928 for the murder of his little boy. He was writing to his wife . . . "It is God's will that I should leave this world of trials. I am reconciled to that fate. . . . I shall remember you, Lizzie, my wife, and I ask you sometimes to remember me in your prayers."

The last few sentences are pathetic: "Kiss the children for me. God bless you all. As I think, I hear you as of old, calling 'Ted, good-bye'."

Another letter written on the threshold of death was that sent by Reginald Haslam to his mother. He was a labourer who was hanged in 1916 for the murder of his sweetheart; but his letters seem to denote an education superior to his calling.

"My darling old Mother," Haslam wrote, "this is my farewell letter to you all. It is now 6.30. I have now only a few hurried moments to live, and then I shall start on the long journey to the new world in which I am about to enter. For, you see, I feel sure that our Lord has forgiven me for all my past sins, and I am anxiously awaiting eight o'clock, which will mean my death. You may rest assured, mother, that your son has gone to his death fearlessly, and, with the kind help of my chaplain, fully prepared to meet my fate.

"You just always think, mother, that the brave lad you once had has not left you for ever, for I shall be ever waiting for you, and I shall have gone to live a far better life than I have been doing in the past. Although the Home Secretary could not see his way to add anything to the jury's strong recommendation for mercy, I have considered this later decision as an act of mercy sent to me from up above. And you know, mother, our Lord's mercy will be more to me than all the mercy our present Home Secretary could ever give me, for I know I am going to a far better place. I will now close these few hurried lines, hoping you will accept my sincerest wishes, and may God Bless you.

"From your ever-loving heartbroken lad,

      x x x x x x x x x x x Reg."

Haslam also wrote very affectionately to his little niece, calling her "his dear little chick," and in an earlier letter to his mother he added some verses of his own composition, giving "a few of my thoughts of home."

> " I turned over an ancient poet's book,
>   And found upon the page
> Stonewalls do not a prison make
>   Nor iron bars a cage,
> Yes, that is true, and something more
>   You'll find where'er you roam,
> That marble floors and gilded walls
>   Do not always make a happy home;
> But every house where mother's love abides.
>   And friendship is a guest,
> Is surely home and home sweet home,
>   For there only my heart can rest."

One of the shortest, and yet the finest, farewell letters ever written before execution was that of Carl Lody, the

German spy, who was shot in the Tower in 1914. He wrote:

"My dear Ones,

"I have trusted in God and He has decided. My hour has come, and I must start on the journey through the Dark Valley like so many of my comrades in this terrible War of Nations. May my life be offered as a humble offering on the altar of the Fatherland.

"A hero's death on the battlefield is certainly finer, but such is not to be my lot, and I die here in the Enemy's country silent and unknown, but the consciousness that I die in the service of the Fatherland makes death easy.

"The Supreme Court-Marshal of London has sentenced me to death for Military Conspiracy. To-morrow I shall be shot here in the Tower. I have had just Judges, and I shall die as an Officer, not as a spy. Farewell. God bless you.

"HANS."

He also wrote a dignified letter in rather broken English, thanking the military authorities for their kind treatment of him during his captivity.

W. F. Edge, a murderer who was executed in January, 1903, like Mrs. Thompson and Bywaters spent his last Christmas in the condemned cell. He wrote to his sister:

"Fancy to think of last Christmas, and then to think of this. . . . The time is very short now, but I have nothing to fear. I am not a felon, but a martyr. I can keep my health and spirits, thank God. . . . I cannot say much more and must conclude now:

' Farewell, dear sister, I must now bid adieu
To those joys and pleasures I've tasted with you.
We've laboured together, united in heart,
But now we must close, and soon we must part.
Though absent in body, I am with you in prayer,
And I meet you in Heaven; there is no parting there.

"From your loving brother, Will.
"P.S. Farewell till we meet in Heaven."

Many convicts in prison pass the time by writing doggerel verse, but this form of helping to while away the last hours is not so common in the condemned cell. There are, however, several instances of it, though none is worth quoting from a literary standpoint.

Occasionally a murderer pens a crude rhyming account of his crime, as in the case of John Selhurst, who was hanged at Taunton in 1877 for the murder of his wife. Here is his version of it:

> " With her a fearful life I led,
>   The drink it did so fly to her head;
>   On the devil's tipple she used to dote,
>   But I cured her with a cut on the throat.
>   I wish I could the deed undo,
>   And so, dear people all, must you."

The apparent cold-bloodedness of this effusion is gainsaid in the last two lines, and is probably due rather to the author's clumsiness in writing verse than to real callousness. But it cannot be said that much sorrow for his crime was shown by the writer of another literary confession, Second-Lieutenant Anastay, who was guillotined at the Roquette Prison, in Paris, in 1892.

In his cell Anastay busied himself with painting, music and literature, and wrote a novel called *The Genesis of a Crime*, in which he figured as the hero and retold his own crime!

When his brother visited him he suggested that Anastay should make his hero a German, instead of a French officer—apparently because murder disgraced his native Army. But Anastay replied with perfect seriousness that his literary conscience would not allow him to choose a setting of which he knew nothing.

In the same prison, three years earlier, another murderer, Fulgence Geomay, showed even more striking literary activity. While occupying the condemned cell his great amusements were to read and write poetry. Each set of verses was signed, dated and written out neatly in a fine military hand. One poem, called "Three Dates" (those of his crime, condemnation and the as yet unknown date of his execution, which in France is not told to the prisoner in advance) was evidently written for self-expression, and shows interesting glimpses of his state of mind while daily expecting death.

When Charles Peace was visited for the last time in the condemned cell by his wife and stepson, he gave the former as a farewell gift perhaps the most unusual literary composition ever penned under sentence of death. This was his own funeral card, which he had worded as follows:

In
Memory
of
CHARLES PEACE
Who was executed in
Armley Prison,
Tuesday, February 25th, 1879
Aged 47
For that I done, but never intended.

The last line referred to the murder of Mr. Dyson, for which he was condemned to death. In his confession the burglar had insisted that he had not contemplated killing Dyson, and that his death was the result of a struggle.

Peace wrote some remarkable letters in the days previous to his execution. On his last day he was busy with correspondence to a number of people. He dated all his epistles for the next day, the fatal February 25th, and asked that they should not be delivered until he was dead. Presumably this was one of the grim jests in which he often indulged in prison.

Many of Peace's last letters were extremely pious, not to say smug, and warned relations, of whom he held a low opinion, to mend their ways and walk in the straight and narrow path of religion.

But there was one missive he wrote quite simply, and that was to his mistress, Sue Thompson. This woman, "Traitress Sue," as she was called at the time, had been adored by Peace, and he had spent the proceeds of many a burglary on her comfort, neglecting his wife for her. Yet she betrayed him to the police for the sake of the £100 reward they offered, telling them many facts which she had learnt when Peace talked in his sleep.

In spite of her treachery, the criminal's love for her never waned.

"A woman of your education and ability must succeed," he wrote to her at the last. "I hope you will be prosperous in this world. My poor, poor Sue. O do forgive me for the trouble and the blows I have given you. God bless you. I am yours, CHARLES PEACE."

H. H. Crippen was a most devoted correspondent to Ethel le Neve. In the condemned cell he was only able to write one letter a day and this was invariably to Miss le Neve, and always breathing the tenderest affection and consideration for her.

When the Home Secretary refused a reprieve, Crippen wrote:

"The Governor brought me the dreadful news about ten o'clock. . . . When he had gone I first kissed your face on the photo, my faithful, devoted companion in all this sorrow. Oh! how glad I was I had the photo. It was some consolation, although, in spite of my greatest efforts, it was impossible to keep down a great sob and my heart's agonised cry. How am I to endure to take my last look at your dear face; what agony must I go through at the last when you disappear for ever from my eyes! God help us to be brave then. . . .

"God help us indeed to be brave. I am comforted at least in thinking that throughout all the years of our friendship never have I passed one unkind word or given one reproachful look to her whom I have loved best in life, to whom I have given myself heart and soul, wholly and utterly, for ever."

Benjamin Tisseau, a French soldier, who was guillotined at Le Mans in 1912, committed to paper in prison a vivid autobiography, tracing his crime to wrong education as a boy and to his passionate belief that there should be no rich and no poor in the world, but that all men should be equal.

Perhaps the most remarkable of all literary output under sentence of death was that of Lacenaire, the criminal-poet-philosopher, who went to the guillotine in 1835. The unusually long period of two months elapsed between his condemnation and execution, and during that time he wrote memoirs and much excellent verse. The notoriety accompanying his trial had set Paris all agog about him, and his writings were never in such demand as during the closing weeks of his life. His literary abilities were praised far beyond their real worth and everything that emanated from his cell had a fancy value. He wrote . . . or is said to have written, for many imitators coolly used his name to bolster up their own lack of reputation . . . an ode to the scaffold he would so shortly ascend. He also left behind a hymn written shortly before his death.

The prison chaplain has a profession which is almost unique. When he enters one of those marked and special doors which lead to the condemned cell, he leaves earthly hope behind him. It is his grim task to prepare the occupant, if he can, for certain death.

Probably no murderer owed more to the ministrations of the prison chaplain than did George Smith, of "Brides in the Bath" fame. The Rev. J. Stott, then chaplain of Maidstone Prison, where Smith was executed in 1915, has recorded that he spent as much as five or six hours a day in Smith's company.

At first the condemned man pretended complete indifference to religion, and on arriving at Maidstone Prison his first act was to demand the removal of the Bible and Prayer Book which, according to rule, had been placed in his cell. Disdainfully he handed them to Mr. Stott.

"I don't want this and I don't want that," he said curtly, viewing each volume in turn. "Send them to the detectives in Scotland Yard. They have far more use for them than I have."

However, this pose of contempt soon left him, especially after he had received a moving letter from Miss Pegler, the "wife" to whom he had returned after each of his crimes. Soon he was present every evening at a very simple little service conducted by Mr. Stott for his benefit, and would occasionally offer up prayer himself.

He spent many hours in reading the Bible, and though one of his warders, used to the ways of criminals, referred contemptuously to this occupation as "the religious dodge," there seems no reason to doubt that Smith's attitude was genuine. Had it not been so he would hardly have ventured to ask, as he presently did, that he might be confirmed and receive the Sacrament before his death.

The Chaplain referred this request to the Archbishop, who sent his suffragan to talk to Smith before giving a decision. Shortly afterwards this same cleric confirmed the murderer.

Smith's confirmation in the condemned cell, though certainly unusual, is not unique. When the Abbé Faure was chaplain of the depot for condemned prisoners at the Roquette Prison, in Paris, he had the moving experience of preparing a young criminal under sentence of death for his first communion.

In France, in the Roman Catholic faith, children are confirmed and first admitted to the Sacrament at the age of eleven. Jeantroux, the applicant for the ceremony, was only seventeen, a tall, slender youth with a gentle face. Yet he had been the remorseless leader of his two confederates in the murder which had brought him to the condemned cell. He told Faure that as a child, when he was just preparing for his confirmation, the secularisation of the French schools had taken place and so his religious education had been abruptly broken off.

Faure suggested that it should be continued in prison, and the unhappy boy was very willing. The Cardinal Archbishop gave his permission for this first communion in a condemned cell and Faure carefully prepared his pupil for it.

In his reminiscences the priest has described the bare, yet imposing scene:

"On the plain deal table," he says, "I spread a little cloth, a corporal (Catholic relic) and the holy pyx. The light consisted of a single candle, stuck to the table. It was a strange setting for confirmation, which usually takes place with so much pageantry and ceremony before a crowded congregation.

"I had often seen solemnisations in all their splendour in the biggest churches, but never one with more grandeur than this in prison, amidst the most austere simplicity, when a boy of seventeen took his first communion under the shadow of the scaffold.

"When it was over, he said to me: 'Now I am ready; whenever they like.'"

Jeantroux was executed shortly afterwards, with his accomplice, Ribot, on March 8th, 1890. When Faure exhorted him, at the last, to have courage, he replied calmly, "Courage, sir? I'll show it," and died bravely. His only grief was that he was not permitted to see and embrace Ribot, who followed him to the guillotine a few minutes later. Ribot, also, begged to say good-bye to his companion in crime, not knowing that Jeantroux was already dead.

During his years of office at the Roquette Prison, Abbé Faure had many sad conversations. But none was sadder than a brief interchange of remarks with Kaps, another murderer, who was almost as young as Jeantroux.

It was barely a week before Christmas, and the chaplain spoke to Kaps about the great festival and how it would be solemnised in prison. The young man looked at him steadily.

"At Christmas, Father," he replied. "I shall be at the Champ-de-Navets!" (the cemetery).

He proved an accurate prophet, for only two days later, on December 19th, he was guillotined.

There is no doubt that a clergyman of the right type, whether the official prison chaplain or not, can do a great deal to comfort the last weeks of a condemned man, and it is all honour to them that so many splendid men undertake work which is so intensely trying.

From old records it appears that in bygone days the ordinary, as the prison chaplain was called, was by no means always so considerate to the unhappy wretches under his spiritual care. In 1849, when executions still took place in public, a good deal of indignation was expressed at the bad taste of a prison chaplain, Mr. Marshall, on the occasion of the execution of Gleeson Wilson.

An immense crowd had assembled to watch the execution, and while they were awaiting the appearance of the condemned man they were electrified to see the priest come forward and put his head under the gallows. He then looked up enigmatically, touched the iron chain across the transverse beam, and with a shrug of his shoulders retired into the gaol. A crowd which can gather to see a man come to a violent end is not particularly humane nor refined, and this piece of pantomime provoked a hearty laugh from the spectators, but it was severely condemned in the Press.

The old time ordinary was sometimes a jovial fellow with a keen sense of liking for the pleasures of the table. In 1763 a man named William Rice was condemned to death for highway robbery, and on the night before his execution he heard one of the warders order a boiled chicken for supper in the condemned cell.

"But," said he, "you need not be particular about the sauce, for you know he is to be hanged to-morrow."

"That is true," replied the second warder, "but the ordinary sups with him and he is a devil of a fellow for butter."

In 1849 much scandal was caused by the Rev. Richard Chapman's treatment of a convict named Mary Ball, who was in Coventry Gaol under sentence of death.

In the absence of the prison governor one day, the chaplain visited Mary Ball's cell and called for a lighted candle. When this was brought he seized the unfortunate woman's hand, and, in spite of her struggles, he held it over the candle flame for what he said was only a few seconds. The assistant matron, however, declared it was fully two minutes. Mary Ball writhed and cried out with pain, but could not release herself from the chaplain's strong grasp.

"If you feel this pain so much," said Chapman sternly, "do you realize what you will suffer in the torments of hell, where your body will burn for a hundred years?"

PIRATE HANGED AT EXECUTION DOCK
(*From an old print*)

Pirates were hanged at East Wapping, in the small inlet known as Execution Dock. Their bodies were allowed to hang until three tides had overflowed them, and the procession from Newgate to Wapping was almost as famous as that to Tyburn.

Execution of William Guest
(*From an old print*)

William Guest was condemned to death for high treason, and was drawn to
Tyburn on a sledge. He was a clerk in the Bank of England, and his high
treason consisted in filing down gold coins and selling the proceeds.

Face page 163]

He actually believed that the best way to save the woman's soul would be to give her a foretaste of the pains which, he declared, were awaiting her after execution. But her burnt and blistered hand aroused much sympathy and indignation. An inquiry was held by the local magistrates, who ordered suspension of the Rev. Richard Chapman from prison duties.

Probably even eighty years ago there were few clergy left who believed so fanatically in hell fire as this gentleman. It was a chaplain of an earlier date who gravely exhorted a condemned man to acknowledge the justice of his sentence and renounce the devil and all his works. To which the poor wretch pithily replied:

"Sir, I beg to be excused, for, as I am going to a strange country when I die, I do not wish to make myself any enemies."

As far back as 1593 chaplains were evidently very cheap, despite the higher value of money in Tudor times, for the municipal documents of New Romney show that one Father Gaskyn was engaged to officiate at a hanging for the modest sum of 6d! This seems little indeed, in view of the arduousness of the work of attending a condemned man, and the high qualifications needed.

Besides possessing wide human sympathies and a great knowledge of erring mankind, a prison chaplain must be a man of very steady nerve, for it is not easy to prepare a prisoner for a violent end at the hands of justice and then to stand by while the sentence is carried out. If anything untoward occurs the chaplain may suffer almost as much mental agony as the unhappy criminal.

Since, rightly or wrongly, modern public opinion feels very strongly regarding capital punishment for women, few nowadays occupy the condemned cell. Edith Thompson, who was executed in January, 1922, with Frederick Bywaters, for the murder of her husband, spent her weeks in the condemned cell in a state almost of numbed trance. When the end came she was so collapsed that it is doubtful if she suffered.

The same condition of broken-down misery characterised Mrs. Sach, who, with Mrs. Walters, was sentenced to death for baby murder in 1903. Her executioner, having the regulation "peep" at her on his arrival at the prison, has recorded that he never saw a poorer wreck of humanity or a more pitiful spectacle than the condemned woman, as she sat in her cell with tears rolling unheeded down her cheeks. For her, too, the end was softened by collapse.

Her fellow-criminal, Annie Walters, was a complete contrast to her behaviour between conviction and death. She was as stout and common as Mrs. Sach was elegant and ladylike, and as talkative as the other was silent and brooding. She often protested her innocence, and accused her accomplice of having betrayed her.

Since everyday human nature does not change greatly even under the shadow of impending death, it is not surprising that dress has played its part in the last days of more than one woman criminal. Eliza Fenning, the poisoner of her master and mistress, in 1815, insisted on going to execution (which was fixed for what was to have been her wedding day) in her white bridal gown. Dress, again, played a curious part in the trial and capital punishment of Mrs. Turner.

She was a woman of great beauty, who had always dressed in the height of fashion. Her sentence was "to be hanged at Tyburn in her yellow Tinny Ruff and Cuff, she being the first inventor and wearer of that horrid garb."

The offending accessories were got up with yellow starch, and in passing sentence Lord Chief Justice Coke told her she had been guilty of all the seven deadly sins, and declared that as she was the inventor of yellow starched cuffs, the fashion should die with her.

As if to ensure the condemnation of yellow starch, the hangman, like his victim, wore yellow cuffs on the day of her execution, which, says a writer of the time, "made many after that day, of either sex, to forbear the use of that coloured starch, till it at last grew to be generally detested and disused."

Since then white starch has always held its own.

Mrs. Manning who, with her husband, murdered O'Connor in 1849, appealed direct to Queen Victoria to save her from the scaffold. The letter went through the usual routine and while waiting for the reply Mrs. Manning grew impatient and made a desperate effort to strangle herself, convinced—and rightly—that clemency would not be shown to her.

It had been suspected that this determined woman would attempt suicide, and three wardresses guarded her. But Mrs. Manning lulled them into a false security. She appeared to be on the friendliest possible terms with them, and often asked them to take a nap and not worry so much about her, as she could not very well escape. The wardresses slept in the condemned cell, at least one being on duty and usually two, while the third took a rest.

One night two were asleep and the other, overcome by the monotony of her task, was fitfully dozing in her chair, in the belief that Mrs. Manning was fast asleep. But the prisoner had been watching for such an opportunity. She had, as it afterwards transpired, allowed her nails to grow inordinately and had deliberately cut them to sharp points. She had determined to kill herself by forcing her sharp-pointed nails into her windpipe.

It is remarkable that anyone should think of such a suicide—but Mrs. Manning was a remarkable woman. The half-dozing wardress woke with a start to find her prisoner in convulsions, her hands dug so deeply into her throat that it took the united efforts of all three watchers to tear them away and control the half-maddened woman.

Previously Mrs. Manning had tried to get rid of the wardresses by pointing out to the chaplain the indignity of being watched while she undressed and prepared for bed. She announced that if she did not get some privacy she would not go to bed at all.

But there is no privacy in the condemned cell.

A very different attitude towards her gaolers was that shown by Kate Webster, who murdered her mistress, Mrs. Thomas, at Richmond, in 1879. Kate was an Irishwoman and a cook, with a nature brutally hard, as she showed by the revolting way in which she dismembered and disposed of the body after death. But in the condemned cell she was overwhelmed with gratitude for all the little attentions paid to her by the wardresses. It was probably the first time in her life that she had been really gently treated, and it was the irony of fate that she should realize what such treatment meant while awaiting death.

One does not think of Mrs. Dyer, the infamous baby-farmer who murdered numerous children, as a poetess. Yet I have already remarked on the way the isolation of the condemned cell drives prisoners to pour out their feelings on paper, and doubtless this accounts for the following verses, written by Mrs. Dyer in 1896, shortly before her execution:

> " By nature, Lord, I know with grief,
>   I am a poor fallen leaf
>   Shrivelled and dry, near unto death
>   Driven with sin, as with a breath.
>   But if by Grace I am made new,
>   Washed in the blood of Jesus, too,
>   Like to a lily I shall stand
>   Spotless and pure at His right hand."

This was signed "Mother"—a title which strikes one as bitterly ironical, in view of her heartless treatment of her poor little foster-children. It seems utterly amazing that a woman who had shown herself as callous and mercenary as Mrs. Dyer did, could write in this highly self-righteous vein; yet in the condemned cell she appears to have shown a certain religious fervour, and it may be that in spite of her terrible crimes, by some odd contradiction in her nature she felt herself assured of salvation.

Speaking of women writers in the condemned cell, there has surely never been a more voluminous one than Mary Blandy, the eighteenth century parricide who, at the instigation of her suitor, Cranstoun, poisoned her father, Francis Blandy.

After conviction she was allowed six weeks before the death sentence was carried out, and they proved none too long for the incessant correspondence and other writing with which she filled her days. Her most important piece of work was " Miss Mary Blandy's Own Account of the Affair between her and Mr. Cranstoun," which has been described by a legal authority as " the most famous apologia in criminal literature."

Probably one of the most curious correspondences ever conducted was the brief one between her and Elizabeth Jeffries; the letters on both sides were written from the condemned cell or its eighteenth-century equivalent. For Elizabeth Jeffries, at about the same time as Mary Blandy was tried, had been convicted, with her lover, of the murder of her master and his uncle.

Newspapers and gossip of the world penetrated into prison in those days, for Mary heard of the case and showed a deep sympathy for the woman whose fate was so like her own.

"It is barbarous," she said, referring to Elizabeth's crime, which, in her experienced opinion, had no " style," " but, poor unhappy girl, I pity her."

She accordingly wrote to her fellow-criminal to express sorrow at her fate, and the correspondence continued till it was cut violently short by the rope.

Mary Blandy possessed both courage and a lurking sense of humour. The latter she showed when a lady visitor to her cell appeared greatly shocked on her expressing her pity for Elizabeth Jeffries.

"Such people," said the lady, pursing up her lips, " fully deserve their dreadful fate."

Mary, naturally, by no means agreed; and her later comment on the incident was:

"I can't bear with these over-virtuous women. I believe if ever the devil picks a bone, it is one of theirs."

She certainly was not over-virtuous herself, but probably no woman has faced a death sentence with greater coolness. A contemporary writer says that after she had been sentenced to death she left the place of her trial and " stepped into the Coach with as little concern as if she had been going to a ball."

On arriving at Oxford Castle, where she was confined, she found that the news of the condemnation had arrived before her, and that the keeper's children were all in tears over her impending fate.

"Don't mind it," said Mary Blandy calmly. "What does it signify? I am very hungry; pray, let me have something for supper as speedily as possible." And without more ado she made a hearty meal of mutton chops and " Apple Pye."

In 1890 Mrs. Pearcey, who was only twenty-four, out of jealousy, murdered the wife and child of a man named Hogg, whose mistress she was. After her conviction her one intense desire was to see him, and she wrote to him begging him to visit her in the condemned cell. He, however, refused to do so.

The unhappy woman would not believe in his unwillingness. She took pains to procure an order that would admit him to see her and sent it to him. Without any comment at all he returned it by post, and on receiving this final declaration of the way in which he regarded her Mrs. Pearcey broke down completely. Before she was executed, however, she wrote to her solicitor saying that she forgave Hogg, and added one last agonised sentence: " He might have made death easier for me!"

CHAPTER VIII

PLACES OF EXECUTION

In a history of capital punishment the actual place of execution plays an important part. Until comparatively modern times executions, in most countries, were public, and they still are officially in some, e.g. France.

"When criminals are executed, the most public places are chosen, where there will be the greatest number of spectators, and so the most for the fear of punishment to work upon them." (Quintillian, Declam. 274.) " The more public the punishments are the greater effect will they produce upon the reformation of others." (Seneca de Ira, Lib. III, cap. 19.) "A gallows or tree with a man hanging upon it was so frequent an object in the country that it seems to have been almost a natural ornament of a landscape." (Wright, *The Homes of Other Days*.)

As far as possible it was customary for an execution to take place as near as possible to the scene of the crime, an old idea which died hard. Little by little executions were held in more or less fixed public places, later in front of prisons, and finally, on the abolition of public executions, within the prisons themselves.

There are many instances of the scene of the crime being the scene of the retribution. And where, owing to the circumstances of the situation or other cause, it was not possible to carry out the execution on the spot, the body of the executed criminal was more often than not hung in chains near the scene of his crime as a warning to all.

"In atrocious cases of murder," says Blackstone in his commentaries, " it was frequently usual for the court to direct the murderer, after execution, to be hung upon a gibbet where the act was committed; but this was no part of the legal judgment; and the like is still sometimes practised in the case of notorious thieves."

Andrews, in his *Old Time Punishments*, quotes the case of Anthony Lingard, tried in 1815 at Derby for the murder of Hannah Oliver, from the *Derby Mercury*. "Before the judge left the town he directed that the body of Lingard should be hung in chains in the most convenient place near the spot where the murder was committed."

Another instance, which I quote from the same work, is of Edward Miles, gibbeted near Warrington for the murder of a post-boy who was carrying the Liverpool mail bag to Manchester in 1791. Miles' body was hung in chains near the scene of the murder, and the gibbet can now be seen in Warrington Museum.

Michael van Berghen, Catherine van Berghen, and a man named Dromelius were executed on July 10th, 1700, for the murder of a Mr. Oliver Norris. They kept a public-house in Smithfield and were executed near the Hartshorn beer house, East Smithfield, being the nearest convenient spot to where the murder was committed. The bodies of the men were hung in chains, between Bow and Mile End, but the woman was buried.

Sarah Malcolm, who murdered Elizabeth Harrison, Mrs. Duncomb and Ann Price in the Temple, was hanged at the bottom of Fetter Lane in Fleet Street, near the scene of her crimes on March 7th, 1733. Houssaint, wife murderer, was executed opposite the end of Swan Alley, Shoreditch, where the murder was committed in 1724. John Hogan, the murderer of Mr. Odell, an attorney who lived in Charlotte Street, was executed opposite Odell's house in 1786. The Gordon rioters in 1780 were executed at various places, Tower Hill, Bishopsgate Street, Coleman Street, Bow Street, Holborn Hill, Bethnal Green, Whitechapel, Old Bailey, Old Street, Moorfields, Bloomsbury Square and St. Georges' Fields. John Brain, who robbed and set fire to his master's house in St. James's Street, was hanged in front of it and afterwards hung in chains near the gravel pits at Acton.

Captain Goodere, who murdered his brother on board his ship while in port at Bristol was hanged at Hotwells within view of the place where the ship lay when the murder was committed.

The last deviation from the usual course of hanging in front of Newgate was that of the sailor Cashman, who was hanged in 1817 in Skinner Street, opposite the house of Mr. Beckwith, the gunsmith, whom he had robbed.

Gradually certain places became to be recognised as places of execution, the most famous of them all being Tyburn. Newgate, Putney and Kennington Commons, St. Thomas à Watering, on the Old Kent Road, and Execution Dock and Smithfield were among the better known execution places at various periods round London.

There are others which deserve a passing mention. In 1413 the gallows was set up at the corner where High Street, St. Giles, Holborn, met Tottenham Court Road. Sir John Oldcastle, Lord Cobham, is the most notable name among the victims who suffered at St. Giles. He was hung in chains and roasted to death over a slow fire at this spot, as a Lollard.

Charing Cross was for many centuries a place of punishment, and its pillory was among the most famous of the many common in London. It was at Charing Cross that Hugh Peters, Chaplain of Oliver Cromwell, Scrope, Jones, Harrison and others of the regicides were executed in the reign of Charles II.

In the Old Palace Yard at Westminster were executed Guy Fawkes and his associates and Sir Walter Raleigh.

Tower Hill was also a place of execution. Of it Stow says: " Tower Hill, sometime a large plot of ground, now greatly straightened by encroachments (unlawfully made and suffered) for gardens and houses. Upon this hill is always readily prepared, at the changes of the city, a large scaffold and gallows of timber, for the execution of such traitors or transgressors as are delivered out of the Tower, or otherwise, to the Sheriffs of London, by writ, there to be executed."

At the last execution which took place here, that of Lord Lovat, April 9th, 1747, a scaffolding built near Barking Alley fell, with nearly 1,000 persons on it, and twelve of them were killed.

Other towns had their recognised places of execution; in front of the prison or castle, or some near by common or waste land where the mob could congregate.

At Aylesbury executions used to take place from the iron balcony in front of the upper floor of the County Hall "before which is a large open space, gradually rising from the level of the building up to the market house, which is about 300 yards distant from it, thus affording to the spectators almost all the advantages of an amphitheatre," to quote a contemporary newspaper account of the execution of the Quaker, Tawell, in 1845, the first man to be arrested following the invention of the telegraph.

Convicts under sentence of death in Maidstone Prison, were usually executed at Penningden Heath, about a mile from the prison, and were drawn there in the usual cart, with the executioner sitting beside them.

In 1769, "Suzannah Loth, for petty treason, in poisoning her husband, was drawn on a hurdle to Penningden Heath, near Maidstone, and fixed to a stake, with an iron chain round her middle, and her body burned to ashes, pursuant to the sentence at the Maidstone Assizes." The same day her lover was hanged for participation in the crime.

Here Nesbitt was hanged in 1824 for the murder of a Mr. Parker and his housekeeper, and James O'Coigley for high treason in 1798.

St. Thomas à Watering, close to the second milestone from London on the Old Kent Road, was the place of execution in Tudor days for the northern parts of Surrey. "Here," says the chronicler in *Old and New London*, "the vicar of Wandsworth, his chaplain and two other persons were hung, drawn and quartered in 1539 for denying the supremacy of Henry VIII in matters of faith."

It is further recorded that a new gallows was erected there in 1559 and five men executed there. It was here that one of the quarters of Sir Thomas Wyatt, beheaded for rebellion in 1554, was exposed, and a younger son of Lord Sandys was executed in 1556 for highway robbery. Franklin, one of the agents implicated in the murder of

Sir Thomas Overbury, was executed here in 1615, and the last persons to be hanged at St. Thomas à Watering were a father and son, in 1740. Seventeen years earlier were hanged together Thomas Athoe and his son for a murder in Pembrokeshire. Their trial raised an interesting point whether a criminal could be tried in any county but the one in which the crime was committed. The trial had taken place in Hereford and the case was referred to twelve judges. An old act of Henry VIII was quoted. "All murders and robberies in or about the borders of Wales shall be triable in any county of England where the criminal shall be taken."

Kennington Common was another regular place of execution. It was a dreary piece of land, covered partly with short grass. It was encircled by tumble-down wooden rails, and consisted of about twenty acres. The common is described in the *Tour round London*, in 1774, as "a small spot of ground on the road to Camberwell, and about a mile and a half from London. Upon this spot is erected the gallows for the County of Surrey." Here suffered the Scottish rebels in 1746, Sir John Wedderburn, John Hamilton Andrew Wood, Alexander Leith, Captain James Dawson and others who were hanged, drawn and quartered.

Here on August 3rd, 1795, the notorious Jerry Avershaw was executed for the murder of Price, who was attempting to arrest him, with a man named Little. The crowd which attended the executions was unusually large. There are many other records of criminals hanged on this once dreary piece of land of whom only a few can be mentioned. In 1749 there was hanged here one Richard Coleman, found guilty of the murder of Sarah Green. To the last he declared his innocence. Two years later three men, Welch, Jones and Nichols, in consequence of an unguarded conversation, were arrested and charged with the murder. Nichols turned King's evidence, admitted his guilt, and that of the other two, and in September, 1751, Welch and Jones were hanged on the same spot where the unfortunate Coleman had already suffered.

The site of the gallows was later occupied by St. Mark's Church, and the common is now Kennington Park and shows no signs of its once notorious character.

Putney Common was another place where the gallows was commonly erected near London. Here John Legee and John Higgs, two notorious thieves, were hanged in 1726.

Opposite to Rotherhithe was Old Gravel Lane, Wapping, and a small inlet there was for many years known as Execution Dock. Here the bodies of pirates were suspended in chains as a reminder to the river folk that piracy was punishable with death. Pepys, in his diary, mentions seeing five pirates hanging in chains "all tarry and vile." Stow says of it, "The usual place for hanging pirates and sea-rovers, at the low-water mark, and there to remain until three tides have overflowed them; was never a house standing within these forty years, but since the gallows being removed farther off, a continual street, or filthy street passage, with alleys of small tenements or cottages built, inhabited by sailors and victuallers, along by the river Thames, almost to Radcliffe, a good mile from the Tower."

According to the *Newgate Calendar* the condemned were taken from Newgate, *via* Cornhill, Whitechapel Road and the Commercial Road to Wapping. They were drawn in a cart preceded by the sheriff's officers on horseback, the city marshalmen and constables. A temporary gibbet was usually erected a few yards from low water mark and the body was allowed to hang until the rising tide reached the feet, when it was cut down and conveyed to Surgeons' Hall for dissection, except in special cases. As a rule the streets and windows and even the house tops were crowded with spectators, and boats and barges and other craft thronged the river within view of the gallows. The time of the executions was in the morning and they were often postponed for some days to fit in with low tide. The execution of Captain John Sutherland, for the murder of Richard Wilson, his cabin boy, was so postponed from the Monday to the Thursday, by order of the court, on account of the tide. He was hanged at low tide on the morning of Thursday, June 29th, 1809, and when the rising tide had reached his feet his body was cut down and taken to the Surgeons' Hall.

Until recently there could have been seen the relics of a once famous house which was, up to 1865, the residence of the Thames Police Magistrate, the last to hold the position being the father of the famous Sergeant Ballantine. The river police were under the control of this magistrate, who had a sea captain to assist him in his duties. Many cases of piracy were tried at the old Thames police court. The last reminder of Execution Dock disappeared in 1920, during the reconstruction of the district.

Pirates were hanged at East Wapping as early as the reign of Henry VI. In a Chronicle of London edited by Sir H. Nicola, it is stated that in this reign two bargemen were hanged beyond St. Katherine's for murdering three Flemings and a child in a Flemish vessel "and there they hangen till the water had washed them by ebbying and floroyd, so that the water beit upon them." In the *Gentlemen's Magazine* for 1775 it is stated "Williams the pirate was hanged at Execution Dock and afterwards in chains at Bugsby's Hole, near Blackwall." The notorious John Gow, or Captain Smith, with seven others were hanged at Execution Dock for piracy on August 11th, 1729, and Gow's friends, anxious to put him out of pain, pulled his legs so forcibly that the rope broke. After his second hanging he was hung in chains on the banks of the Thames. The rope broke also at the hanging here of the notorious pirate Captain Kidd in 1701.

At the execution of William Codlin, hanged for scuttling his ship "off Brighthelmstone" in 1802, an immense crowd gathered. The following account sheds a lurid light on the final execution scenes of those days.

"On Saturday morning, November 27th, 1802, this unfortunate man was brought out of the gaol at Newgate to proceed to undergo the last extremity of his sentence at the Docks at Wapping. On leaving the prison to get into the mourning cart which was to convey him to the place of execution he, in the most gratefully pathetic manner, returned his acknowledgments to Mr. Kirby for his many kind attentions and indulgences to him since his condemnation. He was conducted from Newgate by Ludgate Hill and St. Paul's, into Cheapside. A number of peace officers on horseback were at the head of the melancholy procession. Some officers belonging to the Court of Admiralty, with the City Marshals, followed near. The Sheriffs were in a coach, as was also the ordinary of Newgate, the Rev. Dr. Ford. Codlin was in a cart with a rope fastened round his neck and shoulders. He sat between the executioner and his assistant. He wore a blue coat, a white waistcoat, buff-coloured velvet breeches, and white stockings.

"As he passed down Cheapside, Cornhill, and Leadenhall Street, and onward through Aldgate and Ratcliffe Highway, he continued to read the accustomed prayers with great devotion, in which he was joined by those who sat with him in the cart. . . . The obstructions by the different turnings in the way, and by the concourse of people filling every passage, did not seem to disturb the settled firmness of his mind. As the procession drew near the scene of execution, the difficulties of the passage grew continually greater, so that it was hardly possible for the peace officers to clear the way. At the entrance to the dock it became necessary that the criminal should be moved out of the cart, to walk to the scaffold, which was yet some distance.

"He walked with a steady step, and ascended the ladder to the scaffold without betraying any emotions of terror. . . . The board, upon a signal from the sheriff, who sat in an opposite window, was soon after dropped from under his feet. His body, after hanging for the due length of time, was cut down and carried away in a boat by his friends. . . . The whole neighbourhood to a considerable distance, was filled with one throng; all the decks of the ships round the dock and a multitude of boats on the river, were equally crowded with spectators."

A passing mention must be made of Smithfield. One part was known by the name of The Elms, from a number of those trees that grew on the spot. The Elms was the place of execution until the middle of the thirteenth century, when it was removed to Tyburn. It has been calculated that during the short reign of Mary two hundred and seventy-seven persons were burnt to death for heresy, and of these the great majority suffered in Smithfield. Jack Straw, after whom Jack Straw's Castle on Hampstead Heath is named, the second in command of Wat Tyler's rioters, was hanged at Smithfield.

The most famous of all execution places in London or elsewhere is undoubtedly Tyburn. The history of Tyburn is for many years the main history of the scaffold in London. The Tyburn was a river with two branches, one of which crossed Oxford Street, near Stratford Place, and the other followed the present Westbourne Terrace and the Serpentine. Along its banks grew many elms, the earliest of Tyburn's fatal trees. The now vanished Elms' Lane, Bayswater, for many years commemorated the one time flourishing trees on the banks of the Tyburn.

In 1196 it is recorded that one William FitzOsbert was hanged for sedition at Tyburn, and this is the earliest date which is associated with Tyburn as a place of execution. The account of the execution is given by Ralph of Diceto, a contemporary, who says . . . "his hands bound behind him, his feet tied with long cords, is drawn by means of a horse through the midst of the city to the gallows near Tyburn. He was hanged . . ." In those days the gallows was often known as The Elms, and The Elms, near Tybourne, is frequently mentioned, as The Elms at Smithfield. And among some writers The Elms meant the gallows at Tyburn. It is so referred to, without the added Tyburn, in an order of Henry III, in 1220, to the sheriff of Middlesex to cause two good gibbets to be made in the place where the gallows was formerly erected, namely The Elms.

In that year Constantine Fitz-Athulf was hanged at The Elms, and in 1305 William Wallace, the Scottish patriot, was drawn through the city "usque Elmes" and there executed. In 1330 Roger Mortimer, Earl of March, was executed for treason. In 1388 Sir Robert Tresilian, Sir Nicholas Brembre and others were put to death and these are the only definite records of executions at Tyburn up to that date. But there is no doubt that there were many other executions there of which the records have either been lost or never made. Chaucer makes a very definite reference to the famous scene of execution, speaking of it as though it were well known.

It has been stated that fully 50,000 persons were publicly executed at Tyburn. According to Mr. Alfred Marks, in *Tyburn Tree—its History and Annals*—in 1220 two new gallows were ordered and set up. Thenceforward, down to 1570, many executions are recorded. In 1571 was erected that sinister triangular "tree" which remained there as a fixed apparatus for two centuries. In 1759 that structure was taken down, and during the remaining twenty-four years of the Tyburn period a movable gallows was used.

Many political martyrs, rebels and traitors ended their careers on Tyburn. The infamous Titus Oates, in 1678, brought no fewer than fifteen persons to Tyburn, all innocent of his pretended Popish plot. The Rye House Plot of 1683 and the Assassination Plot against William II in 1696 also added to its victims.

At Tyburn were hanged many famous highwaymen. Claude Duval, who had come to England from Normandy as a page to the Duke of Richmond, and who was a popular hero, was hanged there, and afterwards accorded a "lying in state" in the Tangiers Tavern, St. Giles. Jack Sheppard, the boldest and most resourceful of highwaymen, and prison breaker, was hanged at Tyburn in 1724, and the infamous Jonathan Wild, the unfortunate Dr. Dodd, Elizabeth Barton, the Holy Maid of Kent, Earl Ferrers and many others.

Timbs records a curious privilege with regard to Tyburn. "Formerly," he says, "when a person prosecuted another for any offence, and the prisoner was executed at Tyburn, the prosecutor was presented with a 'Tyburn Ticket' which exempted him and its future holders from having to serve

AN OLD EXECUTION BROADSHEET

Previous to the executions, in front of Newgate and Horsemonger Gaol and other places, hawkers sold many thousands of "the last dying words and confession and copy of the verses," giving a lurid and untruthful account of the crimes.

"Half-hanged Smith"
(*From an old print*)

John Smith, convicted of robbery, was actually hanging on the scaffold at Tyburn, when a reprieve arrived. He was cut down and after a short while recovered consciousness.

on juries. This privilege was not repealed till the sixth year
of the reign of George IV."

It is recorded that after the place of execution was
changed to Newgate in 1783, the gallows at Tyburn was
bought by a carpenter, who made it into stands for beer
butts in the cellars of the Carpenter's Arms public-house
near by.

"Around the gibbet," says Timbs in his *Curiosities of
London*, "were erected open galleries, like a racecourse
stand, wherein seats were let to spectators at executions.
The key of one of them was kept by Mammy Douglas,
'the Tyburn pew opener.' In 1758, when Dr. Henesy was
to have been executed for treason, the price of seats rose
to 2s. and 2s. 6d., but the doctor being 'most provokingly
reprieved,' a riot ensued, and most of the seats were
destroyed."

The last man to be hanged at Tyburn was one John
Austin on November 7th, 1783.

The exact site of Tyburn has been a matter of dispute.
In the first edition of Camden's *Britannia*, 1607, the triangular gallows is shown erected outside the north-eastern
corner of Hyde Park, at the junction of what is now Edgware
Road and Oxford Street. And there is little doubt that
this position was the correct one, most of the evidence to
the contrary being based upon considerably more flimsy
ground than that in its favour. The evidence both for and
against was very ably reviewed by Sir G. L. Gomme in his
pamphlet *Tyburn Gallows*.

In 1909 H.M. Office of Works fixed in the roadway a
triangular device which reads, "Here stood Tyburn Tree
removed 1759." On the railings of Hyde Park close by is
a bronze tablet bearing the following inscription: "Tyburn
Tree. The triangular stone in the roadway sixty-nine
feet north of this point indicates the site of the ancient
gallows known as Tyburn Tree, which was demolished in
1759."

On December 3rd, 1783, the first execution took place at
the Old Bailey, that part of the street opposite Newgate.
The gallows of the Old Bailey was built with three cross-

beams for three rows of victims. In London the front of
Newgate continued to be the place of execution until 1868
when public executions were abolished.

The gallows at Newgate was built with three cross-beams
for as many rows of the condemned, and between February
and December, 1785, 96 persons suffered by the "new drop"
which had taken the place of the cart.

The Newgate gallows was copied from a type used in
Dublin. "It consisted of an iron bar parallel with the prison
wall, and about four feet from it, but strongly affixed thereto
with iron scroll clamps. From this bar hang several iron
loops, in which halters are tied. Under this bar at a proper
distance is a piece of flooring or platform, projecting somewhat beyond the range of the iron bar, and swinging upon
hinges affixed to the wall. The entrance upon this floor or
leaf is from the middle window over the gate of the prison;
and this floor is supported below while the criminal stands
upon it, by two pieces of timber, which are made to slide
in and out of the prison wall through apertures made for
that purpose. When the criminals are tied up and prepared
for their fate, this floor suddenly falls down, upon withdrawing the supports inwards."

It was in front of Newgate that as late as 1788 a woman,
Phoebe Harris, was hanged and then burnt for coining.
One of the objects of the change of venue from Tyburn to
Newgate had been to lessen the number of spectators, but
executions at Newgate attracted as large and disorderly
crowds as ever. As many as 40,000, it is stated, were
present at the execution of Holloway and Haggerty in
1807, when a panic ensued, and scores were trampled to
death.

Following the abolition of public executions the scaffold
at Newgate was erected in a corner of the chapel yard of
the prison, a large open space, with high walls, immediately
behind the house of the Governor.

Horsemonger Lane gaol was a common gaol, and in 1856
it was the only existing common gaol in London, that is
the only place where debtors were still confined under the
same roof as felons. It was for many years the county gaol

for Surrey. Horsemonger Lane was never so well known as Newgate, although many executions took place there. In a contemporary account of the execution of Mr. and Mrs. Manning for the murder of O'Connor, it is stated "the Great thoroughfare leading through Southwark from London Bridge to the Elephant and Castle begins on the north side with High Street, which terminates at St. George's Church, and then the line is taken up by Blackman Street, which runs southward as far as the Borough Road. Almost opposite the spot where it abuts is Horsemonger Lane, a narrow street, leading to the area in which the prison and its outward walls are situated.

"The gaol is a comparatively small one. The roof would be flat, were it not for several large lanthorns or skylights projecting upwards from it."

The scaffold was usually erected on this roof, and here were hanged, among others beside the Mannings, Colonel Despard and his associates for high treason and Youngman for the atrocious murder of his sweetheart at Walworth. At the last execution over 20,000 people were present, an even greater crowd than watched the execution of the Mannings eleven years earlier.

The place of execution within the Tower, on the Green, was reserved for putting to death privately; and the precise spot whereon the scaffold was erected is nearly opposite the door of the Chapel of St. Peter, and is marked by a large oval of dark flints. Hereon many of the wisest, the noblest, the best, and the fairest heads of English men and English women of times long passed away, fell from such a block and beneath the stroke of such an axe, as may now be seen in the armouries.

During the Great War of 1914–18 men who were sentenced to death for espionage in Great Britain were almost all executed by shooting within the precincts of the Tower. Only one, Robert Rosenthal, who was arrested on board an outward bound ship which had almost reached the three-mile limit, which would have meant safety for him, was hanged, and not shot, on July 5th, 1915.

The first to be shot was Carl Hans Lody, who was executed in November, 1914. The spies met their death in the Tower at the hands of a firing party of eight, the execution taking place in the miniature rifle range. The condemned man was bound firmly to a chair very like that used by a barber and blindfolded.

CHAPTER IX

EXECUTION SCENES

EXECUTIONS in the times when they were universally public, were occasions for rioting, revelry and ribaldry, and seldom was the demeanour of the crowd decorous in the face of death. And seldom, too, did a public execution act as a deterrent. More often than not in the crowd would be friends of the criminal who had escaped by the merest accident being in his place and who, the very next day, would continue their criminal practices for which they had watched one of their number hang. In many accounts of the Tyburn and Newgate hangings one reads that pickpockets plied their trade busily among the crowd. It was considered the proper thing to be present at an important execution. Witness the following extract from Pepys' diary:

"January 21st, 1664. Up, and after sending my wife to my aunt Wight's, to get a place to see Turner hanged, I to the 'Change'; and seeing people flock in the City, I enquired, and found that Turner was not yet hanged. So I went among them to Leadenhall Street, at the end of Lyme Street, near where the robbery was done; and to St. Mary Axe, where he lived. And there I got for a shilling to stand upon the wheel of a cart, in great pain, above an hour before the execution was done; he delaying the time by long discourses and prayers, one after another in hopes of a reprieve; but none came, and at last he was flung off the ladder in his cloak. A comely-looked man he was, and kept his countenance to the end; I was sorry to see him. It was believed there were at least 12,000 to 14,000 people in the street."

The high and titled frequently booked windows overlooking the scaffold, as they are now booked for Royal processions, and gave elaborate breakfasts to their friends afterwards. The low gathered in their hundreds to witness a hanging, and the public-houses in the neighbourhood often kept open the whole of the preceding night for their refreshment and enjoyment. At the executions, for example, of Hepburn and White before the debtor's door at Newgate in 1811 it is recorded that among those who attended were the Duke of Cumberland, Lord Sefton, Lord Yarmouth and other noblemen. It was usual at one time for the Governor of Newgate to give a breakfast to those friends whom he had invited to see the hanging, and by established custom devilled kidneys always formed the principal dish, although as Hollingshead relates, nearly everyone was obliged to swallow a glass of brandy first.

In the centre of Newgate was a chapel and in the centre of the chapel was a large pew, painted black, called the Condemned Pew. Those who sat in it were visible to the whole congregation and particularly to the Ordinary, whose desk and pulpit fronted the centre of the condemned pew and within six feet of it.

On the Sunday preceding an execution, the Condemned Sermon was preached, and appropriate hymns sung by the remaining convicts, such as the "Lamentation of a Sinner." If the execution was set to take place the following day the condemned had their final hours thoroughly harrowed by hearing part of the burial service read. On the day of an execution no service was held in the chapel.

The condemned sermon service at Newgate was often attended by the rank and fashion of the day. When, for example, the Ordinary of Newgate, the Rev. Mr. Carver, preached the condemned sermon before the execution of Courvoisier for the murder of Lord William Russell, July 5th, 1840, the sheriffs issued tickets to a large number who wished to attend the service. Among those who were present were Lord Fitzclarence, Lord Coventry, Lord Paget, Lord Bruce, members of the House of Commons and several ladies.

When the famous procession to Tyburn was discontinued

the great Dr. Johnson was one who violently protested. "Sir," he told Boswell, "executions are intended to draw spectators. If they do not draw spectators they do not answer their purpose. The old method was most satisfactory to all parties; the public was gratified by a procession, the criminal is supported by it. Why is all this to be swept away?"

The sheriffs for the year 1784 gave an answer which the following quotation bears out:

"If we take a view of the supposed solemnity from the time at which the criminal leaves the prison to the last moment of his existence, it will be found to be a period full of the most shocking and disgraceful circumstances. If the only defect were the want of ceremony the minds of the spectators might be supposed to be left in a state of indifference; but when they view the meanness of the apparatus, the dirty cart and ragged horses, surrounded by a sordid assemblage of the lowest among the vulgar, their sentiments are inclined more to ridicule than to pity . . . thus are all the ends of public justice defeated; all the effects of example, the terrors of death, the shame of punishment, are all lost."

On the night preceding the execution of condemned criminals, the bell-man of the parish of St. Sepulchre used to go under Newgate, and, ringing his bell, to repeat the following verses, as a piece of friendly advice, to the unhappy wretches under sentence of death.

> All you that in the condemned hold do lie,
> Prepare you, for to-morrow you shall die.
> Watch all, and pray, the hour is drawing near
> That you before th' Almighty must appear.
> Examine well yourselves, in time repent,
> That you may not t' eternal flames be sent;
> And when St. Sepulchre's bell to-morrow tolls,
> The Lord have mercy on your souls!
> > Past twelve o'clock!

Though the verses were repeated by the bellman, the following extract from Stow's *Survey of London*, shows that they should have been repeated by a clergyman.

"Robert Dove, Citizen and Merchant Taylor, of London, gave to the parish church of St. Sepulchre the summe of £50. That after the several sessions of London, when the prisoners remaine in the gaole, as condemned men to death, expecting execution on the morrow following; the clarke (that is the parson) of the church shoold come in the night time, and likewise early in the morning, to the window of the prison where they lye and there ringing certain toles with a handbell, appointed for the purpose, he doth afterwards (in most Christian manner) put them in mind of their present condition, and ensuing execution, desiring them to be prepared therefore as they ought to be. When they are in the cart, and brought before the wall of the church, there he standeth ready with the same bell, and after certain toles rehearseth an appointed praier, desiring all the people there to pray for them. The beadle, also of Merchant Taylors' Hall, hath an honest stipend allowed to see that this is duly done."

On an execution morning crowds gathered to watch the hangings at Tyburn and gathered on the road from Newgate to the end of Edgware Road, where Marble Arch now stands. The crowds were importuned by hawkers to buy the last dying words and confessions of the condemned, "with verses written in the condemned cell." These broadsides, of which many thousands were sold on the occasion of a popular execution, were inaccurate, and the same picture of the condemned man hanging from the scaffold was used for half a dozen different executions. Besides the broadsides and ballads other hawkers moved in and out among the crowds, selling sweatmeats, oranges and other refreshments. When the notorious Greenacre was hanged at a later date in front of Newgate, "Greenacre Tarts," were very popular with the crowd.

The criminals were usually drawn to Tyburn in an open cart, with their arms pinioned and the rope to hang them wound round their bodies. On the crest of Snow Hill a halt was made before the steps of St. Sepulchre's Church, where the bellman stood with a large bell which he rang twelve times before he addressed the convicts and the spectators in the following terms:

"All good people, pray heartily unto God for these poor sinners, who are now going to their death, for whom this great bell doth toll.

"You that are condemned to die, repent with lamentable tears; ask mercy of the Lord for the salvation of your souls through the merits, death, and passion of Jesus Christ, who now sits on the right hand of God, to make intercession for as many of you as penitently return unto Him. Lord have mercy upon you! Christ have mercy upon you!"

Having delivered this address the bellman handed to each of the condemned a bunch of flowers, and occasionally a cup of wine was offered to them.

The procession went down Snow Hill and at the bottom of the steep slope turned sharply to the left, crossing the Fleet river, in those days an open sewer, over a narrow stone bridge, Oldbourne Bridge. A gradual ascent led up Holborn Hill and the gates of St. Andrew's Church. Some historians have pointed out that the route to Oldbourne Bridge from St. Sepulchre's was too narrow for the procession, and that it passed up Giltspur Street, Cock Lane and Hozier Lane, across Smithfield to Oldbourne Bridge, and thence up Holborn Hill, the "heavy hill" and so into Holborn. Either way was through extremely narrow streets.

The cortége was headed by the city marshal on horseback, followed by the under-sheriff with a cavalcade of peace officers, and a body of constables armed with staves. Then came the cart or carts with the condemned, more constables, and finally a company of javelin men. Sometimes a party of javelin men headed the procession, and they were to be seen in all public executions in any part of the country. More often than not the condemned man sat on his own coffin in the cart, and was usually accompanied by the chaplain or ordinary.

All along the route the unhappy man was greeted with varying cries by the mob through which he passed. If he was popular he was cheered on his way, but if his crime was a particularly atrocious one he was met with groans and hisses and ribald shouts and often pelted with mud and garbage.

The procession often stopped for a few minutes at the Crown Inn near St. Giles's Pound, where the prisoners were allowed to drink a last glass, a boon that had been granted since the time when the ancient Lazar house, which stood here, used to present a bowl of ale to them. A popular criminal would even be allowed to stop at the house of any friend he might have on the road, for a farewell drink.

The gallows itself was a permanent triangular affair for the greater part of Tyburn's existence, and was formed by three tall upright posts, joined together at the top by a crossbar. Eight persons could be hanged from each of the beams, or twenty-four in all. The carts were backed underneath, and when the ordinary had finished his exhortations, the nooses were adjusted and the caps drawn. Lashing the horses, the hangman and his helpers put the carts in motion, leaving the condemned dangling and often being slowly strangled, though frequently the hangman or friends shortened the sufferings by pulling on the legs of the hanging man.

Similar scenes on a larger or smaller scale were to be witnessed all over England. The introduction of the ladder and later the drop did much to relieve the agonies of the last moments.

Following the executions at Newgate friends either took the body away when it was cut down, or, pursuant to the sentence, it was beheaded and quartered or anatomised. In London the condemned were publicly anatomised at Surgeons' Hall.

The Surgeons' Hall stood in the Old Bailey, on the site of the New Sessions House, till 1809. Pennant, in his *London* remarks, in connection with the Old Court of Justice, that the erection of the Surgeon's Hall in its neighbourhood was an exceedingly convenient circumstance. "By a sort of second sight," he says, "the Surgeons' Theatre was built near this court of conviction and Newgate, the concluding stage of the lives forfeited to the justice of their country, several years before the fatal tree was removed from Tyburn to its present site. It is a handsome building, ornamented with Ionic pilasters, and with a double flight of steps to the first floor. Beneath is a door for the admission of the bodies of murderers and other felons who, noxious in their lives, make a sort of reparation to their fellow creatures, by becoming useful after death."

The bodies of murderers, after execution, were dissected in the Surgeons' Theatre, according to the Act passed in 1752 and only repealed in the reign of William IV.

The execution of those high in office, political offenders and the like were attended with more ceremony than those of common malefactors. The following is a brief account of the execution of the Earl of Essex, taken from the State papers. He was executed in the Tower.

"The next day, being Wednesday, the 25th of February, 1600–1, about eight o'clock in the morning, he was brought forth from his chamber by Mr. Lieutenant, attended by the three divines exhorting him, with thirteen of the guard, and divers of the lieutenant's men, also following him. He was apparelled in a gown of wrought velvet, a satin suit, and felt hat, all of black, and with a small ruff about his neck. And at his coming forth of the door, and all the way as he went to the scaffold, he earnestly prayed to God to give him strength and patience.

"On a seat near the scaffold were the seven lords mentioned in the letter from the Council as having been appointed by Queen Elizabeth to attend the execution; these were the Earls of Cumberland and Hertford, Lord Viscount Bindon, Lord Thomas Howard, Lord Darcy, Lord Compton, and Lord Morley; several aldermen of London were also present, and other knights and gentlemen to the number of about a hundred. Sir Walter Raleigh, according to his own account, witnessed the execution from the armoury, without being seen by the Earl, and shed tears at the scene (How, *State Trials*, Vol. III, p. 44). Then, being come upon the scaffold, the Earl turned towards the noblemen and others, who sat before him beside the scaffold, and taking off his hat, made a speech acknowledging he deserved death.

"He called the executioner, and asked him how he must dispose himself on the block; and after having given him directions, the executioner kneeled before him, and besought him to forgive him. He turned himself and said, 'I forgive thee with all my heart, thou art the true executioner of justice.'

"Then he called his servant, to whom he gave his gown, and put his shirt-band off, and laid it on the scaffold at his feet. Then presenting himself before the block, and kneeling down, Dr. Barlow encouraged him against the fear of death: he answered 'That having been divers times in places of danger, he had felt the weakness of the flesh, and, therefore, in this great conflict, desired God to assist and strengthen him.' He then laid his neck upon the block, saying, 'Lord Jesus, into Thy hands I commit my spirit.' The executioner, staying the blow longer than the Earl expected, he said, 'O strike, strike.' And so his head was severed from his body at three blows, the first of which absolutely deprived him of all sense and motion. His body and head were placed in a coffin, previously prepared, and carried into the Tower church, where they were buried near to the remains of the Duke of Norfolk and the Earl of Arundel."

Raleigh himself, who had witnessed the execution of Essex, came to the scaffold less than a score of years afterwards. The following account is from that published by Cayley, with some additions made by an eye-witness and preserved in the collection of papers relating to Raleigh in the Records Office.

"Upon Thursday, the 29th of October, 1618, Sir Walter Raleigh was conveyed by the Sheriffs of London to a scaffold, in Old Palace Yard, at Westminster, about eight in the morning. Amongst the spectators were the Earl of Arundel, the Earl of Oxford, the Earl of Northampton, Lord Doncaster, Lord Sheffield, Lord Percy, and a large company of Knights and Gentlemen. When Sir Walter came upon the scaffold, he saluted, with a cheerful countenance, the Lords, Knights, and Gentlemen who were there present. After which a proclamation was made for silence, and he addressed himself to speak in this manner: 'I was yesterday taken out of my bed in a strong fit of

fever, which hath much weakened me, and whose intime-
liness, forbearing no occasion nor place, I likewise expect
to-day.   And I do, therefore, first desire the Almighty
God to keep sickness from me, that I may have time to
deliver my mind; and my next desire unto you all is,
that if disability in voice, or dismayedness in countenance
shall appear, you will ascribe it to sickness rather than
to myself.'

"Then pausing awhile, he directed himself towards a
window where the Lords of Arundel, Northampton and
Doncaster, with some other Lords and Knights sate, and
spake as followeth: 'I thank God, of His infinite goodness,
that he hath brought me hither to die in the light, and
not in darkness; (but by reason that the place where the
Lords and others sate was some distance from the scaffold,
that he perceived they could not well hear him, he said,)
'I will strain my voice, for I would willingly have your
honours hear me.'

"But my Lord of Arundel said, 'Nay, we will rather
come down to the scaffold,' which he and some others did.
Sir Walter Raleigh then saluted them severally, and afterwards began to speak. . . .

"Then the Dean of Westminster asked him in what
faith or religion he meant to die; he said 'In the faith
professed by the Church of England, and that he hoped
to be saved and to have his sins washed away by the precious
blood and merits of our Saviour Christ.'   Then, before he
should say his prayers, because the morning was sharp
the Sheriff offered him to bring him down off the scaffold
to warm him by a fire.   'No, good Mr. Sheriff,' said he.
'Let us despatch, for within this quarter of an hour mine
ague will come upon me, and, if I be not dead before then,
mine enemies will say that I quake for fear.'   So he made
a most divine and admirable prayer, and then rose up
and clasped his hands, saying, 'Now I am going to God.'

"Then a proclamation being made that all men should
depart the scaffold, he prepared himself for death, giving
away his hat, his cap, with some money, to such as he
knew that stood near him.   And then taking his leave

of the Lords, Knights, Gentlemen, and others of his acquaintance, and amongst the rest taking his leave of my Lord of Arundel, he thanked him for his company, and entreated him to desire the King that no scandalous writing, to defame him, might be published after his death; saying further unto him, 'I will now take my leave; for I have a long journey to go, and am assured hope to be quickly there.'

"And then, putting off his doublet and gown, desired the executioner to show him the axe; which not being suddenly granted him, he said, 'I prithee let me see it; dost thou think that I am afraid of it?' So it being given unto him, he poised it in his hand, and felt along the edge of it with his thumb, to see if it was keen; and smiling, spake to Mr. Sheriff, saying, 'This is sharp medicine, but it will cure all diseases.' And then he kneeled down to prayer, and entreated the people to pray for him.

"After that he called for the executioner, who, kneeling down and asking his forgiveness, he laid both his hands upon his shoulders and said he heartily forgave him. And there being some dispute that his face should be towards the east, he made answer and said 'So the heart be straight, it is no matter which way the head lieth.' As he was laying his head on the block, the executioner would have blindfolded him, upon which he rebuked him, saying, 'Think you I fear the shadow of the axe, when I fear not the axe itself?' He gave the headsman a sign when he should strike, by lifting up his hands; and the executioner struck off his head at two blows, his body never shrinking nor moving. His head was showed on each side of the scaffold, and then put into a red leather bag, and his wrought velvet gown thrown over it, which was afterwards conveyed in a mourning coach to his Lady's. The body was interred in the chancel, near the altar, of St. Margaret, Westminster."

The dean of Westminster, Dr. Tounson, who was commanded by the Lords of the Council to be with him both in prison and at his death says (Cayley's *Life of Raleigh*) "He was the most fearless of death that was ever known, and the most resolute and confident, yet with reverence and conscience." An eye-witness wrote, "Every man who saw Sir Walter Raleigh die said it was impossible for any man to show more decorum, courage or piety; and that his death would do more hurt to the faction that sought it than ever his life could have done."

All over England during the Middle Ages and up to the middle of the eighteenth century the scaffold was used not only for the strict legal punishment of murderers and other offenders, but as a vindictive revenge by those in authority. Following the restoration of the monarchy a heavy toll was enacted from those who had supported the Commonwealth, and the following is a brief account of the executions of the regicides at Charing Cross.

"On Saturday the 13th of October, 1660, betwixt nine and ten of the clock in the morning, Mr. Thomas Harrison, or Major-General Harrison, according to his sentence, was upon a hurdle drawn from Newgate to the place called Charing Cross, where within certain rails lately there made, a gibbet was erected, and he hanged with his face looking towards the Banqueting House at Whitehall (the place where our late Sovereign of Eternal memory was sacrificed); being half dead, he was cut down by the common executioner, his privy members cut off before his eyes, his bowels burned, his head severed from his body, and his body divided into quarters, which were returned back to Newgate upon the same hurdle that carried it. His head is since set on a pole on the top of the south-east end of Westminster Hall, looking towards London. The quarters of his body are in like manner exposed upon some of the City gates.

"Monday following, being the 15th of October, about the same hour, Mr. John Carew was carried in like manner to the same place of execution; where having suffered like pains, his quarters were also returned to Newgate on the same hurdle which carried him. His Majesty was pleased to give, upon intercession made by his friends, his body to be buried.

"Tuesday following, being the 16th of October, Mr. John Cooke, and Mr. Hugh Peters, were about the same hour carried on two hurdles to the same place, and executed in the same manner, and their quarters returned in like manner to the place whence they came. The head of John Cooke is since set on a pole on the north-east end of Westminster Hall (on the left of Mr. Harrison's), looking towards London; and the head of Mr. Peters on London Bridge. Their quarters are exposed in like manner upon the tops of some of the City gates.

"Wednesday, October 17th, about the hour of nine in the morning, Mr. Thomas Scott and Mr. Gregory Clement were brought on several hurdles; and about one hour after, Mr. Adrien Scroop and Mr. John Jones, together in one hurdle, were carried to the same place, and suffered the same death, and were returned, and disposed of in like manner.

"Mr. Francis Hacker and Mr. Daniel Axtell were on Friday the 19th of October, about the same time of the morning, drawn on one hurdle from Newgate to Tyburn, and there both hanged. Mr. Axtell was quartered, and returned back, and disposed of as the former; but the body of Mr. Hacker was by His Majesty's great favour given entire to his friends, and buried."

I transcribe the following passage from the *State Trials* in connection with the execution. "Hugh Peters, being carried on a sledge to the scaffold, was made to sit thereon within the rails, to behold the execution of Mr. Cooke. When Mr. Cooke was cut down, and brought to be quartered, Colonel Turner ordered the sheriff's men to bring Mr. Peters near, that he might see it, and bye and bye the hangman came to him all besmeared in blood, and rubbing his bloody hands together, he tauntingly asked, 'Come, how do you like this work, Mr. Peters? How do you like it?' He replied, 'Friend, you do not well to trample on a dying man.'"

The rolling by of years did not lessen very much the horrors of the scaffold. It is customary to quote from accounts of executions on the Continent and in the East, but Merrie England and the eighteenth and nineteenth centuries in this country contain as much material as

EXECUTION OF JOHN PERROTT
(*From an old print*)
John Perrott was executed at Smithfield in 1761 for fraudulent bankruptcy.

[*Face page* 194

Life, Trial, Confession & Execution
OF R. COOPER,

Who was Executed at Newgate, on Monday, November 17th, for the Murder of Anne Barnham, at Isleworth, Middlesex

This morning the sentence of the law was carried into effect on Robert Cooper in front of the Old Bailey. The prisoner has since his condemnation been very attentive to his religious duties, and seemed fully aware of the fearful position in which he was placed. Within the last few days the prisoner had manifested the most intense anxiety and has the time approached for its execution he became more frantic, and all the arguments that could be used failed to convince him that he had no right whatever over the conduct of the unfortunate woman he murdered. The worthy Chaplain attended the prisoner at an early hour and remained in earnest prayer till the Sheriffs arrived. The operation of pinioning having been gone through, the mournful procession proceeded to the scaffold, which having wounded, Calcraft adjusted the rope, the bolt was drawn, and the unhappy man soon ceased to exist.

At the Central Criminal Court, on Wednesday, October 28th, Robert Cooper was indicted for the murder of Anne Barnham, at Isleworth, on the 7th of August. The evidence having been gone through the judge summed up, and the jury found the prisoner "Guilty of Murder."

Mr. Baron Martin said the evidence was quite irresistible, and that it would have been impossible for the jury to have found any other verdict. He advised the prisoner to prepare for the fate that awaited him for he could hold out no hope of mercy. He then passed sentence of death in the usual form. The following Letter was found on the prisoner Isleworth, Wednesday evening.

I am wretched indeed; I am sorely depressed! I love my dear Annie; how can I see her with another man, night after night, and promising me that she do never go with any man? But when I met her on Monday night, at twelve o'clock, or rather one o'clock on Tuesday morning, arm-in-arm with another, and a little the worse for drink, and when I accosted her, and she did not scarcely notice me, my blood at that very moment curdled, my brains were hot with passion, and Satan, that goes about seeking whom he can devour. I am his victim, and may the Lord have mercy upon me. Oh, I cannot bear to see my dear, dearest Annie that I love better than my own life. Yes, I would starve for her. I have fallen on my bended knees while the tears fell like large drops of rain from mine eyes. I have begged time after time for her to be true to me, but she has deceived me, and I am descended, and how can I live when she has trifled with me whom once she loved, one who has knelt on his knees and prayed to his God from his heart to grant her safe through her confinement: yes, I so for her, my dear, dearest Annie, my best friends for you. I am a wretched young man. I find too have deceived me. On Sunday, when I come from the country, you said you were happy to see her. I said, I am overjoyed to see you, and how is your dear babe (Mary Annie? You said, dear Charlie, she is quite well and you immediately kissed me. I gave you 10s. to put into your pocket, and you seemed quite glad, and you said

Behold a man in health and vigour,
Doom'd upon the gallows high,
I must end my days in horror,
For murder I am doom'd to die;
At Isleworth I killed my Annie.
My own, my dear and lawful wife,
And with a dreadful loaded pistol,

A murderer, in health and vigour,
An awful spectacle to view,
I must die in dread November,
In eighteen hundred and sixty-two.

It was on the seventh day of August,
To Isleworth my way I bent,
I was resolved my wife to murder,
My Ann to kill was my intent;
I shot her on that fatal evening,
I took her precious life away,
At Isleworth I was determined,
My darling wife that I would slay

Oh, whatever could possess me,
My darling Annie for to slay,
Oh, whatever could possess me
For to take her life away;
Murder I premeditated,
That day on murder I was bent,
To murder her I had sworn to cherish,
That fatal day was my intent.
Oh! yes, I had the pistol loaded,
I determined was my wife to kill,

Charlie, you are very kind, and you spent the remainder of the day with me; but when I raked you to stop with me till Monday, you said you could not, and I found out you wanted to meet another, and he was the one that you were with on the morning night between twelve and one o'clock Oh, Annie, my dear, dearest sweet Annie, how I love you, and that very day in Brentwood Park you and I walked affectionately together with our lovely babe in your dear arms, and there you

In the dark lane of Isleworth,
I was resolved her blood to spill,
Poor creature, she was not expecting,
Her days on earth, so near, was past,
She little thought that fatal evening
I killed her, was to be her last.

When I had killed my own dear Annie,
And her innocent spirit, haunted me,
From that time by night and day;
I was both wretched and distracted,
I wander'd through the world forlorn
Justice closely did pursue me,
And I must die a death of scorn.

In the midst of health and vigour,
Oh, what a dreadful death to die,
A poor, unhappy, wretched mortal,
On the fatal gallow high;
Farewell, my little darling children,
On earth, no more I shall you see,
I lose my life; I killed my wife,
Oh, what ever could possess me?

Dearly did I love my Annie.
Oh, yes, I loved her as my life,
And I know not what could induce me
For to take away her life,
I am doomed to die at Newgate.
Nothing in this world can me save,
a wret hed and a dreadful murderer,
Who will soon lie in a murderer's grave.

promised me that you would visit the Crystal Palace on the Tuesday, and that I was to come early in the morning. I gave you a sovereign and you went and fetched everything you thought best to that amount out of pledge, and your wearing apparel, and that was all you wanted from me. Your grandmother told me to come and have some supper along with you, and you told me in the park you would go to bed early, as we had not much rest on the Sunday night, for you and I did

not go to bed at your grandmother's till half-past twelve o'clock. How affectionately you acted towards me and promised that day week you would come back to your dear Charlie, but when I went home to supper you told your granny to say that you were gone to Turnham-green, but I myself thought different. Some sudden change came over me, and told me you were with another, and my steps were directed to Hounslow, and it was there that I met you arm-in-arm with another, and your wicked (procuress) of a mother, a bad, bad woman, she brought you to ruin. Many a time hast thou said these words to me, and my dear, dear Annie, it is her that stole you from me, full of deceit. (Read the 7th chapter of Proverbs.) I was driven to commit the fatal deed, oh! what an awful thing it is to commit murder, cut dear babe left behind. Oh! young girls of Brentford; think of the result of tampering with a young feelings that loves you; take my advice and do not forsake a man that loves you. Look at me, poor, wretched, unhappy man, how kind I have been to my Annie; people knew it Brentford. (Mr. Upton down) I told him how unhappy I was he pitied too. How can my Annie respect herself and go on board barges, away down and up the river, for two or three days, but the deed is done. Look to my child. Good bye, farewell all who knew me, God have mercy upon me. I am writing this in a public-house at Isleworth. Annie, dear, dearest Annie, if you had not tampered with me I should not have felt the pangs I now feel. How could you pull her young man's face downwards towards yours and kiss him, time after time in front of me, and tell him you loved him, and yet told me quite different? Did I not send you 10s. and 7s. weekly when I was away from you? I have wronged you, I confess, but I have been forgiven by you, and you told me my kindness made you so that you could not rest away from me. You really did love me but your mother was the serpent. I have suffered for her and had been cruel to her. She is the cause of all this. Good bye, sweet Annie. Oh, that I could lie in your grave with you—that we could be buried together; but I shall lie elsewhere. I have watched and guarded you a long time and my heart has been breaking for you. You remember telling me that your grandmother gave you those bruised eyes you had a few weeks ago; but Annie, I have found you told me a falsehood. It was at Ealing Fair by some man. You have deceived me much-boasted Annie, Thomas Turner, George Lights, (bargeman) James Fribery, at Hounslow, and other too to whom you cohabit with, I hope will persuade you of me. They may live to think of the same you and I met with our death; and all young friends take warning by me, do not deceive me. God bless you. I leave this world a wretched man. God may the Lord have mercy upon my soul through the blood of Jesus Christ our Saviour.

Printed for the Vendors.

BROADSHEET OF R. COOPER

The old time broadsheets, giving the life, trial, confession and execution of notorious criminals, sold by the hundred thousand. The most famous of these sheets, now very rare, were those printed by Catnach in the Seven Dials, London.

can be supplied from the stories of the axe and the guillotine and the rope elsewhere. The following account of the execution of Robert Johnston is abridged from *The Scotsman* of January 2nd, 1819.

"Robert Johnston, aged 23 years, in company with two associates, robbed a gentleman on the highway, near Edinburgh, of a considerable sum of money, but without inflicting any serious violence. Johnston was apprehended and capitally convicted. The place of execution was in the midst of the most public place in the city. The gibbet rested on the wall of the old Cathedral Church of St. Giles, the principal place of the city appropriated to the worship of the God of Mercy, and where the General Assembly of our national church is held.

"Under the gibbet was erected a scaffold, in the centre of which was a quadrangular table. On this table Johnston stood, while the executioner attached to his neck a rope, the upper extremity of which was tied to the gibbet. When the criminal gave the fatal signal, it was intended that the table on which he stood should instantly drop down to the level of the flooring of the scaffold, and leave him suspended. But through the culpable negligence of those concerned in this operation, it really seemed as if the whole had been contrived to produce the shocking consequences which ensued. For, in the first place, the table, which seemed to be elevated only about eighteen inches above the level of the scaffold, was manifestly too low to admit of a sufficient length of rope between the neck and the gibbet, unless it was intended to keep the unhappy man for a long time in torture, by making the rope quite tight before removing the table. In the next place, the table was so clumsily constructed that it could not be removed until some time after the signal.

"Accordingly, nearly a minute of time elapsed after the signal was given, before the table could be forced down; and after it was got down, the perpendicular fall was so short that the unhappy man's toes were still touching the surface, so that he remained half-standing, half-suspended, and struggling in the most dreadful manner.

"It is impossible to find words to express the horror which pervaded the immense crowd assembled round this shocking spectacle, while one or two persons were at work, with axes, beneath the scaffold, in vain attempt to hew down a part of it beneath the feet of the criminal. Meanwhile the cries of horror from the populace continued to increase. Still the magistrates and others on the scaffold did nothing effectual; and it is hard to say how long this horrible scene might have lasted, had not a person, near the scaffold, who was struck by a policeman, cried out Murder. Those who were not aware of this circumstance, which was known only to a very few, imagined that this cry proceeded from the unhappy Johnston. The feelings of the populace could not bear this further laceration, and a shower of stones, taken from the loose pavement on the streets, compelled the magistrates and the police to retire in a moment.

"The populace then took possession of the scaffold, cut down the unhappy man, loosed the rope, and after some time succeeded in restoring him to his senses. They then endeavoured to bear him off, and had proceeded some way down the High Street, when the officers of police (who had abandoned their post of duty on the scaffold) proceeded with their bludgeons to assail all the individuals who were about the half-dead man, of whom they at length recovered possession.

"A spectacle now presented itself which equalled in horror anything ever witnessed in the streets of Paris during the revolution. The unhappy Johnston, half-alive, stript of part of his clothes, and his shirt turned up, so that the whole of his naked back, and upper part of his body was exhibited, lay extended on the ground, in the middle of the street, in front of the Police Office. At last, after a considerable interval, some of the police officers laying hold of the unhappy man, dragged him trailing along the ground, for about twenty paces, into their den, which is also the old Cathedral.

"Johnston remained in the Police Office about half an hour, where he was immediately attended by a surgeon, who bled him in both arms, and in the temporal vein, by which the half-suspended animation was restored; but the unfortunate man did not utter a word. In the meantime a military force arrived from the Castle, under the direction of a magistrate. The soldiers having been ordered to load with ball, were drawn up in the street surrounding the Police Office and place of execution.

"It was now within thirteen minutes of four o'clock, when the wretched Johnston was carried out of the Police Office to the scaffold. His clothes were thrown about him in such a way that he seemed half-naked, and while a number of men were about him, holding him up on the table, and fastening the rope again about his neck, his clothes fell down in such a manner that decency would have been shocked, had it even been a spectacle of entertainment, instead of an execution.

"While they were adjusting his clothes, the unhappy man was left vibrating, upheld partly by the rope about his neck, and partly by his feet on the table. At last the table was removed from beneath him, when, to the indescribable horror of every spectator, he was seen suspended, with his face uncovered, and one of his hands broke loose from the cords with which it should have been tied, and with his fingers convulsively twisting in the noose. Dreadful cries were then heard from every quarter. A chair was brought, and the executioner having mounted on it, disengaged by force the hand of the dying man from the rope. He then descended, leaving the man's face still uncovered, and exhibiting a spectacle which no human eye should ever be compelled to behold. It was at length judged prudent to throw a napkin over the face of the struggling corpse [sic].

"The butchery, for it can be called nothing else, continued until twenty-three minutes past four o'clock, long after the street lamps were lighted for the night, and the moon and stars distinctly visible. How far it was consistent with the sentence of the Justiciary Court to prolong the execution after four o'clock, is a question which the writer cannot answer; but the fact is certain that it was continued until nearly half an hour after, by the magistrates at the head of a military force."

The law is reluctant to give up its victim, however, and over half a century later three determined attempts were made to hang John Lee, and doubtless in this year of grace as many would be made if there were any unexpected hitch at the beginning.

The Cato Street conspiracy, so called because the conspirators met in Cato Street, London, was a plot to murder Castlereagh and other cabinet ministers at a cabinet dinner held in Lord Harrowby's house, on February 23rd, 1820. The chief conspirators, Thistlewood, Ings, Brunt, Tidd and Davidson were hanged in front of Newgate.

The following account of their execution is from "An authentic history of the Cato Street Conspiracy with the Trials at large of the Conspirators for High Treason and Murder, etc., by George Theodore Wilkinson, Esq., editor of the *New Newgate Calendar Improved*. It was published immediately following the executions. The conspirators were executed on Monday, May 1st, 1820.

The trial was presided over by the Lord Chief Justice Abbott.

The sentence on the conspirators was:

"That you, and each of you, be taken from hence to the gaol from whence you came, and from thence that you be drawn upon a hurdle to the place of execution, and be there hanged by the neck until you be dead; and that afterwards your heads shall be severed from your bodies, and your bodies divided into four quarters, to be disposed of as his Majesty shall think fit. And may God of His infinite goodness have mercy upon your souls."

"The Sunday papers had announced the period fixed for the execution, and as this was accompanied by a speculation that a scaffold was to be erected on the top of the prison, upon which the ignominious sentence was to be performed, thousands of persons flocked towards the Old Bailey, and continued to do so during the day, assembling in groups for information, and not infrequently indulging in language disgraceful to themselves, and alarming to

those who felt anxious for the peace of the metropolis.
Among these persons were many who had long been known
as the constant attendants at these factious meetings, the
repetitions of which have been productive of so much
mischief.

"On Saturday evening, Mr. Sheriff Rothwell and Mr.
Under-Sheriff Turner had awaited on Lord Sidmouth to
arrange the mode in which the execution should take
place. The plan at first proposed of erecting a scaffold
on the top of the prison at the near end to Newgate Street
was then considered and abandoned, Lord Sidmouth being
of the opinion that there was no necessity for departing
from the form customary, on like occasions; and on the
suggestion of Sheriff Rothwell, it was further resolved to
dispense with that part of the ceremony which directed
that the culprits should be drawn on a hurdle to the place
of execution, in consideration of the great inconvenience
that might arise in conveying them along the streets in
the manner which had been adopted on former occasions,
namely, from the court-house in front of the sessions house
to the scaffold.

"On the return of Mr. Sheriff Rothwell and Mr. Under-
Sheriff Turner, from the office of the Secretary of State,
with their final instructions, they directed Mr. Montague,
one of the surveyors of public buildings in the city, to
make the necessary arrangements for resisting the pressure
of the crowd which was anticipated, and for enlarging the
ordinary scaffold to such a size as would admit of the
performance of the more awful part of the ceremony—
that of decapitating the criminals.

"To effect these works, a great number of men were
suddenly called into requisition, and during the whole of
Sunday they were actively engaged.

"There were double rows of rails across the top of the
Old Bailey across Newgate Street, Giltspur Street, Skinner
Street, Fleet Lane, and in fact at the mouth of every
approach to the prison.

"In the course of Sunday morning Mr. Sheriff Rothwell
and Mr. Under-Sheriff Turner held a consultation with

the Lord Mayor, as to the necessity of applying to the Secretary of State for the Home Department to direct the attendance of a military force, not alone in the prison, but in its immediate vicinity.

"The result of their deliberations was that such an application was highly proper; and accordingly Mr. Turner was despatched to Whitehall, with a letter to Lord Sidmouth, intimating the wish of the Lord Mayor. In consequence of this application, in the course of the afternoon, one hundred men were ordered to proceed to the gaol of Newgate, and a detachment of fifty was quartered in Giltspur Street Compter.

"Other detachments were on duty at a short distance from the prison. In fact, every possible precaution was adopted to prevent disturbance or disorder.

"As the evening advanced, the throng in front of the prison increased, and at eight o'clock the pressure was so great that it required the utmost exertions of the constables on duty to prevent the interruption of the workmen. Thousands of all ranks and ages congregated in front of the gaol.

"The scaffold had been brought forth from the Courtyard, and the carpenters were busily employed in erecting the additional platform, which was ten feet square, and constructed with great solidity. They continued their operations by torchlight, which seemed as it were to make "darkness visible," and considerably enhanced the solemnity of the scene.

"Such was the anxiety of some to witness the execution, that they literally determined to remain in the neighbourhood all night, and thousands sacrificed their natural rest to the gratification of their curiosity.

"The windows of the houses in the Old Bailey and the streets adjacent, commanding a view of the scaffold, were let out at exorbitant prices. The sums demanded for a view from the windows were from ten shillings to two guineas, but even at these prices there was a superabundance of applicants.

"Between five and six o'clock a great quantity of sawdust

was brought out and deposited beneath the scaffold on which the decollations were to be performed. It was shortly afterwards transferred to the top of it, and at the same time the black cloth was brought, and the scaffold erected in the rear of the drop was completely covered with it. The posts which sustained the chains above it received the same sable attire; and while these preparations were in progress, every avenue leading into the Old Bailey was carefully secured by strong wooden rails fixed across and guarded by constables.

"At seven o'clock, the crowd which was collected about the prison, in every avenue leading to it, or commanding the most distant glimpse of its walls, was beyond all calculation; but still there was not the least appearance of disorder. In fact, such were the formidable preparations to preserve the peace that no possible alarm could exist. In the event of a riot, however, the Lord Mayor was prepared with large boards on poles, ready to be used should it become necessary to read the Riot Act.

"Shortly after seven o'clock the executioner made his appearance on the drop, and placed the steps by which he was to ascend to tie the sufferers to the fatal beam. The sawdust, which had been previously collected in two small heaps on the second scaffold, was now spread over the boards.

"The coffins were then brought out, and placed on the sawdust, the foot of each being put so as nearly to touch the platform, from which those who were to fill them were to be launched into eternity. They had no lids on them. The coffin of Thistlewood was first lifted out. The third coffin brought out appeared to be longer than the others, and was supposed to be intended for Davidson, who was the tallest man; but this conjecture proved erroneous.

"The persons employed to bring the coffins swept out the large one, and then proceeded to throw sawdust into them, that the blood of the sufferers might not find its way through. The block was now brought up, and placed at the head of the first coffin. Most of the spectators were surprised at the shape of the block, as, instead of presenting a flat surface, it was slanted off, so that the top of it was quite sharp.

"The awful moment was now approaching when the ill-fated men were to be removed to another world. Each of them conversed freely with the officers who had them in charge, and severally declared that moment to be the happiest of their lives.

"Thistlewood came out of the condemned cell first; he bowed to the Sheriffs and gentlemen present; he looked very pale, he cast up his eyes, and said 'It appears fine.' He displayed uncommon firmness, and held out his hands for the assistant executioner to bind them. He observed to the persons near him that he never felt in better spirits in his life. He was attired in the same apparel that he wore during his trial. The composure he exhibited was striking; but there was nothing like bravado or carelessness. He now advanced to the block to have his irons knocked off; and, while the turnkey was in the act, Tidd next made his appearance; he came out of the cell into the Press yard with an air of assumed gaiety. He smiled during the time he was being pinioned, and continued quite cheerful during the time his irons *were knocking* off. The moment his legs were free from their burden, he ran towards Thistle-wood, who had taken a seat on a bench (placed in the yard for the purpose), and said, 'Well, Mr. Thistlewood, how do you do?' and they shook hands most heartily. Thistlewood said he was never better. Tidd conversed in the most gay and cheerful manner with the turnkey, while he was driving the rivets out of his irons, and composedly assisted the man in taking them off.

"Ings then came out of the cell, and danced as he came down the steps along the yard. He was dressed in his usual clothes as a butcher, a rough pepper-and-salt coloured worsted jacket, and a dirty cap. During the time his hands were being tied he became thoughtful, afterwards he seemed *hurried* and in great mental pain; but before his irons were knocked off he began to laugh and shout, and afterwards took a seat by the side of his fellow sufferers.

"Brunt was then brought into the Press yard; he was perfectly composed, but looked round eagerly to see his wretched companions. He nodded to them, and then held out his hands to have then tied. He said nothing during the time he was being pinioned and having his irons taken off; but afterwards he addressed Thistlewood, Tidd and Ings; he told them to keep up their spirits, and to one of his companions he said, 'All will soon be well.'

"Davidson was then brought out of his cell; he seemed a little affected at the sight of his companions, but soon regained that composure which he evinced during the trials. His lips moved; but he did not betray much anxiety till his irons were knocked off. He then looked wildly at the Rev. Mr. Cotton, and appeared to be in prayer, very devoutly; the others declared they were about to die in peace with all mankind, but that they had all made up their minds on religious matters, and were determined to die Deists.

"When the awful ceremony of pinioning the culprits by the yeoman of the halter was concluded, they each shook hands, and most fervently exclaimed, 'God bless you.' The Reverend Mr. Cotton then began to read the burial service, commencing at the words, 'I am the resurrection and the life,' etc. and, the arrangements being completed, the procession advanced through the dark passages of the gaol, led by the Sheriffs and the Under-Sheriffs. The Rev. Mr. Cotton moved first. Thistlewood followed, with his eyes fixed, as it were, in abstract thought, and apparently lost to his situation. A vacant and unmeaning stare pervaded his countenance, which seemed unmoved by the devotions of the pious Ordinary. Tidd walked next, and although somewhat affected by his situation, his manner was collected, manly, and unaffectedly firm. Ings came next, and was laughing without reserve, and used every forced effort to subdue the better feelings of nature, which might remind him of his awful situation; his conduct was more like a delirium of fear than an effect of courage. Brunt, in fixed and hardened obduracy of mind, next advanced, and with a sullen and morose air of indifference surveyed the officers who were conducting him to his fate. The unhappy Davidson came last, with clasped hands and uplifted eyes, praying most devoutly; and the officers of the goal closed the mournful procession.

"On their arrival at the Lodge, from which the Debtor's Door leads to the scaffold, a moment's pause took place, while the dreadful paraphernalia of death were adjusted without. Thistlewood, who stood first, clasped his lips, and with a frown surveyed, from the doorway in which he stood, the awful preparations for his fate.

"Those opposite the prison saw in the next moment the procession from the interior of it reach the door through which the culprits were to pass to expiate their crimes with their blood.

"The Ordinary ascended the platform, and at a quarter before eight Thistlewood made his appearance on the scaffold. His step faltered a little as he mounted the platform, and his countenance was somewhat flushed and disordered on being conducted to the extremity of the drop. His deportment was firm, and he looked round at the multitude with perfect calmness. He had an orange in his hand. On the cap being placed on his head, he desired that it might not be placed over his eyes. While the executioner was putting the rope round his neck, a person from the top of the houses exclaimed, 'God Almighty bless you.' Thistlewood nodded. The Rev. Mr. Cotton by whom he was preceded, endeavoured to obtain his attention; but he shook his head, and said 'No, no.' He looked round repeatedly, as expecting to recognise someone in the crowd, and appeared rather disconcerted at observing the distance to which the populace were removed.

"Some of those to whom the face of Thistlewood was not familiar, imagined that he gave proofs of the fear of death upon the scaffold, but in this supposition they were much mistaken. At the moment that he has been uttering his dangerous politics in safety, and declaring his determination to stand or fall by them, the expression of his features was the same; and Thistlewood with the rope round his neck was the same Thistlewood that appeared so conspicuous at Smithfield.

"Mr. Cotton approached him while the executioner was making his awful arrangements and spoke to him upon the subject of his thoughts hereafter. Thistlewood shook his head, and said he required no earthly help upon that subject. He then sucked his orange, and, looking down at the officers who were collected about the scaffold, said, in a firm voice, 'I have but a few moments to live, and I hope the world will be convinced that I have been sincere in my endeavours, and that I die a friend to liberty.'

"The figure of the miserable man, which naturally was not good, had undergone a change for the worse; in consequence of the pressure of the rope with which his arms were fastened behind, his shoulders were raised to a degree that closely approached deformity. The executioner having placed the cap upon his head, and fastened the rope round the beam, looked towards the Sheriff as a signal that his duties towards Thistlewood were completed.

"While the executioner was performing his last offices without to this wretched man, the scene within the Lodge was almost beyond the power of description. The dreadful obduracy of Brunt and Ings filled with horror the small assemblage of persons among whom they stood. Ings, with a hardihood almost indescribable, sucked an orange, and sung, or rather screamed, in a discordant voice, 'Oh, give me death or liberty!' Brunt rejoined, 'Aye, to be sure. It is better to die free, than to live slaves.'

"Tidd, who had stood in silence, was now summoned to the scaffold. He shook hands with all but Davidson, who had separated himself from the rest. He ran towards the stairs leading to the scaffold. In his hurry his foot caught the bottom step, and he stumbled. He recovered himself, however, in an instant, and rushed upon the scaffold, where he was immediately received with three cheers from the crowd in which he made a slight effort to join. The rope having been put round his neck, he told the executioner that the knot would be better on the right than on the left side, and that the pain of dying might be diminished by the change.

He than assisted the executioner, and turned round his head several times for the purpose of fitting the rope to his neck. He also desired that the cap might not be put over his eyes, but said nothing more. He likewise had an orange in his hand, which he continued to suck most heartily. He soon became perfectly calm, and remained so till the last moment of his life.

"Ings followed and rushed to the platform, upon which he leaped and bounded in the most frantic manner. Then, turning himself round towards Smithfield, and facing the very coffin that was soon to receive his mutilated body, he raised his pinioned hands, in the best way he could, and leaning forward with savage energy, roared out three distinct cheers to the people, in a voice of the most frightful and discordant hoarseness.

"Davidson walked up the platform with a firm and steady step, but with all that respectful humility becoming the condition to which he had reduced himself. He bowed to the crowd, and instantly joined Mr. Cotton in prayer.

"Brunt was the last summoned to the fatal platform, and he rushed upon it with impetuosity. Some of the people cheered him, which evidently gratified and pleased him. It brought a sort of grin on his countenance, which remained till his death. While the rope was being adjusted he looked towards St. Sepulchre's Church, and perceiving or affecting to perceive, some one with whom he had been acquainted, he nodded several times, and then made an inclination of the head towards the coffins, as if in derision of the awful display. His conduct was marked by the same irrational levity to the last. His last act was to take a pinch of snuff from a paper which he held in his hand. He also threw off his shoes.

"The executioner was now proceeding to adjust the ropes, and to pull the caps over the faces of the wretched men. When he came to Ings the unhappy man said, 'Now, old gentleman, finish me tidily. Tie the handkerchief tight over my eyes. Pull the rope tighter; it may slip.' Tidd's lips were in motion just before he was turned off, as if in prayer. Davidson was in the most fervent prayer.

"The executioner having completed the details of his awful duty, walked down the ladder, and left Mr. Cotton alone upon the scaffold. The reverend gentleman, standing closer to Davidson than to any of the rest, began to read those awful sentences which have sounded last in the ears of so many unhappy men. Suddenly the platform fell, and the agonies of death were exhibited in the view of the crowd in their most terrific force. Thistlewood struggled slightly for a few minutes. The struggles of Ings were great. The assistants of the executioner pulled his legs with all their might; and even then the reluctance of the soul to part from its native seat was to be observed in the vehement efforts of every part of the body. However, in the course of five minutes all was still.

"Exactly half an hour after they had been turned off, the order was given to cut the bodies down. The executioner immediately ascended the scaffold, and drew the legs of the sufferers up, and placed the dead men, who were still suspended, in a sitting position, with their feet towards Ludgate Hill. This being done, the trapdoor was again put up, and the platform restored to its original state. The executioner proceeded to cut Thistlewood down; and, with the aid of an assistant, lifted the body into the first coffin, laying it on the back, and placing the head over the end of the coffin, so as to bring the neck on the edge of the block. The rope was then drawn from the neck, and the cap was removed from the face.

"The last convulsions of expiring life had thrown a purple hue over the countenance, which gave it a most ghastly and appalling appearance; but no violent distortion of features had taken place. An axe was placed on the scaffold, but this was not used. When the rope had been removed, and the coat and waistcoat forced down, so as to leave the neck exposed, a person wearing a black mask, which extended over his mouth, over which a coloured handkerchief was tied, and his hat slouched down, so as to conceal part of the mask, and attired in a blue jacket and dark grey trousers, mounted the scaffold with a small knife in his hand, similar to what is used by surgeons in amputation, and, advancing to the coffin, proceeded to sever the head from the body.

"When the crowd perceived the knife applied to the throat of Thistlewood, they raised a shout, in which exclamations of horror and reproach were mingled. The tumult seemed to disconcert the person in the mask for the moment; but, upon the whole, he performed the operation with dexterity; and, having handed the head to the assistant executioner, who waited to receive it, he immediately retired, pursued by the hootings of the mob.

"The assistant executioner, holding the head by the hair over the forehead, exhibited it from the side of the scaffold nearest Newgate Street. A person attended on the scaffold, who dictated to the executioner what he was to say; and he exclaimed with a loud voice, 'This is the head of Arthur Thistlewood, the traitor!' A thrilling sensation was produced on the spectators by the display of this ghastly object, and the hissings and hootings of part of the mob were vehemently renewed.

"The same ceremony was repeated in front of the scaffold, and on the side nearest Ludgate Street. The head was then placed at the foot of the coffin; while the body, before being lifted up to bring the neck on the block, was forced lower down, and, this done, the head was again put in its proper place, at the upper end of the coffin, which was left open.

"The block was then moved by the hangman, and placed at the head of the second coffin, and the same ceremony performed on Tidd. The execution lasted an hour and eight minutes. It was a quarter before eight when Thistlewood walked up the steps leading to the fatal platform; and it wanted seven minutes to nine when the head of Brunt was placed in the coffin.

"The person who wore the mask, and who performed the ceremony of decapitation, is said to be the same person who beheaded Despard and his associates. This, however, may be doubted, as from the quickness and spring of his motions, he seemed to be a young man. His mode of operation showed evidently that he was a surgeon. On performing his dreadful duty, the edge of the first knife was turned by the vertebrae of Thistlewood, and two others became necessary to enable him to finish his heart-appalling task.

"At a late hour in the evening, the wives of the executed men were informed by the keeper of Newgate that the bodies of their husbands were buried. In the course of the afternoon a channel had been dug alongside of the subterraneous passage that leads to the cells, and, about seven in the evening, after the coffins had been filled with quicklime, they were strongly screwed up, placed in a line with each other, strewed over with earth, and finally covered with stones, and of course no trace of their end remains for any future public observation. On this circumstance being communicated to their unhappy wives, they were entirely overcome by the poignancy of their feelings."

The execution of the Mannings for the murder of O'Connor in 1849 brought forth a famous protest from Charles Dickens, which, however, had no immediate result. "I was a witness of the execution at Horsemonger Lane this morning," he wrote to *The Times*, . . . "I believe that a sight so inconceivably awful as the wickedness and levity of the immense crowd collected at that execution this morning could be imagined by no man, and could be presented in no heathen land under the sun. The horrors of the gibbet and of the crime which brought the wretched murderers to it faded in my mind before the atrocious bearing, looks and language of the assembled spectators. I came upon the scene at midnight. . . . As the night went on, screeching and laughing, and yelling in strong chorus of parodies on negro melodies, with substitutions of 'Mrs. Manning' for 'Susannah' and the like were added to these. When the day dawned, thieves, low prostitutes, ruffians and vagabonds of every kind, flocked on the ground, with every variety of offensive and foul behaviour. . . . When the sun rose brightly it gilded thousands upon thousands of upturned faces, so inexpressibly odious in their brutal mirth or callousness that a man had cause to feel ashamed of the shape he wore. When the two miserable creatures who attracted all this ghastly sight about them were turned quivering into the air there was no more emotion, no more pity, no more thought that two immortal souls had gone to judgement, than if the name of Christ had never been heard in this world."

The following is a condensed account of the execution taken from *The Times* :

"On Tuesday morning, at nine o'clock, Frederick George Manning and Maria Manning, his wife, were hanged in front of Horsemonger Lane Gaol, for the murder of Patrick O'Connor. . . . For some days previous to the execution the place was visited by thousands of persons, and, perhaps, on no previous occasion was ever such indecent eagerness exhibited by persons moving in a respectable class of life to witness a public execution.

"On Sunday and Monday the whole space in front of Horsemonger Lane Gaol was crowded with people, while all the windows in the neighbourhood whence a view of the execution could be obtained were let at prices of one guinea and two guineas for each seat for spectators. The housetops were also let out in seats for spectators, who paid exorbitant prices for the unenviable privilege of taking their stand there; and every patch of enclosed land where a glimpse of the drop could be had was employed for the erection of scaffoldings fitted up with seats, as on the occasion of some grand national solemnity.

"The prices rose as the demand increased and towards the evening of Monday large premiums were offered for places in favourable positions overlooking the gallows.

"A meeting of the visiting justices was held at the gaol at ten o'clock on Monday, in order to make the final arrangements for the execution. During the day preparations made in the erection of the gallows were watched with intense eagerness by the assembled crowd; and towards evening large bodies of the refuse of London arrived on the ground determined to make a night of it. The itinerant hawkers of provisions were in great force in the neighbourhood, hoarsely bawling their respective commodities; and the whole place had the aspects of the outskirts of Bar-

BELLMAN AT ST. SEPULCHRE'S
(From an old print)

Criminals on the way to execution at Tyburn were halted before the steps of
St. Sepulchre's church, where the bellman addressed an admonition to them,
ending "Christ have mercy upon you!"

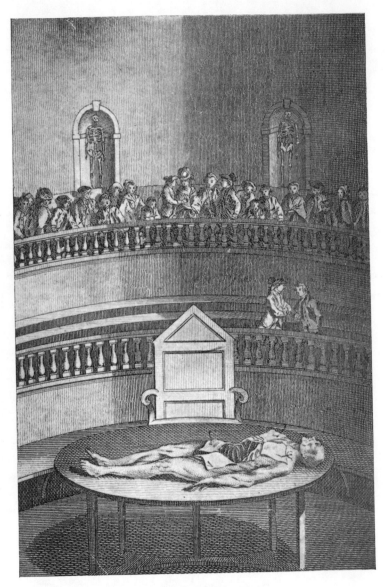

MURDERER IN SURGEONS' HALL
(*From an old print*)

Murderers were not only sentenced to death, but they were often sentenced to be publicly dissected. This public dissection took place in the theatre of the Surgeons' Hall, Old Bailey, and the galleries were crowded with spectators.

Face page 211]

tholomew Fair when that venerable nuisance flourished in high prosperity under the protection of the London corporation.

"As the evening drew on the excitement outside the prison walls increased, and when night had closed upon the scene the road in front of the gaol and all the thoroughfares leading thereto were thronged with spectators. The erection of strong barriers in double lines along the front of the gaol, with cross rows at short intervals, was completed early in the evening. . . . The current of human life once set in that direction never ceased to flow until the morning sun was well up in the sky. The number of people present probably exceeded thirty thousand. Taking up their stations on the carriage way, in front of and rather to the westward of the entrance of the gaol, were the dregs and offscourings of the population of London, the different elements that composed the disorderly rabble crew being mingled together in wild and unsightly disorder, the 'navvy' and Irish labourer smoking clay pipes and muzzy with beer, pickpockets plying their light-fingered art, little ragged boys climbing up posts. . . . From that great seething mass there rose a ceaseless din of sounds and war of tongues—voices in every note, shrill whistles and slang calls. Occasionally the roar of voices swelled into a chorus to the burden of some vulgar doggerel—a sort of 'gallows Marseillaise' which the depraved multitude caught up with avidity.

"The sight of the drop (a huge, gaunt, and ominous-looking structure) raised on the flat roof of the gaol, failed to put the least check on the uproarious tendencies of the mob. Now it was a fainting, then a fight, and again the arrest of a thief. Even the dreadful sight of two human beings—husband and wife—hurried into eternity for the crime of murder, failed to solemnize for one moment or to check perceptibly the disgusting levity of the crowd. On the outskirts of this great mass of human beings were, grouped in smaller numbers, a very different class of people —men and women too—who had paid their two or three guineas to gratify a morbid curiosity, and who, from the fashionable clubs of the West End, and from their luxurious homes, came to fill the windows, the gardens and the housetops of a few miserable little houses. The eye could detect among the spectators a number of fashionably-dressed women who levelled their lorgnettes towards the scaffold.

"At a quarter past eight Manning and his wife entered the chapel. The Sacrament was then administered to them when the governor appeared and said that time pressed. Calcraft also came forward and the wretched pair were conducted to different parts of the chapel to be pinioned. That operation was performed upon the male prisoner first and he submitted to it with perfect resignation. In the pinioning of Mrs. Manning a longer time was occupied. When the cords were applied to bind her arms her great natural strength forsook her for a moment, and she was nearly fainting, but a little brandy brought her round again, and she was pinioned without any resistance. She drew from her pocket a black silk handkerchief and requesting that she might be blindfolded with it her request was acceded to. Having had a black lace veil fastened over her head, so as to completely conceal her features from the public gaze, she was conducted to the extremity of the chapel, where the fatal procession was at once formed and in a slow and solemn manner moved forwards towards the drop, the prison bell tolling.

"The procession passed along a succession of narrow passages, fenced in with ponderous gates, side rails and *chevaux de frise* of iron. In its course a singular coincidence happened. The Mannings walked over their own graves, as they had made their victim do over his. Mrs. Manning walked to her doom with a firm, unfaltering step. Being blindfolded she was led along by Mr. Harris, the surgeon. She wore a handsome black satin gown.

"At last nine o'clock struck and shortly after the dreadful procession emerged from a small door in the inner side of a square piece of brickwork which rests on the east end of the prison roof. To reach this height a long and steep flight of stairs had to be climbed, and it is only wonderful that Manning, in his weak and tottering state, was able to ascend so far. As he ascended to the steps leading to the drop his limbs tottered under him, and he appeared scarcely able to move. When his wife approached the scaffold he turned round with his face towards the people, while Calcraft proceeded to draw over his head the white nightcap and adjust the fatal rope. The executioner then drew the nightcap over the female prisoner's head and all the necessary preparations being now completed the scaffold was cleared of all its occupants except the two wretched beings doomed to die. In an instant Calcraft withdrew the bolt, the drop fell, and the sentence of the law was fulfilled. They died almost without a struggle, and the bodies, having been allowed to hang for an hour, were cut down, and in the evening buried in the precincts of the gaol.

"Scarcely a hat or cap was raised while the drop fell; and the bodies of the murderers had hardly ceased to oscillate with the momentum of their fall before the spectators were hurrying from the spot."

The execution of William Bonsfield on March 31st, 1856, before Newgate, was attended by a peculiarly horrifying scene.

When Calcraft, the executioner, was admitted to the room where the condemned man was confined Bonsfield was sitting on a sort of couch that formed his bed, with his head buried on his chest, and apparently utterly unconscious of what was passing round him. Calcraft at once proceeded to pinion the culprit, and the unhappy man had to be carried by four warders to the scaffold. As he appeared totally unable to stand, it was considered wise to place him on a chair under the beam and he was held in that position by one of the assistants while Calcraft fixed the rope.

When the signal was given the chair on which Bonsfield was still seated gave way with the drop, but the fall was not nearly so great as it is under ordinary circumstances. And at this moment the prisoner began a desperate struggle for life. "The sound of the falling drop had scarcely passed away," said one contemporary account, "when there was a shriek from the crowd 'He's up again!' and, to the horror of everyone, it was found that the prisoner by a powerful muscular effort had drawn himself up completely to the level of the drop, that both his feet were resting upon the edge of it, and he was vainly endeavouring to raise his hands to the rope. One of the officers immediately rushed upon the scaffold, and pushed the man's feet from their hold, but in an instant, by a violent effort, he threw himself to the other side, and again succeeded in getting both his feet on the edge of the drop. Calcraft, who had left the scaffold, imagining that all was over, was called back; he seized the criminal, but it was with considerable difficulty that he forced him from the scaffold, and he was again suspended. The short relief the wretched man had obtained from the pressure of the rope by these desperate efforts had probably enabled him to respire, and, to the astonishment and horror of all the spectators, he for a third time succeeded in placing his feet upon the platform, and again his hands vainly attempted to reach the fatal cord. Calcraft and two or three other men then again forced the wretched man's feet from their hold, and his legs were held down until the final struggle was over. While this fearful scene was being enacted the bells of the different neighbouring churches were ringing merrily" (for the conclusion of the Crimean War).

The last public execution to take place in England was that of Michael Barrett in front of Newgate, on May 26th, 1868. The following is taken from the account of the scene at his execution in *The Times* for May 27th, of that year.

"Yesterday morning, in the presence of a vast concourse of spectators, Michael Barrett, the author of the Clerkenwell Explosion, was hanged in front of Newgate. In its circumstances there was very little to distinguish this from ordinary executions. The crowd was greater, perhaps, and better behaved; still, from the peculiar atrocity of the crime for which Barrett suffered, and from the fact of its being probably the last public execution in England, it deserves more than usual notice.

"On Monday the barriers were put up, and on Monday night a fringe of eager sightseers assembled, mostly sitting beneath the beams, but ready on a moment's notice to rise and cling to the front places they had so long waited for. There were the usual cat calls, comic choruses, dances, and even mock hymns, till towards two o'clock, when the gaiety inspired by alcohol faded away as the public-houses closed, and popular excitement was not revived till the blackened deal frame which forms the base of the scaffold was drawn out in the dawn, and placed in front of the door from which Barrett was to issue.

"Its arrival was accompanied with a great cheer, which at once woke up those who had been huddled in doorsteps and under barricades, and who joined in the general acclamation. The arrival of the scaffold did much to increase the interest, and through the dawn people began to flock in, the greater portion of the newcomers being young women and little children. Never were these more numerous than on this occasion, and blue velvet hats and huge white feathers lined the great beams which kept the mass from crushing each other in their eagerness to see a man put to death. The crowd was most unusually orderly, but it was not a crowd in which one would like to trust.

"It is said that one sees on the road to the Derby such animals as are never seen elsewhere; so on an execution morning one sees faces that are never seen save round the gallows or near a great fire. Some laughed, some fought, some preached, some gave tracts, and some sang hymns; but what may be called the general good-humoured disorder of the crowd remained the same, and there was laughter at the preacher or silence when an open robbery was going on. None could look on the scene, with all its exceptional quietness, without a thankful feeling that this was to be the last public execution in England.

"Towards 7 o'clock the mass of people was immense. A very wide open space was kept round the gallows by the police, but beyond this the concourse was dense, stretching up beyond St. Sepulchre's Church, and far back almost, into Smithfield—a great surging mass of people which, in spite of the barriers, kept swaying to and fro like waving corn. Now and then there was great laughter as a girl fainted, and was passed out hand over hand above the heads of the mob, and then there came a scuffle and a fight, and then a hymn, and then a sermon, and then a comic song, and so on from hour to hour, the crowd thickening as the day brightened, and the sun shone out with such a glare as to extinguish the very feeble light which showed faintly through the glass roof above where the culprit lay.

"It was a wild, rough crowd, not so numerous nor nearly so violent as that which thronged to see Muller or the pirates die. In one way they showed their feeling by loudly hooting a magnificently attired woman, who, accompanied by two gentlemen, swept down the avenue kept open by the police, and occupied a window afterwards right in front of the gallows. This temporary exhibition of feeling was, however, soon allayed by coppers being thrown from the window for the roughs to scramble for.

"The Sheriffs, with the Under-Sheriffs arrived at the prison shortly after seven o'clock, and, according to custom, spent the interval until eight o'clock in their official apartment connected with the Court-house. There they were joined by the Governor of Newgate, the prison surgeon, and the Ordinary, the Rev. F. Lloyd Jones. A few representatives of the Press to whom tickets of admission had been given were also present. The convict Barrett had retired to rest about ten on the previous evening, and having spent a somewhat restless night, rose at six yesterday morning, dressed himself, and engaged in prayer. Shortly afterwards he was joined in his cell by the Rev. James Hussey, attached to the Roman Catholic chapel in Moorfields, who had attended him regularly since his conviction, and who remained with him to the last. It is understood that he received the Sacrament one day last week, and again yesterday morning. Towards eight o'clock the Sheriffs paid him a visit, accompanied by the Governor, and then retired to a part of the prison leading to the scaffold, where the rest of the authorities and the public representatives had already assembled. By a pre-determined arrangement, and contrary to the usual practice, the convict was not pinioned in the Press room, as it is called, but in his own cell, and, this process over, he was conducted to the drop by a private way, accompanied by his priest and attended by the executioner and three or four warders, the prison bell and that of St. Sepulchre's Church, hard by, tolling the while. The Sheriffs and Under-Sheriffs, who, with others, stood in a group in a gloomy corridor behind the scaffold, just caught a glimpse of the doomed man as he emerged with his attendants from a dark and narrow passage, and turned a corner leading to the gallows. He was dressed in the short claret-coloured coat and the gray striped trousers, both well worn, by which he had become familiar to all who were present during his protracted trial. His face had lost the florid hue it then wore, and in other respects he was an altered man.

"With the first sound of the bells came a great hungry roar from the crowd outside, and a loud, continued shout of 'Hats off,' till the whole dense, bareheaded mass stood white and ghastly-looking in the morning sun, and the pressure on the barriers increased so that the girls and women in the front rank began to scream and struggle to get free. Amid such a scene as this and before such a dense crowd of white faces, Barrett was executed. His clergyman came first. Barrett mounted the steps with the most perfect firmness. This may seem a stereotyped phrase, but it really means more than is generally imagined. To ascend a ladder with one's arms and hands closely pinioned would be at all times difficult, but to climb a ladder to go to certain death might try the nerves of the boldest.

"Barrett walked up coolly and boldly. His face was as white as marble, but still he bore himself with firmness, and his demeanour was as far removed from bravado as from fear. We would not dwell on these details, but from the singular reception he met as he came out upon the scaffold. There was a partial burst of cheers, which was instantly accompanied by loud hisses, and so it remained for some seconds, till as the last moment approached the roars dwindled down to a dead silence. To neither cheers nor hisses did the culprit make the slightest recognition. He seemed only attentive to what the priest was saying to him, and to be engaged in fervent prayer.

"The hangman instantly put the cap over his face and the rope round his neck. Then Barrett turning spoke through his cap and asked for the rope to be altered, which the hangman did. In another moment Barrett was a dead man. After the bolt was drawn and the drop fell with the loud boom which always echoes from it, Barrett never moved. He died without a struggle. It is worthy of remark that a great cry rose from the crowd as the culprit fell—a cry which was neither an exclamation nor a scream, but it partook of the sound of both. With the fall of the drop the crowd began to disperse, but an immense mass waited till the time for cutting down came, and when nine-o'clock struck there were loud calls of 'Come on, body snatcher!' 'Take away the man you've killed!' etc. The hangman appeared and cut down the body amid a storm of yells and execrations as has seldom been heard even from such a crowd. There was nothing more to be seen, so the concourse broke up with its usual concomitants of assault and robbery.

"The body on being taken down was placed in a shell and removed to an adjoining building in the presence of the Sheriffs and under-Sheriffs, the Governor, the prison surgeon, and the Ordinary. There the rope having been removed from the neck, and the leathern straps by which the legs and arms had been pinioned, the surgeon certified that life was extinct. The expression of the face was marvellously serene and placid, and the features composed to a degree irreconcilable at first sight with the notion of a violent death, though the lips and parts of the forehead were unusually livid. Towards the evening the body was buried in the accustomed place within the precincts of the prison, in a grave upwards of five feet deep, in the presence of the Governor and other officers of the gaol."

Nowadays there are no spectators other than the chaplain and the necessary officials. Nothing remains for the morbid-minded but the doubtful satisfaction of loitering outside a prison on the morning of an execution to see the death notice posted. With the adoption of the long drop method of hanging, and the careful training every hangman receives before

JONATHAN WILD ON HIS WAY TO TYBURN
(From an old print)

Jonathan Wild was executed at Tyburn on May 24, 1725. He was the head of a gang of thieves, the forerunner of similar present-day organisations in America. He was reviled and pelted by the mob all the way to Tyburn.

[*Face page* 218

EXECUTION OF THE CATO STREET CONSPIRATORS
(From an old print)

The Cato Street conspirators were hanged and afterwards decapitated. Their coffins were placed in front of them before the execution, and as each head was taken off it was held up to the watching mob by the assistant executioner; who cried "Behold, the head of a traitor!"

he is allowed to officiate, the proceedings are very quick, to the infinite relief of all concerned.

At an execution inquest in 1922 evidence was given that only ten seconds elapsed between a murderer quitting the condemned cell and being hanged. Human justice could hardly be more considerately brief.

CHAPTER X

MISCELLANEOUS FORMS OF EXECUTION

THE ingenuity of man to make his fellow beings suffer has never been more fearfully exemplified than in his methods of inflicting the punishment of death. It is only within the last hundred years that the least attempt has been made to make that punishment swift and humane, and even now, in the most enlightened countries, it is still surrounded by forms and ceremonies which needlessly add to the mental torture of the condemned.

In Chapter I many of these forms of execution of the past were touched upon. Cutting, burning, boiling, breaking and tearing to pieces of the human frame have been practised in all countries at some time or another. The pious pioneers held up their hands in righteous horror at the Red Indians' custom of burning at the stake, but they did not hesitate to practise such atrocities themselves upon those who differed from them in religion. No tortures of savages, indeed, can approach those devised by the leading brains of the Middle Ages throughout Europe. There were many unofficial forms of execution which only added to the fear of death in the " good old times."

The walling up of the condemned alive; embedding them in cement which, as it set, slowly crushed them to death; impalement on a stake; eating alive by ants; the cutting off of the flesh in strips; these and a thousand other methods reveal the pitiless fertility of the mind of man.

When Rome was at the height of her power executions became degraded to ingenious forms of death to satisfy the blood lust of Roman citizens. In the great arena of the Colosseum, Christian martyrs, captured enemies and criminals fought one another to delight citizens of a degraded empire and the mistress of an emperor; were torn to pieces by maddened wild beasts; or gored to death by bulls.

STONING TO DEATH.

The ancient law of Moses contains a long list of offences, each of which was punished by stoning. The mode of execution was as follows. The culprit was led outside the town to a place set apart for such grim ceremonies. The scene of execution was easily recognisable by the piles of stones, each telling a tale, which covered it. An open space was selected and the unfortunate victim led to it.

A crowd formed round the condemned, each individual holding in his hand a heavy stone. Through a gap in the ranks, at last, came one dressed in white, with a deep coloured fringe to his garments. He advanced to the edge of the ring and took a small stone in his hand. He was the first to accuse the condemned man and the law was that he should be the one to cast the first stone. If it were his own daughter he was compelled to throw this stone. Following its casting a shower followed until the condemned is struck to the ground unconscious. The stones continued to fall until they are piled high on the corpse to form another execution mound. The execution did not always end with the malefactor. His property was confiscated, and in some instances all his beasts and relatives were stoned to death as well.

CRUCIFIXION.

Lt.-Col. Cecil Powney, in the *Transactions of Metropolitan College*, 1922, gives an excellent summary of this terrible form of punishment.

"The punishment of crucifixion," he says, "emanated from the Phoenicians. It is known to have been used in Assyria, Egypt, and Persia, and by the Greeks, Carthaginians and Romans. For instance, we find the Carthaginian general, Malcus, invested his son Cartalo in royal raiment with a crown on his head and then crucified him in order to get a special favour from Baal.

"It is more probable that the Romans introduced crucifixion into Palestine, but there is no word in classical Latin for crucifixion. At the time of our Lord's death crucifixion was regarded as most degrading, as well as the most painful death, and was only reserved for slaves and the worst of malefactors, any who had been sentenced to death, even for the most heinous crimes, if he could prove his Roman citizenship, being executed in a different manner.

"The method of crucifixion was as follows. Originally the cross, as it was even then called, consisted of a single stake. To this the criminal was bound and left to die by thirst and starvation, while sometimes he was impaled on it. Later the cross, of which there were three varieties, was used.

"These were, the *crux immissa*, consisting of four arms; the *crux commissa*, consisting of three arms, and the *crux decussata* or St. Andrew's cross, the proper Greek cross, being in the form of the Greek letter chi. There was also the three-sided cross, like an association goal post, to which the victim was hanged by one leg and an arm.

"The criminal was first scourged with a whip into the several points of which were inserted small pieces of bone, or even bones, to increase the suffering. Sometimes the application was so severe that his entrails almost gushed out. He was then forced to bear to the scene of execution the transverse beam of the cross, it being a physical impossibility for anyone, unassisted, to bear the whole cross. Arrived at the place of execution, he was stripped naked, with only a loin cloth, and the transverse beam fixed on the upright one which was laid on the ground. He was then nailed through the hands and the insteps as being the most sensitive parts of the extremities, or else tied by cords, the feet resting on a small block of wood or horn called the *suppedanem*. This was to prevent the weight of the body tearing the hands from the nails and so causing it to fall. The cross was then fixed in a previously prepared socket driven into the ground, and the sufferer sometimes remained alive for two or three days. A board was sometimes carried in front of the criminal from the Judgement Hall to the place of execution where it was tied above the cross.

"The feet were close to the ground; in the pictures of St. Andrew's crucifixion on the Greek cross, the feet are on the ground. Myrrh and vinegar were handed to the crucified on a pole to allay their sufferings and their limbs were broken to hasten their death. It was customary to bury the cross with the victim.

"Crucifixion in the Roman Empire was abolished by the Emperor Constantine in A.D. 315 or 345. The date is uncertain."

The punishment was never popular in Rome itself, though it was common throughout the provinces and conquered States. It was quite usual to postpone any individual execution until a batch of unfortunates were waiting and all were crucified together, to add to the spectacle. The heat, the flies and the dust added intensely to the sufferings of the unhappy wretches, lingering to their slow deaths on the cross, and only nightfall brought any relief to their tortured bodies. In some cases an order was given that those who had not died by sundown should receive their quietus. One form of crucifixion occasionally practised was that of fastening the victim upside down on the cross. Happily he quickly passed into a state of unconsciousness, and though this form of crucifixion was looked upon as being far more terrifying than the usual form, it was in reality much more merciful, for the agony was quickly over.

In Japan there was, till the nineteenth century, a form of crucifixion which was particularly ghastly. The condemned were tied to a cross by ropes and then transfixed by light spears by the executioner. If the latter had been bribed heavily enough the first spear transfixed the heart. If not, the condemned passed through exquisite agony before death released them, the spears often being passed *slowly* through the body, so as to miss any immediately vital part.

As late as 1127 Louis the Bulky ordered Bertholde, the murderer of Charles the Righteous, to be crucified, and this punishment was also inflicted in France on Jews and heretics at different times.

Smith, in his *Dictionary of the Bible*, states with regard to the seven sons of Saul "the victims were not, as the Authorised Version implies, hung, they were crucified. The seven crosses were planted on the rock on the top of the sacred hill of Gibeah. . . . The victims were sacrificed at the beginning of the barley harvest—the sacred and festal time of the Passover—and in the full blaze of the summer sun they hung till the fall of the periodical rain in October". Thus the practise of gibbeting on a cross was in use at least as early as in the days of King David.

THE WHEEL.

It was in Germany and France that the wheel was most used. Traitors and parricides were the chief sufferers.

Executions by the wheel generally took place in the morning, so that the spectacle of the scaffold and its great object-lesson might be before the populace as long as possible. Before he was led out to the place of execution the convict was stripped save for a pair of linen drawers. He was then wrapped up in a cloak and placed in the cart which was to take him to where the execution was to take place—generally the public square of the town—and where a scaffold was erected. On the scaffold was a huge oak wheel, and a block of wood for it to rest against, while on the ground were several bars of iron and a bundle of ropes. The assistant executioners seized the condemned man and laid him on the wheel, which rested on the ground. A stout rope was placed round his waist, and he was attached firmly to the spokes and hub of the wheel. This was but the preliminary of the actual work of the executioner-in-chief who advanced, bearing in his hand a thick bar of iron. Seizing one of the arms of the doomed man, he drew it out along one of the spokes, and fastened it at the elbow with a cord. Then he proceeded to make the rest of the arm fit the rim of the wheel. As it would not do so naturally, the limb was broken by several blows with the iron bar. The other arm was then similarly treated, and the legs likewise attached to the wheel. It was a test of the skill of the executioner to avoid actually breaking the flesh when he smashed the limbs.

When the victim was thus attached to the instrument the great wheel was lifted up and propped against the block of wood, so that all could see the writhing convict. At first the execution ended at this point, the malefactor being permitted to linger until he succumbed to sheer exhaustion.

In other words, the punishment of the wheel was but a modification of crucifixion.

Then it became customary to deal a number of heavy blows on the chest with the iron bar, care being taken that too much force was not used, lest unconsciousness should supervene. Every breath thus was made excessively painful, and the wretched man died in agony.

THE GAROTTE.

With the advent of later ideas of humanity a modification was introduced. Through one of the spokes a hole was bored, through which a double cord was passed. The loop of this went round the culprit's neck, and as soon as the officer in charge of the punishment thought that the victim had suffered enough the assistants pulled on this cord and thus strangled the criminal. From this cord sprang two modern methods of execution, namely the process which is called hanging in Austria, and the garotte of Spain, both of which are merely modifications of the same principle.

It is said that when Patkul, the envoy of Peter the Great, was put to death on the wheel by order of Charles XII of Sweden, the latter cashiered the officer in command of the guard for permitting the head to be stricken from the mangled body of the victim before life was extinct. Breaking on the wheel was abolished in France during the Revolution.

The first garotte was undoubtedly merely an upright post with a hole in it, through which passed a double cord. The loop of this went round the victim's neck, and when the free ends were pulled the windpipe was constricted, and death ensued from strangulation. Later the free ends of the cord were tied together, a stick was inserted, and thus the cords were twisted until sufficiently constricted. Here we have the simplest form of garotte proper. One man was sufficient to do the necessary twisting, and when he judged that the loop had been drawn sufficiently tight, he fastened the stick with another cord in such a way that the twisted rope could not unwind. Death resulted from slow strangulation.

An improvement was introduced in the form of an iron collar, to pass round the neck and the upright post. At the back of the pillar a screw, operated by means of levers with heavily-weighted ends, passed through the collar, its end pressing against the upright post. The neck of the culprit is thus squeezed until life is extinct. Till comparatively recent times this form of garotte has been in force. At present there are two kinds in use, both of which are more humane than the one just described. In one of these the collar is in two pieces, an upper and a lower ring. There a very powerful screw operated mechanism, by means of which the upper collar is drawn towards the pillar and the lower thrust from it. If the screw be turned quickly and the double collar so adjusted that one of the rings presses on one vertebra and the other on an adjoining one, then the spinal column is dislocated and almost instantaneous death follows.

The other is less truly a garotte. It has a collar and screw and in outward appearance is similar to those just described. The screw presses against a narrow blade, which projects through the pillar. If the instrument be properly adjusted, when the executioner turns the great levers the collar tightens, as in the ordinary garottes, but at the same time the sharp knife advances, and, passing between two of the bones of the neck, divides the spinal column, thus causing death.

In some forms the collar and lever are fixed into the back of a chair, to which are attached manacles and fetters for the proper securing of the condemned, but in general, and especially where the execution is to be public, the old pattern of single post, with a shorter pillar for the culprit to sit on, is adhered to.

About nightfall on the evening preceding an execution the Spanish condemned man is taken from his cell to the prison chapel. Before he leaves his cell he is bidden to say farewell to it, for he will never re-enter it. Attended by a couple of priests, and carefully guarded by warders, the convict enters the chapel and is told to kneel before the high altar. On each side of this are the clergy, and around him, though out of earshot, stand the armed guards. Prayer succeeds prayer for a time, and then a move is made to a pew to rest for a short while. Then again to the altar steps, the priests never

EARL FERRERS IN HIS COFFIN
(*From an old print*)

Earl Ferrers was executed at Tyburn, May 5, 1760, for the murder of his steward.
The coffin containing his body was afterwards taken to Surgeons' Hall, where
he was publicly dissected.

[*Face page* 226

EXECUTION OF WILLIAM CORDER
(From an old print)

William Corder was famous as the author of the "Red Barn Mystery". He was executed at Bury St. Edmunds, on August 11, 1828, for the murder of Maria Marten, whose body he had buried in the Red Barn.

Face page 227]

allowing the doomed man's mind to stray from the awful nearness of death and from the necessity for repentance.

Towards the morning he is asked if he confesses his crime, and the poor wretch generally is ready enough then to admit that he has been justly condemned. The law of Spain would not permit his execution to take place until he had confessed his guilt.

In theory the garotte can cause instant death. In practice it does not do so in the great majority of cases, and is only slow strangulation.

Following the Spanish-American war the Americans were left with the legacy of the garotte, and in 1902 four men were executed by this method in Porto Rico. From time immemorial executions on the island had been observed as gala events by the populace, but the American governor allowed only twenty witnesses, mostly officers and priests, to be present.

Official photographs were taken of the garotting, and the following is a description of this form of execution which ended this method of capital punishment for ever under American administration.

Four posts were erected, each fitted with a crude wooden seat and set up in the yard of the gaol. The condemned could hear all the preparations being made, for they were kept awake all night by the prayers of the priests in their cells. Each man was draped at the execution in a long black robe, pinioned, and fastened to the upright post. A black cloth was thrown over the head of each when the brass collar was fixed round his neck. One turn of the heavy screw by the executioner punctured the spinal column and death was instantaneous. But the whole proceedings were too reminiscent of the Inquisition for the century and have been replaced by hanging.

In Austria slow strangulation was the method of execution, and in the *St. James's Gazette* for August 8th, 1893, appeared the following:

"In the presence of a hundred spectators a dangerous convict named Emi Brunner, was executed by strangulation, the method practised in Austria, in the courtyard of the prison at Krems on Saturday. The process of strangulation, which was accomplished partly by the noose of a rope and partly by the compression of the wind passages by the hands of the executioner, occupied five minutes, and it was not until two minutes afterwards that the prison doctor certified the extinction of life."

The Mazzatello

In the Papal States the mazzatello flourished as late as the nineteenth century.

Accompanied by a priest the criminal was led out to the public square, where a scaffold had been erected. On the platform was a coffin, and by it stood the executioner, garbed in black and masked, who leant on a heavy mallet or poleaxe. This instrument was the mazza or mazzatello.

On to the scaffold the culprit was led and, after a few final prayers from the priest, he was asked it he was ready. Standing behind the condemned, the executioner then raised the awful mallet, swung it once or twice in the air, as if to test its strength, and then, with a resounding thud, brought it down with his full force on the head of the condemned man. To make his work complete the executioner drew a knife across the throat of the unconscious man. The whole method of execution was most revolting, but it was not until the coming of Garibaldi and of a United Italy that this form of execution was abolished.

Pressing to Death

Peine forte et dure, the strong and slow torture, was a species of torture formerly applied by the law of England to those who, on being arraigned for felony, refused to plead, and stood mute, or who were guilty of equivalent contumacy.

In the reign of Henry IV it had become the practice to load the offender with iron weights, and thus press him to death, and until nearly the middle of the eighteenth century pressing to death was the regular and lawful mode of punishing persons who refused to plead. Though not a legal form of execution in theory, in practice it becameso.

Among instances of the infliction of the *peine forte et dure* are the following: Juliana Quick, in 1442, charged with high treason in speaking contemptuously of Henry IV; Margaret Clitheron, the martyr of York, in 1586, for her constancy to the Catholic faith; Walter Calverly of Calverly, of Yorkshire, arraigned at the York Assizes in 1605, for murdering his two children and stabbing his wife; and Major Strangways, in Newgate, in 1657, for refusing to plead when charged with the murder of his brother-in-law. In 1720 a person of the name of Philips was pressed in Newgate for a considerable time, till he was released on his submission; and the same is recorded in the following year of one Nathaniel Hawes, who lay under a weight of 250 lbs. for seven minutes. A statute of 1772 virtually abolished *peine forte et dure*, and a later statute of 1828 made standing mute equal to a plea of not guilty.

The following are the words used by the judge who sentenced Henry Jones in 1672 at the Monmouth Assizes for refusing to plead:

"That the prisoner shall be remanded to the prison, and laid there in some low and dark house, where he shall be naked on the bare earth, without any litter rush or other clothing, and without any garment about him, and that he shall lie upon his back, his head uncovered and his feet, and one arm shall be drawn to one quarter of the house, and the other arm to another quarter, and in the same manner shall be done with his legs, and there shall be laid upon his body iron and stone as much as he can bear, and more, and the next day following he shall have three morsels of barley (bread) without any drink, and the second day he shall drink thrice of the water that is next to the house of the prison (except running water) without any bread, and this shall be his diet until he is dead."

The sentence was carried into execution in a cellar belonging to the gaoler, whose name was George Sadler. Henry Jones was placed under the pressure on the Saturday, the day after his sentence, and only expired at midday on the following Monday.

The penalty of *peine forte et dure* was publicly put into force at the Kilkenny Assizes as late as 1740, when one Matthew Ryan was tried for highway robbery. He pretended to be mad and dumb, and would not plead. The judges ordered a jury to be empanelled to inquire and give their opinion whether he was mute and lunatic by the hand of God or wilfully so. The jury returned in a short time and brought in a verdict of " Wilful and affected dumbness and lunacy."

No. 674 of the *Universal Spectator* records two instances of pressing in the reign of George II: " Sept. 5th, 1741—On Tuesday was sentenced to death at the Old Bailey, Henry Cook, the showmaker, of Stratford, for robbing Mr. Zachary on the highway. On Cook's refusing to plead there was a new press made, and fixed to the proper place in the Press Yard; there having been no person pressed since the famous Spiggot, the highwayman, which is about twenty years ago. Barnworth, alias Frasier, was pressed at Kingston, in Surrey, about sixteen years ago."

These horrible details have often been discredited; but records of pressing so late as 1770, exist; with the addition, however, that " the punishment was seldom inflicted, but some offenders have chosen it in order to preserve their estates for their children. Those guilty of this crime are not now suffered to undergo such a length of torture, but have so great a weight placed on them that they soon expire."